THOMAS AQUINAS:
BASIC PHILOSOPHICAL WRITING

broadview editions
series editor: Martin R. Boyne

THOMAS AQUINAS:
BASIC PHILOSOPHICAL WRITING:
FROM THE *SUMMA THEOLOGIAE*
AND *THE PRINCIPLES OF NATURE*

edited and translated by Steven Baldner

broadview editions

BROADVIEW PRESS – www.broadviewpress.com
Peterborough, Ontario, Canada

Founded in 1985, Broadview Press remains a wholly independent publishing house. Broadview's focus is on academic publishing; our titles are accessible to university and college students as well as scholars and general readers. With over 600 titles in print, Broadview has become a leading international publisher in the humanities, with world-wide distribution. Broadview is committed to environmentally responsible publishing and fair business practices.

Library and Archives Canada Cataloguing in Publication

Thomas, Aquinas, Saint, 1225?–1274
[Works. Selections. English]
   Thomas Aquinas : basic philosophical writing : from The summa theologiae and The principles of nature / edited and translated by Steven Baldner.

Includes bibliographical references and index.
Translated to English from the original Latin.
ISBN 978-1-55481-372-8 (softcover)

   1. Thomas, Aquinas, Saint, 1225?–1274. 2. Philosophy, Medieval. I. Baldner, Steven Earl, 1951–, editor, translator II. Thomas, Aquinas, Saint, 1225?–1274. Summa theologica. Selections. English. III. Thomas, Aquinas, Saint, 1225?–1274. De principiis naturae ad fratrem Silvestrum. English. IV. Title. V. Title: Basic philosophical writing : from The summa theologiae and The principles of nature.

B765.T52E5 2018   189'.4   C2018-905032-2

Broadview Editions
The Broadview Editions series is an effort to represent the ever-evolving canon of texts in the disciplines of literary studies, history, philosophy, and political theory. A distinguishing feature of the series is the inclusion of primary source documents contemporaneous with the work.

Advisory editor for this volume: Juliet Sutcliffe

Broadview Press handles its own distribution in North America:
PO Box 1243, Peterborough, Ontario K9J 7H5, Canada
555 Riverwalk Parkway, Tonawanda, NY 14150, USA
Tel: (705) 743-8990; Fax: (705) 743-8353
email: customerservice@broadviewpress.com

Distribution is handled by Eurospan Group in the UK, Europe, Central Asia, Middle East, Africa, India, Southeast Asia, Central America, South America, and the Caribbean. Distribution is handled by Footprint Books in Australia and New Zealand.

Broadview Press acknowledges the financial support of the Government of Canada for our publishing activities.

Typesetting and assembly: True to Type Inc., Claremont, Canada
Cover Design: Aldo Fierro

PRINTED IN CANADA

Contents

Acknowledgements

I am pleased to acknowledge the huge support I have unfailingly received from Broadview Press: from Brett McLenithan, whose gentle but persistent encouragement got me to do this at all and kept me at it; from Stephen Latta, an excellent editor who combines good sense, efficiency, and tact; and from Juliet Sutcliffe, who has been a meticulous copy editor and a literate reader. I am also most appreciative of the anonymous reviewer, all of whose careful suggestions have made the translation better. I would like to thank numerous but here nameless students, including my dear friends from Classics for Classics, who read parts of this in draft and said nice things to me. Finally, I would like to thank Frances, my second most favourite philosopher, who read the entire draft and did not always say nice things but always said the things that I needed to hear.

Introduction

Biographical Sketch of Thomas Aquinas[1]

Thomas Aquinas was born in 1224 or 1225, the youngest son of nine children in a family of noble standing in southern Italy. Thomas, as was customary for a youngest son in such a family, was expected to have a life in the Church; his family wanted him to become the abbot in the nearby Benedictine monastery at Montecassino. Thomas was sent there as a child for early schooling (1230–39), where he participated in the monastic life. At the age of 14 or 15, he was sent to the university in Naples, which was founded by Emperor Frederick II and which would later become part of the University of Bologna. In Naples, Thomas received what we would regard as an undergraduate education, especially in the philosophy of Aristotle. In addition to his university studies, Thomas also benefitted from the presence of Dominican friars, who had established a house of study there.

The Dominican influence led to a momentous decision: at the age of 19 or 20 in 1244, Thomas entered the Dominican life by taking the habit of the Order from the Dominicans in Naples. In Thomas's day, the Dominicans, along with the Franciscans, were a new order of friars and nuns who were committed to following the Gospel with a radical purity. Both orders were committed to a life of poverty, and this meant a life at odds with what one would find in much of the established Church. The Dominicans emphasized the importance of preaching, especially in the growing cities of Europe, and both orders soon developed an important commitment to university teaching and scholarly work. The intellectual life of the great universities (Oxford, Cambridge, Paris, Bologna, and so forth) soon came to be dominated by Dominicans and Franciscans, a dominance that lasted for nearly 300 years.

---

1 I have drawn material in the following from three sources primarily: Pasquale Porro, *Thomas Aquinas: A Historical and Philosophical Profile*, translated by Joseph C. Trabbic and Roger W. Nutt, Catholic U of America P, 2016; Jean-Pierre Torrell, *Saint Thomas Aquinas*, vol. 1: *The Person and his Work*, translated by Robert Royal, Catholic U of America P, 1993; and James A. Weisheipl, *Friar Thomas D'Aquino: His Life, Thought and Work*, Doubleday, 1974.

From the family point of view, however, young Thomas was doing something that was radical and unacceptable. The family wanted a strong alliance with a powerful institution within the Church, such as a large monastery, not with a ragtag fraternity of itinerant, mendicant preachers. Thomas's mother sent his brothers to kidnap Thomas, and for some months in 1244 and 1245 Thomas was held in friendly captivity by his own family. The story is told that a prostitute was engaged to try to tempt young Thomas to a worldlier life, but this attempt, so the story goes, went nowhere with the resolute young man. Eventually, the family realized that Thomas's intentions were unshakeable, and Thomas was released to begin his Dominican career.

The Dominicans, fortunately, had the best possible mentor and teacher for Thomas: Albert the Great (Albertus Magnus, 1200–80). Albert was a man of extraordinary learning and one of the earliest to see the immense value of the philosophy of Aristotle for Christian theology. In the thirteenth century the works of Aristotle, along with works of great Muslim and Jewish thinkers (Avicenna, Averroes, and Maimonides, to name only three), were being translated for the first time into Latin and studied in the new universities—but not without significant controversy.[1] On several occasions, Aristotle and his expositors were banned from the university curriculum by nervous bishops, especially at the University of Paris. Albert, however, spent 20 years producing paraphrases of all of the major works of Aristotle so that the new philosophy could be assimilated, albeit critically. The revolutionary effect of the introduction of Aristotelian philosophy in the thirteenth century is somewhat analogous to the explosive introduction of the new mathematical physics and astronomy in the seventeenth century. Aristotelian philosophy was in effect the new science, and Albert, against more conservative reactions, welcomed this new science, as did his brilliant disciple.

From 1245 to 1248, Thomas studied at the University of Paris, living in the Dominican house of studies, St. Jacques. In 1248, Thomas was sent with Albert to Cologne, where Albert founded a new Dominican house of studies, a *studium generale*, in which Thomas studied for four years. In Cologne, Thomas lived with other students, and then as now student nicknames were common. Thomas was tall, corpulent, and, though friendly, very quiet. From these characteristics, the students began to call

---

1 See the end of the Introduction (pp. 33–38) for a guide to these philosophers, and to all the other philosophers that Thomas mentions.

Thomas "the dumb ox." When Albert was told this, he is said to have replied, "We call him the dumb ox, but he will make resound in his doctrine such a bellowing that it will echo throughout the entire world."[1]

In the years 1252–59, Thomas again returned to the University of Paris. Between 1252 and 1256, he completed what might be the analogue (though bigger) of the modern PhD thesis: a four-book commentary on the *Sentences* of Peter Lombard, which is a collection of theological opinions on all major theological topics, compiled by Lombard in the mid-twelfth century. Thus, at this stage of his academic career, while also beginning to lecture on the Bible to other students, Thomas wrote a vast synthesis of theology. This commentary on the *Sentences* was standard practice for all scholastic theologians from Thomas's day until the sixteenth century, and samples of writings from this genre by other authors are included in Appendices B, C, F, H, and I. Thomas also at this time wrote two important short philosophical works at the request of his confreres: *The Principles of Nature* and *On Being and Essence.* The first is included as Chapter 1 of this volume and provides an introduction to the basic terms of natural philosophy, including form and matter and the four Aristotelian causes. The second is a primer in metaphysics, containing many of Thomas's fundamental metaphysical insights. In 1256, Thomas began to teach as a Master of Theology, or "Regent Master," composing, in addition to his teaching, commentaries on books of the Bible, a commentary on Boethius's *De Trinitate* (containing texts on methodology in science, philosophy, and theology), and the huge *Disputed Questions on Truth,* with important texts in epistemology, metaphysics, and theology.

After serving in this professorial role, Thomas was sent by his Order to Italy in 1259, perhaps to Naples, and then to Orvieto (1261–65). At this time, Thomas composed his second major theological synthesis, the *Summa contra Gentiles* (the "Summa against the Non-Believers").[2] This four-volume work is remarkable because the first three volumes contain entirely philosophical arguments, given of course for an ultimate theological purpose. This work contains Thomas's most extensive arguments

---

1 Torrell, *Saint Thomas Aquinas,* vol. 1, p. 26.

2 The word "Summa" was commonly used by scholastic theologians as a title for a major synthetic work. Thomas and others wrote a "Summa of Theology" (*Summa theologiae*), William of Ockham wrote a "Summa of Logic" (*Summa logicae*), and so forth. The term "summa" would indicate that the topic was covered comprehensively.

for the existence of God, the doctrine of God's creative causing of all being, the nature of the human soul, including its immortality, and so forth. It is an example of what is so characteristic of Thomas's theology: the generous use of philosophical arguments in the service of theology. At this time Thomas also wrote a commentary on the *Divine Names*, a fifth-century neo-Platonic work that enjoyed a special status for scholastic theologians because it was believed to have been written by Dionysius (or Denys), who was a companion of St. Paul.[1] Though he himself was fundamentally Aristotelian in philosophy, Thomas always regarded the Platonic tradition as making important contributions to philosophy and theology.

From 1265 to 1268, Thomas taught in Rome, where he wrote the first part of his masterpiece, the *Summa theologiae*.[2] The *Summa theologiae* is divided into three parts: the First Part discusses God, the Trinity, and God's creation, including the human person. Texts in Chapters 2 and 3 of this volume are taken from the First Part. The Second Part concerns ethics, and it is itself divided into two parts: the First Part of the Second Part, and the Second Part of the Second Part. The First Part of the Second Part deals with general problems in ethics (what today might be called metaethics); the Second Part of the Second Part deals with all of the specific virtues and vices in great detail. The texts in Chapter 4 are all taken from the First Part of the Second Part. They concern the goal for human life, the moral relevance of human action, the nature of virtue, and natural law. The Third Part of the *Summa theologiae* contains Thomas's Christology and discussion of the sacraments, but the Third Part is incomplete, with only four of the seven sacraments treated. In this Roman period, Thomas also wrote the *Disputed Questions on the Power of God*, a major text on God's nature, power, creation, providence, and so forth.

Typically, a professor would serve only once as Master of Theology, but, as a testimony to his extraordinary prestige, Thomas was called for a second time and served in the role of Regent Master at the University of Paris from 1268 to 1272. What Thomas accomplished during this second time in Paris defies the imagination. In addition to his teaching and public disputations, he composed the massive Second Part of the *Summa theologiae*, he wrote a dozen important philosophical and theological works,

---

1 On Dionysius, see p. 35.

2 *Summa theologiae* ("Summa of Theology") or *Summa theologica* ("Theological Summa").

and he completed book-length commentaries on eleven major works of Aristotle. Thomas wrote mostly by dictating to secretaries. It is said that he could dictate to three or four secretaries at the same time, in rotation, an account that seems true, given his extraordinary output at this time. One of the philosophical works of this period was a commentary on the *Book of Causes* (the *Liber de causis*). This work, which in fact includes material from the fifth-century neo-Platonist Proclus, had been thought by Thomas's contemporaries to have been composed by Aristotle. Thomas argued, however, on doctrinal grounds, that the work could not have been written by Aristotle, a fact that was later confirmed, in the Renaissance, based on textual evidence.

At the end of this Regency, Thomas was again ordered by the Dominicans to return to Naples, where he wrote most of the Third Part of the *Summa theologiae* (1272–73). On 6 December 1273, Thomas underwent some sort of powerful experience—spiritual, psychological, and/or physical—the result of which was that he ceased all writing and academic work. We do not know the nature of this experience. According to legend, Thomas had a mystical experience, after which he claimed that in comparison to his vision, his writings amounted only to so much straw. We do not know whether this actually happened, or whether Thomas passed such a judgement on his work. He did, however, cease all writing, leaving the great *Summa theologiae*, and a number of other works, incomplete.[1]

In early 1274, Thomas was summoned to the Council of Lyon, which was to deal with relations with the Greek churches. He suffered a blow to the head en route to the Council, eventually became fatally ill, and died on 7 March 1274, never having made it to the Council, where he would have met his old colleague and friend Bonaventure.[2]

The accounts of Thomas's personality and character are consistent: he was quiet, serious, constantly working or praying, charitable, generous, kind, and (occasionally) humorous with his students. He was fair to his intellectual adversaries and had the

---

1 There is a supplement to the *Summa* that treats the missing topics in the Third Part, written by Thomas's students and taken from material in Thomas's commentary on the *Sentences*.

2 St. Bonaventure (1221–74) was the great Franciscan contemporary of Thomas. Like Thomas, he was a university professor and a great theologian and philosopher. His philosophy is built upon the scholastic vocabulary that is derived from Aristotle but has a more neo-Platonic cast than would be found in Thomas.

ability to state objections to his own positions in clearer, more forceful language than the objectors could do themselves. He argued often and brilliantly against opposing positions but was never personal. His intellectual and spiritual energy was legendary: he wanted nothing other, he said, than to speak to God and about God. His sanctity was recognized by those who knew him, and by the Church when he was canonized in 1323. Thomas's academic career lasted only 21 years, but during this time he wrote enough to fill 50 folio volumes in the modern critical edition. In this short time, he also travelled much: from Naples, to Paris, to Cologne, back to Paris, back to Naples, to Orvieto, to Rome, back to Paris, back to Naples, and, then, finally, part of the way to Lyon—all of this on foot. It is calculated that Thomas walked some 15,000 kilometres in order to take up the various academic posts to which he was assigned.[1]

A word should be added about two famous condemnations, in 1270 and again in 1277. The Bishop of Paris, Stephen Tempier, condemned 13 philosophical theses in 1270 and 219 philosophical and theological theses in 1277. These condemned theses concerned a wide range of topics: the nature of God and how he can be known, God's knowledge and power, angels, creation and the eternity of the world, the human soul and immortality, human knowledge and will, the Eucharist, and Christian morality. No one was named in the condemnations, and none of the theses in the 1270 condemnation were held by Thomas. Some of the theses condemned in 1277, however, were held by him, but even this admits of some uncertainty. The condemnations forbade the teaching of the theses they covered only in the University of Paris, but the effect, especially of the larger condemnation, was felt throughout Europe. In 1325, a later bishop of Paris, Stephen Bourret, rescinded any condemnations particularly applicable to Thomas.

Reading Thomas: Some Important Terms

Thomas Aquinas wrote for a university audience familiar with Aristotelian and Scholastic terms. We, however, do not use these terms, or, if we do, we often mean something different. In order to prepare today's reader for this mediaeval text, the following distinctions and definitions might be helpful.

---

1 Torrell, *St. Thomas Aquinas*, vol. 1, p. 280. As part of their commitment to apostolic poverty, Dominicans were required to walk, if they were able, rather than ride or travel by carriage.

1. Substance and Accident. One of the basic facts about the world is that some things exist independently and other things exist dependently. Independently existing things are things like rocks, water, plants, animals, and human beings. They can be understood and defined on their own, and they are the principal agents in our world, acting and interacting with each other. These independently existing natural units are called substances. On the other hand, there are myriad dependent realities, such as shape, size, colour, texture, position, activity, and so forth. These realities necessarily belong to substances, and none of them could exist without a substance. The shape is always the shape *of* something, the colour is the colour *of* something, and so forth. These dependent realities are called accidents. Accidents modify substances: substances differ by being big or small, heavy or light, located here rather than there, and so forth. Some accidents will always belong to some substances (granite is always hard; a plant always respires); other accidents come and go (I am tanned in the summer and pale in the winter; water can be hot or cold). The accidents that always belong to a substance are sometimes called "proper" or "essential" accidents. All substances have some accidental modifications.

In the strict sense, substances are natural things: salt, gold, geraniums, dogs. An artefact like a table or a computer is really not one substance but rather a collection or aggregate of a number of different substances.

Aristotle taught that there were nine ultimate categories of accidents: quantity (number, length, etc.), quality (colours, tastes, smells, dispositions, etc.), relations (taller than, slower than, etc.), actions, being acted upon, time when, place where, position, and possession.

2. Essential and Accidental. The idea of accident, given above, suggests that some accidents might or might not belong to something else. So what a thing does not have to have in order to be what it is is accidental; what it must have to be what it is is essential. In order for a triangle to be a triangle, it is essential that it have three sides and that the sum of its interior angles equal 180 degrees. On the other hand, it is accidental to the triangle that it be blue or red or that it be made of wood or drawn on paper. Whenever we talk about what is intrinsic to the thing, what the thing has in itself, or that without which the thing could not be what it is, we are talking about what is essential. Whenever we talk

about what is extrinsic to the thing, what does not belong to the thing as such, or what the thing could lose and still be what it is, we are talking about what is accidental.

Notice that the distinction between essential and accidental is not the same as the distinction between substances and accidents. Accidents (as defined above) have essential properties; we can talk about the essence of a colour, for example. It is essential to the colour red that it reflect light in a certain wavelength band; it is accidental to the colour red that it be the colour of an apple or the colour of my shirt. Both substances and accidents have essential natures, and hence we can talk about what is essential to either and also what is accidental to either.

3. Act and Potency; Actuality and Potentiality. One of Aristotle's fundamental insights is that everywhere in the world there is a distinction between what is actually the case and what is potentially the case. I am actually in my office but potentially at the pub; the water is actually cold but potentially hot; we are actually learning but potentially forgetful, and so forth. The point about this distinction is that it applies everywhere in the world, because it applies to everything that can change—and that means everything in our world. Thus everything in our world is a combination of act and potency, or of actuality and potentiality. These two fundamental parts of reality are essential to all material, natural things in order to include both the change and motion in our world and also the intelligibility of it. If a philosopher denies potentiality and insists that all reality is actual, the result is a denial of change or motion. On the other hand, if a philosopher denies actuality and insists only on the reality of potentiality and change, an ever-flowing change is unknowable. The fact that change is real is attributable to potency; the fact that the world is intelligible is attributable to actuality.

4. Form and Matter. Act and potency as the two fundamental parts of all reality correspond to the two metaphysical principles, form and matter. Form makes something actual and intelligible, while matter is the source from which the thing can change and is individual. All of the things in our world are composites of form and matter. For everything that we encounter, we can ask what is it, by which we mean, what is its nature or essence? The answer to that question will be rooted in the form, for the form makes the thing to be what it actually is. On the other hand, we may ask what the thing is made out of, what it might be made into, how

it might change, and these questions are about the matter. Hence everything, both substances and accidents, are *composites* of form and matter; form is the principle of actuality, and matter is the principle of potentiality.

Form and matter, as they have been just described, are both *parts* of the essence or nature of any natural substance. If we wish to understand the essence or nature of a thing, that is, if we wish to define it, we must include both form and matter. Thus, in the concrete existing thing, form and matter are its two ultimate metaphysical constituents. When we try to understand the essence of the thing as a whole and define it, we must include both of these parts, because the essence or nature includes both form and matter.

5. Soul and Body. In living things, the form is called the *soul*, to distinguish it from the forms of non-living things, which are much less complicated and have many fewer operations. Similarly, the matter of living things is much more complicated, because living matter must be a precise combination of specifically distinct and differentiated organs. The matter of the living organism is called the *body*. Soul and body, thus, are the form and the matter of living things.

Thomas thought that *all* living things are composites of soul and body (geraniums, mosquitos, lions, and human beings), but this is merely his way of saying that all things are composed of form and matter. We tend to think of "soul" as something human, religious, and immortal, but this is not the fundamental sense of the word for Thomas or for Aristotle.

6. Knowledge: Sensation and Understanding. One of the most important things about human beings is that we have knowledge. Fundamental in this is the distinction between the two ways of knowing: sensation and understanding. Sensation is through our five external senses and also in our interior feelings, imaginations, and emotions. The crucial mark of sensation is that we always sense individual, unique things. I see this exact shade of blue, I taste this particular apple, and I remember just what I felt like this morning.

Understanding, on the other hand, is the human ability (not shared by animals, Thomas would say) of recognizing what is generally, abstractly, or universally true. By understanding, I grasp, not what Fido looks like, but what it means to be a dog, any dog. Because I can understand, I can think about abstract concepts like justice or government. Understanding allows me to come to understand even things that cannot be sensed in any way, like logical relationships, metaphysical terms, or God.

Texts in this Volume

Chapter 1: The Principles of Nature

The first text in this volume is a translation of a complete work, *The Principles of Nature (De principiis naturae)*, which Thomas wrote early in his academic career, when he was still commenting on the *Sentences* of Peter Lombard, or perhaps even earlier.[1] This work was written by Thomas at the request of one of his Dominican confreres, named Sylvester, about whom we know nothing. We may surmise that Thomas, who was always recognized for his advanced understanding, was asked to provide an explanation of basic Aristotelian philosophical terms that were troublesome to his fellow students. The short work that he produced amounts to a primer in Aristotelian natural philosophy, drawn especially from Books I and II of Aristotle's *Physics*.

The Principles of Nature includes three major topics. First, in sections 1 and 2, Thomas explains the fundamental terms of *potency* (matter), *actuality* (form), and *privation* (the lack of form). As I have indicated above, these are the basic terms for explaining all change and motion and also for explaining the being of natural things. All change is change from some prior potency (matter) to some realized actuality (form), and it presupposes the initial lack of that realized form (privation). All natural substances are composites of matter and form; and all accidents are forms that inhere in substances as in their matter. In the first two sections of *The Principles of Nature*, Thomas develops the important principle of privation, explaining that it is a principle needed to explain change or motion but that it is not a principle of being. He also explains the crucial but hard to understand idea of *prime matter*. Prime matter is not a *thing* or any formal reality, but it is matter at its most basic: that is, a pure potentiality for change. Any material thing could, ultimately, become any other material thing, and this omni-potentiality of matter is the fundamental fact about matter. A world of nothing but forms would be a static world; matter, at its root, is restless and thus an ultimate source of change.

---

1 Torrell, *Saint Thomas Aquinas*, vol. 1, pp. 48–49, 349.

The second major topic in *The Principles of Nature* is that of causality. In sections 3 to 5, Thomas explains that a complete account of any natural thing—a scientific account—must include four kinds of causal explanations: what a thing is made out of (its matter, the material cause); what a thing is (its definition, the formal cause); what produced the thing (the efficient cause); and what the goal or purpose of it is (the final cause). Let me note two things about this discussion of causality. First, since the advent of modern philosophy (at least since Descartes), philosophers and scientists have spoken about causality in a much more restricted sense. Modern philosophers will recognize an efficient cause, and perhaps a material cause, but formal and final causes are generally rejected. A second thing to note is the distinction between actual causes and potential causes. Actual causes, Thomas argues, must be temporally simultaneous with their effects; actual causes and actual effects are *not* thus two separate events, as modern philosophers since the time of Hume have supposed. Rather, Thomas regards cause and effect as two simultaneous parts of one event; the effect is occurring if and only if the cause is simultaneously causing.

A third major topic is that of analogy, or the problem of how, when we use our language, we recognize both sameness and difference. The principles of form and matter are used to determine a nature, that is, a kind of being. Whenever we have the same kind of matter and the same kind of form, we have one kind of being: all dogs have the same kind of matter and the same form. We recognize different individual dogs (which have different individual matter), but we say that both Fido and Rover are dogs. The term "dogs," thus, is predicated *univocally* of both Fido and Rover— the term has the same meaning for both individuals. The same is also true when we group together various species under one genus, as when we say that dogs and horses are "mammals." Here, again, the similarity of matter and form is close enough to allow the term "mammal" to be predicated with the same meaning. On the other hand, if we talk about the "bark" of a dog and also the "bark" of a tree, we are now using the same term but with completely different and unrelated meanings. In this case, the use of the term "bark" is *equivocal* when used to talk about dogs and trees—there is no real sameness, even though the word is the same. There is, however, a third possibility, and a very important one. It can happen that we talk about things that are in very different categories but still have closely related, though different, meanings. For example, food, colour, and a human being are all in different logical categories, which seem to have nothing to do with one another. They can, however, all be importantly related to one common reality, namely, health. We might say that a diet is "healthy," that the colour of a complexion is "healthy," and that a human being is "healthy." The word "healthy" means something different in each case: food is the cause of health, a complexion is a sign of health, but the human being is the one who is properly healthy in the principal sense of the word. This is an example of *analogous* predication of terms: different but closely related meanings. Thomas thinks that the analogous use of terms and concepts is essential to philosophy, theology, science, and everyday knowledge, because there are real and important relations that connect beings outside of the natural categories of being.

Chapter 2: God

The texts in this chapter are all taken from the *Summa theologiae*, Part I. I will identify these texts by references to questions (Q) and articles (A). In this chapter, four major topics are treated. First, very briefly, there are two short texts on the broad problem of faith and reason (Q. 1, AA. 1 & 2). The goal of human life goes beyond what philosophers can know, and hence both revelation and the theology that is based on it are necessary in order for us to know fully and reliably our ultimate happiness and how to achieve it. This collection of introductory texts is philosophical, but it is important for the reader to know that the truths of philosophy carry us only so far; revelation and theology are needed to complete the story.

The second topic (Q. 2, AA. 1–3) is the existence of God. Thomas's philosophical claims about God are modest. We do not in this life know the essence of God, and hence we cannot conclude that God exists from a consideration of God's essence or from what it means to be God. To argue from the essence of God to God's existence is to offer what philosophers call an ontological argument, two versions of which are given in the Appendices.[1] Thomas rejects such arguments, pointing out that they are not

---

1 Anselm's argument from the *Proslogion* is given in Appendix A, and Descartes's argument from the *Meditations on First Philosophy* is given in Appendix E. Briefly, an ontological argument is one that argues from the idea or definition of God to the existence of God. From an understanding merely of the nature or essence of God, so ontological arguments go, we will see that God necessarily exists.

properly "arguments" at all but mere claims that God's existence is "self-evident" (Q. 2, A. 1). He insists that the only philosophical way to know about God is by way of arguments from effects to cause (Q. 2, A. 2). Such arguments necessarily tell us very little about the cause. From fossil evidence of bones, for example, palaeontologists conclude that certain species of dinosaurs once existed, which is an argument from effect to cause, but we recognize that we can know very little about such animals compared to those that we can observe now. Likewise, Thomas tells us, to know that God exists from the effects he has caused is to know some important but very restricted truths about God.

Thomas's famous Five Ways to prove the existence of God are given in Q. 2, A. 3. Two of these are condensed versions of arguments given at length elsewhere.[1] They all presuppose an understanding of Thomas's philosophical principles generally. Still, the beginning student can get some idea from them of why there must be a first cause. The First Way (and the Second, which is similar) rests on two essential claims. First, nothing can move or cause itself. Whenever something is being moved or being caused, the cause is something other than itself. Motion is always the actualizing of some potency, but the moving thing as such is in a state of potency and not yet actuality. Some source or cause is required for this actualizing to take place, and it must be other than the thing that is moved. Second, if one thing is moved by another, that mover may also be moved by something else; the second mover may also be moved by a third, and so forth. The chain of causes, however, cannot be infinite. To say that the chain of causes is infinite is to say that all causes receive their causal power or efficacy from something else, but that no cause is actually the source of such causal power. Since Thomas finds that this is absurd, he concludes that there must be some cause that is uncaused, that is, the unmoved mover.

In the Third and Fourth Ways, Thomas shifts the focus to the being or existence of things. In both of these Ways, Thomas is arguing that the being of everything in the universe requires a cause and that only God can be the cause of that being. In the Third Way, the problem is that everything other than God is contingent, that is, all creatures might exist or not exist. Their being is not a necessary product of their natures, and hence is some-

---

1 For a greatly expanded version of the First Way, see *Summa contra Gentiles*, Bk. 1, Ch. 13. For an expanded version of the Third Way, see *Summa contra Gentiles*, Bk. 1, Ch. 15–16, or *Disputed Questions on the Power of God*, Q. 5, A. 3.

thing distinct from their natures and in need of a cause. In the Fourth Way, this fact is realized from a consideration of grades of being; there must, Thomas argues, be a first instance of being, an instance that is being itself and not, like everything else, something that receives its being. The first instance or pure being will be the source of being in all creatures, which receive their being from some cause other than themselves.

The Fifth Way is a teleological argument. The fact that nature and natural beings act regularly to achieve goals that are good is an indication, Thomas argues, that nature is intelligently ordered. The regular achievement of goals that are good does not happen by chance, and since non-intelligent nature is so ordered, some intelligent cause for the whole of nature is required.

To be the first cause of the universe and thus to be uncaused entails a series of predicates that Thomas will explore in Questions 3–10, which form the third major topic of Chapter 2. God must be perfectly simple (not bodily, not different from his nature, or different from his being, Q. 3, AA. 1, 3, 4), he must be perfect and the source of all perfections (Q. 4, AA. 1–2), and he must be infinite (Q. 7, A. 1), immutable (Q. 9, A. 1), and eternal (Q. 10, A. 1). God, Thomas argues, is *in* all things, insofar as God is causing the being of all things (Q. 8, A. 1). As long as any creature exists, God must be causing the being of the creature, for otherwise the creature would cease to exist. God is thus completely intimate to all creatures, for he is the ongoing cause of their being, but he is distinct from them, and they have their own operations from their own natures.

The fourth major topic of Chapter 2 is Thomas's explanation of how terms from human language can be used meaningfully about God (Q. 13). The general problem is that human beings are suited by nature to know the material things of this world, which are known first and best. How, then, can human concepts and words be extended to apply meaningfully to God? Thomas explains that our concepts and words do not indicate God's essence, just as it is in itself (A. 1). They do, however, really indicate God—"substantially," as Thomas puts it (A. 2). That is, they do not indicate merely what God is not or merely that God is the cause of things that we do know. Further, even though God's nature is perfectly simple and without any parts or composition, the different words that we use of God are not mere synonyms (A. 4). The solution to the problem is found in the doctrine of the analogous use of words and concepts (A. 5), which Thomas already introduced in *The Principles of Nature*.[1] This doctrine allows Thomas to distinguish between words or concepts that are used *properly*, though *analogically*, about God from words that are used *improperly* and, hence, *metaphorically* about God (A. 6). Metaphorical language provides an important access to the reality of God for finite creatures whose knowledge starts with material things, but metaphorical language about God presupposes non-metaphorical language, that is, language used analogically about God.

Chapter 3: Human Nature

This chapter contains texts on three related topics. The first topic, how a human person is a composite of soul and body, is one on which Thomas attempts a very delicate balance (QQ. 75–76). On the one hand, he rejects the materialist position that a human being can be reduced to a mere assembly of bodily parts (Q. 75, A. 1). On the other hand, he rejects the dualist position of Plato that a human being is really a soul that resides in or uses a body (Q. 75, A. 4; Q. 76, A. 1). Thomas's middle position is that a human being is, like any other natural, material substance, a composite of matter and form. In the case of living substances, the matter is called the body and the form is called the soul. Body and soul, thus, are two essential parts of the human person, but neither by itself is a complete human person. The body without a soul is not a human person at all: it is a corpse that will decay immediately into various chemical elements. The human soul without the body would not corrupt or go out of existence (Q. 75, A. 6), but it is impossible to explain philosophically how a human soul without a body could perform *any* normal human operation, including the operations of understanding or of willing. Matter and form are not independent *things* but are co-dependent *principles* of naturally existing material substances. The same is true for the human body and soul: they are the co-dependent parts of a single, united entity, called a human person.

It so happens, Thomas argues, that the human soul will not degenerate or corrupt into elemental constituents, as the body will, because in fact the soul is a *form* that is itself not composed of anything. Although it is a form and not a *mover* of the body (Q. 76, A. 1), this form is unusual because it has operations that are

---

1 See the discussion of this above on pp. 19–20.

not reducible to bodily operations (Q. 75, A. 2). The soul makes the body to be *actually* human, that is, alive as a human being, and thus gives rise to a whole range of different operations, such as growth, metabolism, digestion, repair of tissue, respiration, sensation, and so forth. Most of the operations made actual by the soul are necessarily operations of various bodily organs, which can be identified. Two operations, however, willing and understanding, are *not* operations of any bodily organs, although they do require the human body and its organs to operate (Q. 75, A. 2, Reply to Obj. 3). Understanding is an immaterial operation and not the operation of some organ such as the brain, but this operation requires (in its natural operation) a brain that can produce sense images in order that the intellect have some objects to think about. Here, again, is another of Thomas's balancing acts: the intellect is a power of the soul and not a power of some bodily organ, but this same intellect requires human sensation that can only occur in a living, bodily person. What is true about understanding is also true about willing.

The second topic in Chapter 3 is that of free will and choice (QQ. 82–83). The will is understood by Thomas to be an appetite, a kind of desire that is characteristic of human beings. Sense desires are obvious: we have appetites for food, for drink, for sexual union, and so forth. In each case the appetite is an appetite for some object, and the object taken in general is good. The will is an *intellectual* appetite, and this means that it is a desire for what is intellectually understood to be good. We desire, or should desire, things like justice, virtue, and what is ultimately good for us. The problem is whether this intellectual appetite is free or not. Thomas solves this problem by making a distinction between the goal and the means to the goal. If the will is considered as a natural appetite, it is naturally, and necessarily, ordered to its goal, which is the ultimate good for human beings, or happiness (Q. 82, A. 1). Put another way, *every* human act of the will is a choice for something that is good, and all human beings by nature necessarily will their own happiness. On the other hand, if we consider the question of what sorts of things will make us happy, we find that there are many, many possible *means* to choose from. We can consider the various possibilities (wealth, power, pleasure, virtue, etc.), and, since we can never see a necessary connection between any of these possibilities and our happiness, the will is not necessarily ordered to any one of these. The will is, therefore, free insofar as it is concerned mostly with making choices about good things that might or might not make us really happy (Q. 82, A. 2).

The will is the general power by which human persons desire things that are understood to be good. Choices are acts of the will by which individual good things are chosen, always as a means to some other good. The will always sets the goal, and choices are always about means to reach the goal. These choices, Thomas explains, are free insofar as we can rationally consider a range of possible things to choose (Q. 83, A. 1). Animals, too, make choices, but their choices are always driven by an instinct in one way rather than in another, and hence they are not free. The rational ability to consider freely among possible good things is the essence of free choice.

The third topic in Chapter 3 is that of knowledge or episte- ·mology (QQ. 84–85). Here, again, Thomas wishes to steer a middle course, this time between the materialists, who reduced all knowledge to sensation (that is, they were strict empiricists), and the Platonists, who held that the true object of human knowledge was a separate Form. The principal problem with the materialist position is that it fails to recognize that our intellec- tual knowledge is universal in character; the senses are deter- mined to sense only single, unique things, but the intellect is able to grasp what is common. In order that this happen, the opera- tion of understanding must be an immaterial operation and must abstract from sense knowledge (Q. 84, A. 2). This is so because any material thing is necessarily singular or individual, and hence any material process is determined in one way. Intellectual understanding, however, is not determined to one but is univer- sally inclusive of all individuals. Intellectual understanding is, therefore, possible only to the extent that it is an operation sepa- rate from any material organ. Plato correctly recognized that understanding is radically different from sensation, and he understood that the act of understanding must be an immaterial act. Plato, however, mistakenly thought that, because the act of understanding results in concepts that are universal, stable, and immaterial, the *objects* of such concepts must also have the same characteristics; that is, the objects of understanding must be Forms that are completely separate from the material things of this world (Q. 84, A. 1).

Plato's position, according to Thomas, generates a number of unsolvable problems. If Plato is correct, human science is not about the things in this world but, rather, about Forms that exist in some other realm (Q. 84, A. 1). Natural science, however, should give us knowledge about things in *this* world. Further, Plato's position implies a doctrine of innate ideas, but Thomas insists that all knowledge comes initially from sensation; if we did have such innate ideas, it is inexplicable that we should have forgotten them and it should be the case that we could have knowledge completely without sensation, but that is not the case (Q. 84, A. 3). Finally, the Platonic doctrine of knowledge of separate Forms fails to explain the natural and necessary role of sensation and the human body (Q. 84, A. 4). If the Platonic theory of knowledge were true, the human body and sensation should not be necessary for human knowing, but Thomas always insists on the naturalness and importance of sensation. In fact, Thomas argues that our abstract understanding would be impossible without sense images (Q. 84, A. 7). This is true even when the intellect gains some understanding of things that are completely immaterial and cannot be sensed in any way, such as God or the soul.

The correct position, according to Thomas, is that of Aristotle (Q. 84, A. 6). Aristotle agrees with empiricists that all knowledge must start with sensation and that without sensation intellectual knowledge is impossible. Aristotle, however, does not think that our knowledge *ends* with sensation. Rather, he agrees with Plato that the intellect understands abstractly in an immaterial way that allows for universal concepts that go far beyond sensation. Plato, however, mistakenly eliminated the essential role that sensation plays in human knowledge. On Thomas's account, Plato would allow for sensation to take place in the human soul on the basis of the Forms, even without functioning sense organs. Aristotle's middle position is that sensation through the sense organs is essential to human knowing and that the intellect abstracts universal concepts from the data of sense images.

Thomas explains the meaning of abstraction in Q. 85, A. 1. Essentially, abstracting is the operation of knowing the intelligible forms that exist in material things but to know them not *as individual*; it is to recognize what is common among many individuals. In this article, Thomas explains that abstracting does not mean *separating* form from matter (as though a material form existed separately from the material object, as Plato would have thought), but rather it means *considering* what is common and leaving what is individual out of consideration. Importantly, Thomas explains in this text three different levels of abstraction: the level of natural, material objects, the level of mathematical objects, and the level of metaphysical objects.

Finally, Thomas makes a small but crucial point. The mental equipment of our understanding is called intellectual concepts (or ideas). These concepts allow us to know what is universal or in common among innumerable individuals. It is tempting, but wrong, to think that our concepts are the *objects* of our knowing. Thomas, therefore, insists that intellectual concepts are not *that which we know* but rather *that by which we know* (Q. 85, A. 2). When I know an apple, I do not in the first instance know the *concept* of apple in my mind; I know, instead, really existing apples, or apples that I imagine as real, though the *means* of my knowing is indeed the concepts in my mind. If we suppose, as nearly all modern philosophers do, from Descartes through Kant, that concepts are the objects of our knowledge, we have the terrible (and unsolvable) problem of modern philosophy: how to explain that our knowledge is really about things in the material world of our immediate experience. Thomas would tell us that we should not make the mistake of thinking that our concepts are the objects of our knowledge.

Chapter 4: Ethics

The entire Second Part of the *Summa theologiae* is concerned with what we would call ethics and what Thomas would think of as the way of finding our ultimate happiness. The Second Part is huge and is divided into two parts: the First Part of the Second Part, from which all of the texts in this chapter are taken, concerns what we might call general ethics; the Second Part of the Second Part concerns, in great detail, all of the individual virtues and vices that make up the moral life.

The texts in Chapter 4 concern five topics: happiness, voluntariness, what is morally good or bad in human action, habits and virtues, and natural law. The first topic, happiness, is treated in the selections from Questions 1, 2, 3, and 5. Thomas argues in these passages that happiness must be *completely* satisfying. It is necessary, Thomas says, "that the ultimate goal so fulfil the whole human desire that nothing be left over to be desired" (Q. 1, A. 5). He will accept no candidate for happiness that promises only partial or temporary happiness: wealth (Q. 2, A. 1), honour (Q. 2, A. 2), power (Q. 2, A. 4), health (Q. 2, A. 5), and pleasure (Q. 2, A. 6) are all rejected. In fact, no created good can satisfy the human desire for happiness, because humans want what Thomas calls the "universal good," which is God (Q. 2, A. 8).

The argument is straightforward: humans want what is perfectly and unfailingly good; only God is perfectly and unfailingly good; and, therefore, only God can satisfy the human desire for happiness. Ultimately, this happiness is attained only in the immediate enjoyment of God, which is the heavenly vision of God (Q. 3, A. 8). Perfect happiness, therefore, cannot be attained in this life, but Thomas does think that there is a real, though imperfect, happiness that is attainable in this life and through natural human effort (Q. 5, AA. 3 & 5). Following Aristotle, Thomas understands this partial human happiness to be a life of virtuous activity.

The second topic, "voluntariness," is really the problem of when and under what circumstances human persons are morally responsible for their actions (QQ. 6 & 13). The mark of truly human action, according to Thomas, is that it is *voluntary* (Q. 6, A. 1). Coughing or inadvertently scratching are acts performed by human beings, but they are not *human* acts because they do not stem from the conscious, voluntary attempt to achieve some goal. When we know the goal and are consciously acting to achieve it, our actions are human and voluntary, and we are morally responsible for them. Sometimes, also, our actions are voluntary when we do not actively act but when we refrain from acting in a situation in which we could have acted (Q. 6, A. 3). The will by its very nature is a rational inclination to what is good, and this interior rational inclination is inherently voluntary (Q. 6, A. 4). Human actions, however, that are commanded by the will might in some cases be taken over by some external force. A walker, for example, might be blown by the wind and thereby bump into someone else. Force of this sort, in effect, negates the commands of the will and removes voluntariness and hence responsibility from what otherwise would be a human act.

If force renders an action involuntary, does fear similarly force an action that otherwise would not occur (Q. 6, A. 6)? Thomas concedes that, out of fear, humans will do things that otherwise they would not do, but he points out (following Aristotle) that, in the concrete circumstances of the actual, individual choice, to act out of fear is to make a choice for what is preferable. It is, thus, to act voluntarily and to be morally responsible. In fearful situations, an option may be desirable only in those circumstances, but in those circumstances, it *is* desirable. When the robber's gun is pointed at me, my choice is to give him my money, which, given the other option, is genuinely preferable at that particular time. Similarly, acting for the sake of pleasure does not render an action involuntary; in fact, in the normal course of events, it makes actions more voluntary (Q. 6, A. 7). Pleasure is not some external force that takes over our actions but something we choose.

Ignorance raises a special problem (Q. 6, A. 8). Sometimes, as Thomas points out, we act out of ignorance, but it is an ignorance that we have caused, either because of negligence or because of behaviours that have rendered us ignorant (as, for example, from excessive drinking). In such cases, ignorance does cause the action, but the ignorance itself is voluntary, and for this reason we are morally responsible for the ignorance and for the action. On the other hand, there are times when we act in ignorance of individual circumstances that we could not reasonably have known. In such cases, when we do what otherwise we would not have done, our actions are involuntary and we are not responsible for them.

For the most part, human actions are free because they are *choices* that we make as a result of free deliberation among various possible means to some goal (Q. 13, A. 6). If we were confronted with absolute, unlimited good, there would be no other choices to rival the obvious one. Human life, however, is entirely concerned with making choices about things that are limited goods, and usually there are options. When there are options, we can rationally consider what is good and what is not, or what is better and what is worse, and we can make choices on this basis. Herein lie human action and moral responsibility.

From this, then, follows the third topic: precisely what is it about human action that is morally good or morally bad, or what is morally relevant in human action (QQ. 18 & 19)? For Thomas, four considerations here are relevant. First, in a very general way, an action is good to the extent that it has being (Q. 18, A. 1). This is not so much a criterion by which to judge actions as a metaphysical consideration of the convertibility of goodness and being. Second, an action is good or bad depending on the *kind* of action it is, viewed as an external action that tends to accomplish one object rather than another (Q. 18, A. 2). In this sense, an action of giving money to a poor person is objectively good, and an action of taking the life of an innocent person is bad. Third, the circumstances under which the action is performed are morally relevant: the time, place, frequency, health or strength, financial state, age or time of life, and so forth are all morally relevant (Q. 18, A. 3). What might be properly done in private, for example, might not be properly done in public. Fourth, the internal intention of the person doing the action is morally relevant: is this action being done to help someone in need, or is it being done to gain praise and recognition (Q. 18, A. 4)? Thomas insists that an action must be good in all four of these ways for it to be considered a morally good action (Q. 18, A. 4, Reply to Obj. 3). Thus, if one is performing an objectively good exterior action (giving alms to the poor, for example) but doing it for a bad intention or doing it in the wrong circumstances (when one had insufficient money, for example), this would make an otherwise good action bad. Or an action done for the best of intentions might be objectively a bad action: stealing, for example, cannot be justified by the intention of using stolen goods for some good purpose.

Moral responsibility is involved any time that a human being is making a decision and performing a human act. It is true that some actions, considered in general, are morally indifferent (Q. 18, A. 8). In any concrete situation, however, in which one makes a choice, the choice will always be either morally good or morally bad (Q. 18, A. 9). To put this another way, for Thomas, all human actions are, by the very fact that they are human actions, either morally good or morally bad. *Every* choice that human beings make is morally relevant.

Thomas thinks that the moral agent should always follow what reason dictates (Q. 19, A. 5). The dictates of reason are what we call "conscience," and we should always follow our conscience, according to Thomas. Sometimes, of course, conscience is wrong, but even in that case, we should obey it, because to do otherwise is to act irrationally. The person with the mistaken conscience does not think that the conscience is mistaken, and such a person should follow reason as well as he or she knows it. A moral agent, however, has an obligation to have a well-formed conscience; thus, if the conscience is mistaken because of ignorance that could and should have been avoided, then the agent is morally guilty, not for following conscience, but for having a defective conscience (Q. 19, A. 6).

The fourth topic is that of habits and virtues (QQ. 51, 55, & 61). The texts in this brief section give the barest glimpse at what is a huge topic in Thomas's writings on ethics. These texts bring out two main points. First, the moral life requires the development of good habits, and these habits are called virtues (Q. 55, A. 1). In particular, the human emotions and the intellect both require the development of good habits, and this requires repeated practice (Q. 51, A. 3). The habits are needed to perfect and regulate human abilities, which, without habits, are hard to regulate.

The second point is that there are four main, or cardinal, virtues (Q. 61, AA. 2–3). The doctrine of the four cardinal virtues is an ancient one that can be found in almost every major moral philosopher from the time of Plato until the early modern period. Thomas builds on the philosophy of Aristotle in providing an explanation of why there are the four cardinal virtues because of the relevant powers in human nature. The relevant powers are the intellect that reasons about moral decisions; the will; the sense appetite involved in desires for bodily goods (the concupiscible appetite); and the sense appetite involved in fear and anger (the irascible appetite). Since these are the four relevant human powers, there must be a different virtue to perfect each power. Prudence is the virtue that perfects the intellect, as the habit of sound moral reasoning; justice is the virtue of the will, by which we will to give to other people what they deserve; temperance (or self-control) is the virtue of the concupiscible appetite, regulating our desires for pleasures; and courage is the virtue of the irascible appetite, regulating our responses to dangers. From a philosophical consideration, setting aside theological virtues and the life of faith, the cardinal virtues are the essence of the moral life. For the imperfect happiness that can be had in this life and philosophically known, happiness is a life lived in accord with these four, main virtues.

The fifth topic is the natural law (QQ. 90 & 94), which Thomas presents as a way of explaining the source of moral precepts.[1] Moral precepts, Thomas says, amount to various expressions of the natural inclinations of human persons. These natural inclinations tend to goals that are good and fulfilling for human persons, and a careful reflection on these inclinations shows the basic human goods that moral precepts try to foster.

There are, Thomas tells us, three basic inclinations, giving rise to three basic sorts of human goods (Q. 94, A. 2). First, there is the very common inclination to self-preservation; this inclination is shared in a way with all substances, since everything tends to maintain its own existence and to avoid destruction. Second, there is the inclination to the goods shared among animals and human beings. Like animals, we procreate and raise our young in families, and there are thus goods of marriage, of education, of

---

1   Other moral philosophers provide such a source of moral precepts: for a Kantian, the moral precepts follow from the imperative of duty; for a utilitarian, the moral precepts follow from the goal of maximizing pleasure. Virtue ethicists, like Aristotle, have not always seen fit to offer such an explanation of where the precepts come from; natural law is Thomas's attempt to provide an answer to this question.

family obligations, and so forth. Third, there is the inclination to good things that are specifically human insofar as we are rational, intelligent persons. This third category includes a very wide range of goods, from the goods of knowledge and science to the goods of living together in human societies.

At the more general levels, natural law is unchanging and is the same for all people (Q. 94, AA. 3–4). As we descend, however, from general moral truths down to more and more specific cases, we find that what is generally true is not specifically true in all concrete cases. Thus, it is generally true that borrowed goods should be returned, but we may find some exceptional cases in which this is not true, as when the returned goods might be expected to be used by the owner for a crime. As well, natural law can be added to or subtracted from in the more specific cases, according to changes in needs and circumstances. Traffic laws may be regarded as part of the natural law, insofar as they are ordered to protect life, which is a part of the first general class of goods. Obviously, however, such rules have not always been needed, and they may not be needed in the future, and the specifics of them are not dictated by any goods of human nature. Driving on the right side of the road, for example, rather than on the left side, is not itself a dictate from human nature, but the good of preserving human life and health requires *some* such rule for safety.

Two general comments about Thomas's doctrine of natural law are in order. First, this text on natural law is *extremely* general. Thomas in this text is only laying down the principle of natural law, that moral laws are justified insofar as they help to realize the goods of human nature. The working out of specific moral precepts involves the careful consideration of individual virtues and specific conditions. This kind of moral reasoning can be found in many places in the long Second Part of the Second Part of the *Summa theologiae.* Anyone looking for a clear guide to individual moral precepts just from reading this question on natural law will be disappointed.

Second, the ethics of Thomas is often described as a "natural law ethics," and this claim is true to an extent. It is worth noting, however, that this one Question on natural law is the *only* formal treatment of natural law anywhere in Thomas's vast writings. By contrast, any other important topic in Thomistic philosophy has usually been treated formally in five to ten different locations, as Thomas treated all important topics repeatedly at different times in his life and in different kinds of writing. The natural law, however, was explained formally by Thomas only in this one question with its six articles. By contrast, the treatment of virtues and vices requires more than 100 questions in the Second Part of the Second Part of the *Summa theologiae*. The doctrine of natural law is fundamental to Thomistic ethics, but this ethics may be more accurately called a virtue ethics.

The Appendices provide a series of *contrasting* texts from mediaeval authors (and one from Descartes) on important problems dealt with by Thomas. These texts show opposing positions or arguments against Thomas's position. Appendices A–E deal with the existence of God. Anselm (Appendix A) and Descartes (Appendix E) provide ontological arguments for the existence of God, arguments based on an understanding of the essence of God or what it means to be God. Bonaventure (Appendix B) argues that the existence of God is so certain that it really cannot be thought that God does not exist. John Duns Scotus (Appendix C) gives an argument that combines both ontological arguments and an argument from effect to cause. William of Ockham (Appendix D) argues from effects to cause that there must be *some* cause of our world, but not necessarily a transcendent God. Appendices F and G provide contrasting arguments on the problem of the human soul and immortality. In Appendix F, Scotus argues that if the soul is taken as the form of the body (as Thomas claims) it cannot also be shown to be immortal. In Appendix G, Ockham argues (against both Thomas and Scotus) that the soul cannot be known to be the form of the human body. Appendices H and I show contrasting views on the human will. Scotus, in Appendix H, argues that the fundamental source of human wrongdoing is the excessive love of our own happiness, something Thomas would have found impossible, and in Appendix I, Ockham argues that the human will wills nothing necessarily, not even its own happiness.

Philosophers and Theologians Referred to by Thomas Aquinas

The following list includes all of the philosophers and theologians to whom Thomas refers in the texts included in this volume.

Alan of Lille (c. 1128–1202/03). Alain de Lille or Alanus ab Insula was a French theologian and poet. He was philosophically influenced by neo-Platonism and had a broad range of theological and moral interests.

Anaximines (c. 585–c. 528 BCE). Anaximenes of Miletus was a pre-Socratic philosopher who, like Thales, identified a fundamental material source or underlying element. He thought that it was air and that a process of condensation and rarefaction can explain change and different kinds of substances.

Anselm (1033–1109). St. Anselm was a Benedictine monk who became abbot of the monastery at Bec (in Normandy) and Archbishop of Canterbury. In his *Proslogion* (1077–78) he devised the famous "ontological argument" to prove the existence of God. See Appendix A.

Aristotle (384–322 BCE). Aristotle, a student of Plato for 20 years, was the most influential philosopher on the scholastic period, 1200–1600. His works in logic, natural philosophy, metaphysics, and ethics provided the starting point of all scholastic philosophy. Aristotle's philosophy differed sharply from Plato's on many points. Aristotle was much more oriented to the empirical, to this world, and to natural science, of which he may be regarded as the founder.

Augustine (354–430). St. Augustine was enormously influential on all of Western theology, both Catholic and Protestant, on a range of topics: creation, the Trinity, sin, free will, grace, Christian morality, biblical exegesis, and so forth. His *Confessions* is a classic of autobiography and theology. In philosophy, he was heavily influenced by neo-Platonic thinking, especially the philosophy of Plotinus.

Averroes (1126–98). Averroes, or Ibn Rushd, was a philosopher who lived most of his life in the Muslim-controlled southern part of Spain. His most important philosophical works were long commentaries on all of the major works of Aristotle. These commentaries were translated into Latin and read by Thomas and other scholastics. For this reason, Averroes was called the Commentator, and his interpretations of Aristotle at times were in conflict with Christian teaching.

Avicenna (980–1033). Avicenna, or Ibn Sina, was a philosopher from Persia who achieved a synthesis of Aristotelian and neo-Platonic philosophy. His works in metaphysics and epistemology were translated into Latin and read by scholastic thinkers like

Thomas. Avicenna's doctrine of being was particularly influential on Thomas.

Boethius (c. 475–524/25). Boethius was a Roman senator and consul who eventually fell into disfavour with the Ostragoth King, Theodoric, and was put to death for treason. He translated most of Aristotle's logical works into Latin, wrote some influential theological treatises (one of which prompted an important commentary by Thomas), and, while in prison, wrote his famous *The Consolation of Philosophy*, a great meditation on the problem of evil and God's providence.

Democritus (c. 460–c. 370 BCE). Democritus was a pre-Socratic philosopher who was understood by Thomas to have been a materialist (believing that the only real things are material things) and an atomist (believing that the ultimate building blocks of all material things are indestructible and invisible material units).

Dionysius (5th–6th century). Pseudo-Dionysius the Areopagite, or Pseudo-Denys, may have been a Syrian Christian. He claimed to have been the Dionysius who was with St. Paul at the Areopagus in Athens. He was neo-Platonic in philosophy, probably influenced by Proclus. He wrote a number of works in mystical theology, on one of which, *On the Divine Names*, Thomas wrote a commentary.

Empedocles (c. 490–c. 430 BCE). Empedocles was a pre-Socratic philosopher who is remembered chiefly for having first developed the theory that all natural substances are made up of four primary elements: earth, water, air, and fire. This theory was adopted by Aristotle and Thomas and had a very long life, lasting into the early modern period.

Gregory of Nyssa (c. 335–c. 395). St. Gregory of Nyssa was, along with his brother, Basil, and friend, Gregory Nazianzus, known as one of the Cappadocian Fathers. He was a Greek Church Father whose influence was extensive in the Catholic and Protestant West. See also Nemesius.

Heraclitus (c. 535–c. 475 BCE). Heraclitus of Ephesus was a pre-Socratic philosopher who was taken by Aristotle and Thomas to have held that the primal element of all material substances was fire. He was also understood to have held a doctrine of constant flux: all things were changing all the time.

Hugh of St. Victor (c. 1096–1141). Hugh of St. Victor was a French theologian who became the head of St. Victor, a school in Paris. He reflects the great influence of the theology of St. Augustine.

Isidore of Seville (c. 560–636). Isidore became Bishop of Seville; his writings are a great effort to preserve ancient learning at a time when this was most difficult. He wrote an etymological encyclopaedia, called *Etymologiae* (*"Etymologies"*), sometimes going by the title *Origines* ("Sources").

John of Damascus (675/76–749). St. John of Damascus was a Syrian monk and priest who was a polymath. His systematic account of Orthodox theology, *De fide orthodoxa* ("On the Orthodox Faith," as it was known to the scholastics) was very influential on scholastics like Thomas. This work incorporates material from Nemesius's *De natura hominis*.

Lombard, Peter (c. 1096–1160). Peter Lombard was an early scholastic theologian who compiled (c. 1150) four books of "Sentences," that is, opinions or judgements of theological authorities. It contains quotations from all of the major Church Fathers and other theological writers, arranged according to topic. All theology students had to compose a commentary on the *Sentences* of Peter Lombard. These commentaries would be roughly the equivalent of our PhD thesis.

Maimonides (1135–1204). Moses ben Maimon, or Moses Maimonides, was born in Cordoba and eventually lived in Morocco and Egypt, where he died. He was a Rabbi, one of the greatest mediaeval scholars of the Torah. His *The Guide of the Perplexed* was enormously influential on Thomas regarding problems of creation and biblical interpretation. Thomas called him Rabbi Moses.

Melissus (fl. 5th century BCE). Melissus of Samos was a philosopher of the Eleatic school, along with Parmenides and Zeno. Aristotle associates Melissus's teaching with that of Parmenides.

Nemesius (fl. c. 390). Nemesius was a Christian philosopher who lived in present-day Syria. He wrote a work on human nature, *De natura hominis* (*On the Nature of the Human Person*) that drew upon Aristotle. This work was believed by Albert the Great and Thomas to have been written by Gregory of Nyssa; it had, therefore, great philosophical and theological authority with them. Parts of this work were also incorporated into the major work of John of Damascus, *De fide orthodoxa* (*On the Orthodox Faith*).

Parmenides (fl. late 6th–early 5th century BCE). Parmenides of Elea was a pre-Socratic philosopher and the first of the Eleatic philosophers, including also Zeno and Melissus of Samos. His philosophical poem *On Nature* was a metaphysical *tour de force*, arguing that changing realities were matters of opinion and ultimately illusory. What could really be known was being, and this was thought to be transcendent, eternal, and unchanging.

Plato (427–347 BCE). Arguably the most influential philosopher of all time, Plato wrote dialogues that are fresh and lively philosophical discussions even in modern translations. He founded his famous Academy, where Aristotle studied for 20 years, which existed for almost 900 years. Plato's doctrines included separate Forms, innate ideas and recollection, the immortality of the human soul, the identification of virtue with knowledge, and so forth. Thomas regarded Plato as the most important philosopher to answer, as he did extensively in his discussions of human nature (see Chapter 3). It must be remembered that Thomas probably never read Plato's actual dialogues but gained his knowledge of Platonic doctrines from other sources, such as Augustine, Boethius, the Pseudo-Dionysius, and others.

Pythagoras (c. 570–c. 495 BCE). Pythagoras of Samos was a mathematician and philosopher. A number of mathematical discoveries are attributed to him (such as the Pythagorean Theorem), and he was influential on Plato.

Speusippus (c. 410–335/34 BCE). Speusippus was Plato's nephew. A philosopher like his uncle, he became head of the Academy after Plato died (347 BCE).

Thales (c. 623–c. 546 BCE). Thales of Miletus is generally regarded as the first philosopher in the entire Greek tradition. It is he who began the attempt, carried on by other philosophers from Asia Minor, to identify the basic element of all material things. According to Thales, that basic elemental source was water.

Thomas Aquinas: A Brief Chronology[1]

1216	The Order of Preachers (Dominican Order) founded.
1224/25	Thomas born at Roccasecca (region of Naples).
1230–39	Becomes oblate at Benedictine Abbey of Montecassino.
1239–44	Studies at university in Naples.
1244	Becomes a Dominican.
1244–45	Detained by family at Roccasecca.
1245–48	Studies in Paris under guidance of Albert the Great.
1248–52	Studies with Albert in Cologne at *Studium Generale*.
1252–56	Teaches at Paris as a Bachelor of the *Sentences* (the equivalent roughly of being a graduate assistant, completing the PhD).
1256–59	Regent Master in Paris (a professorial appointment).
1261–65	Lector at Dominican Convent of Orvieto.
1265–68	Teaches as Regent Master in Rome.
1268–72	Regent Master for a second time in Paris.
1270	Condemnation of 13 Propositions of Radical Aristotelianism by Bishop Stephen Tempier of Paris.
1272–73	Teaches as Regent Master in Naples.
1274	Dies at Fossanova (7 March).
1277	Condemnation of 219 Propositions by Bishop Stephen Tempier of Paris (some propositions included were held by Thomas).
1323	Canonization in Avignon (18 July).
1325	Revocation of Condemned Propositions held by Thomas (Stephen Bourret, Bishop of Paris).
1567	Proclaimed "Doctor of the Church" (*Doctor Ecclesiae*). A Doctor of the Church is a saint whose teaching has been recognized by the Church to be reliably sound. There are 36 such recognized doctors, including saints such as Augustine, Anselm, Bonaventure, and Albert the Great.
1879	Proclamation by Pope Leo XIII of encyclical *Aeterni Patris* (indicating a special place in the Church's teaching for the thought of Thomas Aquinas).

---

1 See also the excellent Chronology in Porro 439–44.

A Note on the Texts

The texts of Thomas are taken from two sources. Chapter 1, "The Principles of Nature," is taken from the critical edition of this work.[1] It is a short expository work that I have translated as a whole. The texts in Chapters 2, 3, and 4 are taken from the Ottawa edition of the *Summa theologiae*.[2] These texts have been taken out of their original context, shortened, and rearranged. Each part of the *Summa theologiae* is divided into questions, and each question is divided into articles. Each article treats a topic that is often given in the form of a question (e.g., "Does God exist?"). In the original texts, the format of each article is as follows: first, there are initial objections (usually three or four) that present apparent or real objections to the position that Thomas will take. Second, there is usually one argument given against these objections, often an argument from some authority. Third, there is Thomas's answer to the problem of the article, sometimes called the body of the article. Fourth, Thomas responds to the initial objections, sometimes, with needed qualifications, accepting the objections. In this translation, I have taken the liberty of rearranging and abridging the articles. In Chapters 2, 3, and 4, I have begun each article with Thomas's answer. After it, I have usually given only one or two objections, followed by Thomas's response to those objections; in some cases, I have given no objections at all. I have rearranged the material of the articles in this way with the goal of making Thomas's meaning and arguments clearer. Once his own position is stated and argued for, the objections and replies should make more sense.

Whenever Thomas quotes an author verbatim, I have translated the given quotation from the Latin that Thomas gave. I have not attempted to provide an original or authoritative translation from a printed source. I wanted to reflect the quotations as Thomas gave them, not as they might be in an original source. I have done this for all sources: philosophical, theological, and biblical.

References to the *Summa theologiae* are given thus: *ST* I, Q. 2,

---

1   Thomas Aquinas, *De principiis naturae* in *Opera omnia*, ed. Leonine Commission, vol. 43, Santa Sabina, 1976, 39–47.

2   *S. Thomae de Aquino Summa theologiae*, ed. Mediaeval Institute of Ottawa, 5 vols., Commissio Piana, 1941.

A. 3, where "*ST*" stands for *Summa theologiae*, "I" indicates First Part, "Q. 2" indicates Question 2, and "A. 3" indicates Article 3. When the First Part of the Second Part is referred to, the Roman numerals appear thus: I-II.

I have also endeavoured to provide a *translation into English* and not a literal, word-for-word, transposition of Latin terms into English. Purists may find my translation too free. So be it. I have tried to capture the literal meaning of the text but in the idiom of contemporary English so that a first-time reader today can actually make sense of the text just from reading it. Whenever an addition to the translation was needed that seemed to go beyond the bounds of a translation, I have indicated the addition in square brackets. Thomas had a remarkable ability to write clearly, simply, and concretely. I hope that I have reproduced those qualities.

BASIC PHILOSOPHICAL WRITING

Chapter 1: *The Principles of Nature*

Section 1: The Three Principles

Notice the difference between what *can exist*, although it does not, and what *exists*. That which *can exist* we call *being in potency*; that which already *exists* we call *being in actuality*. There are, furthermore, two kinds of being: a thing's essential or substantial being, for example, being a human person, which is being absolutely; the other is accidental being, for example, being pale, which is being in a qualified way.

Something is in potency to every kind of being. For example, the human sperm or ovum is in potency to being a human person; likewise, the person is in potency to being pale. Both that which is in potency to substantial being and that which is in potency to accidental being can be called matter, as the sperm and ovum are the matter of the human person, and the human person is the matter of paleness. There is, however, a difference, because the matter that is in potency to substantial being is called the matter "out of which" the thing arises, whereas the matter that is in potency to accidental being is called the matter "in which" the accident arises.

To speak accurately, what is in potency to accidental being is called the "subject," and what is in potency to substantial being is called the "matter." As an indication of this, we say that accidents "belong in a subject," whereas the substantial form does "not belong in a subject." The difference between "matter" and "subject" is that the subject does not gain its being from any accidents it happens to have, for it has complete being in itself; a human person, for example, does not have being from a pale colour. Matter, on the other hand, *does* have its being from something else, because all by itself its being is incomplete. Hence, we can say as a general truth that form gives being to matter, and a subject gives being to its accidents, but not the other way around. Nevertheless, we sometimes use one term in place of the other, as "matter" may be used in place of "subject," or vice versa.

Just as whatever is in potency can be called matter, so whatever gives rise to being can be called form, whether the being in question is substantial or accidental. A human person, for example, who is potentially pale becomes actually so through the form of paleness, and the sperm and ovum, which are potentially a human person, become an actual person through the soul.[1] Since the form makes actual being, the form is thereby called actuality. Further, what makes substantial being actual is the substantial form, and what makes accidental being actual is called the accidental form.

Because generation occurs when a form is acquired, there are two kinds of generation that correspond to the two kinds of form: generation in an absolute sense corresponds to substantial form, and generation in a qualified sense corresponds to accidental form. When a substantial form is brought into being, we say that something has simply come into being. When, however, an accidental form is brought into being, we do not say that something has simply come into being, but that, while already existing, it has come to be *this modified thing*. For example, when someone becomes pale, we do not say, absolutely, that the person comes into being or is generated, but rather that he or she becomes pale or is changed in colour. Furthermore, two kinds of corruption correspond to the two kinds of generation, namely, corruption absolutely and corruption in a qualified sense. Absolute generation and corruption belong only in the category of substances, but generation and corruption in the qualified sense belong to all the different kinds of accidents.

Since generation is a kind of change from non-being to being, and, contrariwise, corruption is a change from being to non-being, generation does not come about from just any non-being but only from the non-being that is being-in-potency. The statue, for example, comes into being from the bronze, which is a statue in potency, not in actuality.

In order that generation take place, therefore, three things are required: being-in-potency, which is *matter*; non-being-in-actuality, which is *privation*; and that through which the new reality becomes actual, namely, *form*. When, for example, a statue is sculpted from a piece of bronze, the bronze which is in potency to the form of the statue is the matter; the fact that the bronze is unshaped or not sculpted is called privation; and the shape by which the bronze is recognizably a statue is the form. This is not, however, *substantial* form, because the bronze before the coming of form or shape is an actual being, and its being does not depend upon that shape, which is an accidental form. All artificial forms,

---

1 The soul is the substantial form of the human being, and paleness is the accidental form of being pale.

in fact, are accidental forms, because art operates only on that which is already naturally constituted as a complete being.

Section 2: Privation and Matter

There are, therefore, three principles of nature, namely: matter, privation, and form. One of these, form, is that which generation achieves, and the other two are those from which generation comes. Hence, matter and privation are the same in subject but different in meaning. Before it receives its form, that which is bronze is the same thing as that which is unshaped, but by one meaning it is called bronze and by another it is called unshaped. Hence, privation is called, not an essential principle, but an accidental principle, because it is an accidental feature of matter. If we say, for example, "the doctor is building," this is accidental, for a person builds not by being a doctor but by being a carpenter, but it just so happens—accidentally—that this one person is also a doctor.

There are two kinds of accident: the necessary accident, which is not separated from the thing, like the ability to laugh in a human being; and the non-necessary accident, which is separable, like having a pale complexion. Accordingly, although privation is an accidental principle, it is still necessary for generation, because matter is never found without privation. Insofar as matter exists under one form, it has the privation of some other form, and vice versa. In fire, for example, there is the privation of air, and in air there is the privation of fire.[1]

Although generation occurs from non-being, we say that *privation*, and not *negation*, is the principle of generation, because

---

1 Thomas refers here to the chemistry of his day, according to which there were four elements—earth, air, fire, and water—and each of these elements can be changed into others. Air, when consumed, can be changed into fire, and fire, when extinguished, into air. Air, thus, is the matter out of which fire can come into existence, and fire is the matter out of which air can come into existence. Air, thus, has the actual form of air and simultaneously the *privation* of fire, and likewise, fire has the actual form of fire and simultaneously the *privation* of air. A contemporary example might be water. Hydrogen and oxygen, as separate gases, are not water but may become water; as gases they have the privation of water. When they undergo the chemical change and become water, the resultant water now has the privation of hydrogen and oxygen. The water is *not* hydrogen and oxygen, but it may be decomposed into hydrogen and oxygen.

the term "negation" does not imply a specific subject. The term "does not see" can be said even of non-beings, as, one might say, "the chimera does not see," or also of beings which are not naturally able to see, for example, of rocks. Privation, however, is only said of some definite subject in which the quality can naturally be found, as blindness is only said of those things which can by nature have the ability to see.

Privation is called a principle of generation, because generation does not come about from just any non-being but from the non-being that is in some pre-existing specified subject. Fire, for example, does not come into being from just anything that is not fire but only from the sort of thing which is not fire but could naturally become fire. Privation, however, is a principle that is different from the other two (matter and form), because the others are principles both of being and of becoming. For example, in order that a statue come to be, there must be bronze (the matter) and there must be the final shape of the statue (the form), and these two must also be present when the statue is completely finished. Privation, however, is a principle of becoming but not of being, because while the statue is coming to be it must not yet be a statue, for if it were a statue, it would not be *becoming* a statue. What comes to be exists only in successive stages. In the completed statue there is no privation of the statue, because, just as there cannot be an affirmation and a negation at the same time, so there cannot be at the same time a privation and a possession. Furthermore, privation is an accidental principle, as was explained above, whereas form and matter are essential principles.

From what has been said, therefore, it is clear that matter differs in meaning from form and from privation. Matter is that in which form and privation are recognized, as *shaped* and *unshaped* are recognized in the bronze. Sometimes matter is considered with privation and other times without privation. Bronze, for example, as the matter of the statue does not indicate privation, for when I say "bronze" I do not necessarily imply that it is unshaped or not made; on the other hand, flour, which is the matter for the making of bread, implies in itself the privation of the form of bread, because when I say "flour," I imply what is not yet made or is disordered, in relation to the form of bread. Since, in generation, the matter as subject remains but the privation does not, and since the composite is not made of matter and privation, the matter that does not imply privation is matter that remains [as the subject], but that which does imply privation is transient.

Note that matter in one sense is composed with form, in the sense that the bronze is the matter of the statue, but the bronze itself is composed of matter and form, and for this reason it is not called *prime matter*, because it *has* matter. The matter, however, that is understood to be without any form or privation, but is the subject of all form and privation, is called *prime matter*, for the reason that before it there is no other matter. This is also called in Greek *hylé* [ΰλη]. Because every definition and all knowledge comes from form, prime matter cannot be known or defined through itself, but it can be known or defined in comparison to other things. For example, prime matter is called that which is related to all forms and privations, just as bronze is related both to the actual statue and to the unshaped statue. Prime matter in this sense is matter without qualification. Something can also be called prime matter with respect to some category, as water is the prime matter of all liquid things, but it is not prime matter absolutely, because it itself is composed of matter and form and hence has a prior matter.[1]

Note, furthermore, that prime matter and also form are neither generated nor corrupted, because all generation is *from* something *to* something. That, however, *from which* generation takes place is matter; that *to which* it goes is form. If, then, matter or form were generated, there would be a matter of the generated matter, and a form of the generated form, and so on, infinitely. Hence, to speak properly, generation only belongs to the composite.

We say that prime matter is *numerically one* in all things. There are, however, two ways in which we understand "numerically one." Whatever has one individual form, like Socrates, is numerically one, but prime matter is not understood to be numerically one in this way, since in itself it has no form. Something is also understood to be numerically one when it is without the characteristics that would make it numerically different. In this way we say that prime matter is numerically one, because it is understood without any characteristics that would result in something numerically different.

Finally, it is important to understand that, although matter does not have in its nature any form or privation, as, for example, the meaning of bronze includes neither *shaped* nor *unshaped*, nev-

---

1 Any liquid, in the chemistry of Thomas's day, would be a liquid because it contains water as an elemental constituent. In this sense, water is *prime* with respect to all liquids, but water is not *prime matter*, because prime matter is matter without *any* form.

ertheless it is never found without form and privation. Matter exists at one time under one form, and at another time under another form. Just in itself, however, matter cannot exist at all, because actual being comes only from form, and matter does not include any form in itself or in its definition. It is being only in potency, and hence nothing actual can be called prime matter.

Section 3: The Four Causes

From what has been said, therefore, it is clear that the principles of nature are three: matter, form, and privation. These, however, are not enough for generation. What is in potency cannot bring itself into actuality, as the bronze which is potentially a statue cannot make itself into a statue, but it requires an agent that can draw the form of the statue from potency into actuality. As well, the form cannot draw itself from potency into actuality. I am speaking here about the form of a completed thing, which is the goal of any process of generation. Form, in fact, belongs only to the completed being, but the agent operates on the becoming, that is, it operates while the thing is coming to be. Beyond form and matter, therefore, there must be something that acts, and this is called the *efficient cause, moving cause, agent,* or *that from which the beginning of motion comes.*

Since, as Aristotle says in Book 2 of the *Metaphysics*,[1] whatever acts does so by intending something, there must be a fourth thing, namely, that which is intended by the agent, and this is called the *goal.* Every agent, whether natural or voluntary, intends a goal, but this does not mean that every agent knows the goal or deliberates about it. Voluntary agents must have a knowledge of the goal, because their actions are not determined and can be done in opposite ways. It is, thus, necessary that such beings know the goal and determine their actions accordingly. The actions of natural agents, however, are determined, and hence it is not necessary that such agents choose actions to achieve a goal. Avicenna gives the example of a kithara[2] player who strikes the notes of the chords without deliberating, since the notes are determined for him. If it were not so, then there would be delays in the striking, which would cause discord. Since even a voluntary agent, such as a kithara player, can operate without deliber-

---

1 Aristotle, *Metaphysics* 2.2, 994b9–16. On Aristotle, see p. 34.
2 A kithara is a stringed musical instrument that was played in ancient Greece.

ating, it is all the more obvious that a natural agent can intend a goal without deliberating. For the natural agent, "to intend" means nothing other than to have a natural inclination toward something.

From what has been said, therefore, it is clear that there are four causes, namely, the material cause, the efficient cause, the formal cause, and the final cause. Although the terms "principle" and "cause" may be used synonymously, as is said in Book 5 of the *Metaphysics*,[1] nevertheless in the *Physics* Aristotle distinguishes the four causes from the three principles.[2] By "causes" he understands both the intrinsic and the extrinsic: matter and form are intrinsic to the thing because they are constituent parts of the thing; the efficient cause and the final cause are extrinsic because they are outside of the thing. By "principles," however, he understands only the intrinsic causes. Privation, however, is not considered a cause, because it is an accidental principle, as has been said.[3] When we speak of the four causes, we understand them to be essential causes, in relation to which the accidental causes are understood derivatively, because whatever is accidental is derivative from what is essential.[4]

Although Aristotle uses "principles" for intrinsic causes in Book 1 of the *Physics*, nevertheless, as he says in Book 11 of the *Metaphysics*, to speak most properly, "principle" is used of extrinsic causes, while "element" can be used of the intrinsic causes, which are the parts of a thing, and "cause" can be used of both. At times, one term may be used for another, for every cause can be called a principle, and every principle can be called a cause. Still, "cause" seems to add something beyond the general meaning of principle, because whatever is first can be called a principle, whether what follows depends upon it or not. For example, a knife grinder may be called the "principle" of the knife he or she makes, since from his or her work the knife comes into being. On the other hand, when a cloth is bleached from black to white, blackness is the principle of that change, and in general anything from which motion begins is called the principle, even if the whiteness of the cloth does not depend upon the prior blackness. "Cause," however, is said only of that upon which an effect primarily depends; in other words, a cause is that upon which the

---

1 Aristotle, *Metaphysics* 5.1, 1013a17.
2 Aristotle, *Physics* 2.7, 198a22–31; 1.7, 191a12–21.
3 See pp. 47–48.
4 On the difference between essential and accidental causes, see pp. 15–16.

being of another depends. Therefore, that first condition from which change starts, i.e., privation, cannot be called the essential cause, even though it is called a principle. For this reason, privation is reckoned among the principles but not among the causes, because privation is that from which generation begins but the resultant being does not depend upon it. It can, however, also be called an accidental cause, insofar as it belongs to matter, as was explained above.

"Element," however, is the proper term only for those causes that compose the thing, and these are properly material causes. It is not, however, used for just any material cause, but only for what is primary in the composition. Hence, for example, the limbs are not the elements of a human being, because the limbs themselves are composed of other more primary things. We say, instead, that earth and water are the elements, because these are not composed of other bodies, but from these the first composition of natural bodies derives. Aristotle, accordingly, says in Book 5 of the *Metaphysics* that "the element is that from which a thing is composed first and it remains in the thing and it is not formally divisible."[1]

In the quotation just given, the meaning of the first phrase, "that from which a thing is composed first," is clear from what we have said. The second phrase, "and it remains in the thing," shows the difference between an element and the matter that entirely corrupts in generation; for example, the food that is eaten is the matter of blood, but blood is only generated after the complete corruption of food, and hence food as such does not remain in blood. Food, therefore, cannot be called an element of blood. An element, however, must remain in some way in the thing that it belongs to, since it is not corrupted, as is said in *On Generation and Corruption*.[2] The third phrase, "and it is not formally divisible," shows that elements are different from the parts of a thing that can be divided into specifically recognizable parts, like the parts of the hand, which are flesh, blood, bones, etc. The element,

---

1 Aristotle, *Metaphysics* 5.3, 1014a30–33.
2 Aristotle, *On Generation and Corruption* 1.10, 327b29–31. Just *how* the elements remain is, however, a difficulty. They do not remain *actually*, for they do undergo a substantial change when they become part of a thing, but their powers or their natural tendencies do remain. Thomas uses the term *virtus* to describe the way in which the element remains in the thing of which it is an element: the element remains *in virtute*, in its power, in the thing. See Thomas's *Metaphysicam Aristotelis Commentaria* 5.4, ¶ 795–807, ed. M.R. Cathala (Turin: Marietti, 1935), pp. 262–64.

however, cannot be divided into parts that are specifically different; all of the parts of water, for example, are water. The being of an element can be divided quantitatively, but it cannot be divided into specifically different parts. If it is not divisible, it is called an element, as the letters are called the elements of writing. It is clear, therefore, that "principle" is a wider term than "cause," and that "cause" is a wider term than "element." This is what Averroes says in Book 5 of the *Metaphysics*.[1]

Section 4: Relations among the Four Causes

Having seen that there are four kinds of causes, it should be clear that it is possible for the same thing to have more than one cause. The causes of the statue, for example, are both the bronze and the sculptor—the sculptor as efficient cause, and the bronze as material cause. It is also possible for the same thing to be the cause of contrary effects, as the captain can be the cause both of saving and of sinking the ship, for the captain causes the latter by his or her absence and the former by his or her presence.

Note also that it is possible for the same thing to be both the cause and the effect in relation to some other thing, although this can only be true in different respects. Walking, for example, is the cause of health as its efficient cause, but health is the cause of walking as its final cause, for walking is sometimes done for the sake of health. Again, the body is the matter for the soul, but the soul is the form of the body. The efficient cause is called the cause of the goal to be achieved, since the goal would not actually exist without the operation of the agent; the goal, however, is called the cause of the efficient cause, since the efficient cause only operates because the goal is intended. Hence, the efficient cause (walking, for example) causes the goal to be realized (health, for example), but it does not make health to be a desired goal. The efficient cause thus does not give the final cause its causal power, that is, it does not make the goal to be a final cause. The doctor, for example, causes health to exist in actuality, but he or she does not make health a goal to be sought. The goal, on the other hand, does not cause the efficient cause to exist, but it does cause the efficient cause to act as an efficient cause. The health that a doctor can cause, for example, does not make the doctor to be a

---

1 Averroes, *Commentary on Aristotle's Metaphysics*, Book 5, Commentary Text 4 (Aristotle, *Metaphysics* 5.3, 1014a26–1014b15). On Averroes, see p. 34.

doctor, but it makes the doctor actually treat patients. Hence, the goal is the cause of the causality of the efficient cause, because it makes the efficient cause to be actively causing. It also makes the matter to be matter and the form to be form, since the matter only acquires the form because of the goal, and the form only perfects the matter because of the goal. Hence, the goal is called "the cause of causes," because it is the cause of the causality in all causes.

Matter is called the cause of form because form only exists in matter,[1] and likewise form is the cause of matter because matter only exists actually through form. Matter and form are spoken of in relation to each other, as is said in Book 2 of the *Physics*.[2] Matter and form are understood in relation to the composite, just as parts are understood in relation to the whole, and as what is simple in relation to what is complex.

Because every cause insofar as it is a cause is naturally prior to its effect, it must be seen that "prior" has two meanings, as Aristotle says in Book 16, *On the Generation of Animals*.[3] Because of this, the cause can be prior to the effect in one sense, but the effect can be prior to the cause in another sense. In one sense, one thing is prior to another *in generation and in time*, but in another sense one thing is prior to another *in substance and in completeness*. Since the operation of nature proceeds from the imperfect to the perfect, and from the incomplete to the complete, what is imperfect is prior to what is perfect in generation and in time, but on the other hand, what is perfect is prior to what is imperfect in substance and completeness. For example, the adult is prior to the child in substance and completeness, but the child is prior to the adult in generation and time.

In generable things the imperfect is prior to the perfect and potency is prior to actuality, and in any given thing the imperfect stage is prior to the perfect stage and its potency is prior to its actuality. Nevertheless, properly speaking, actuality and perfection must be prior, because what brings potency into actu-

---

1 "Form only exists in matter." This is true for the forms of physical, material things, which is the subject of this work. There are, however, instances of forms that exist without matter; angels, for example, are pure forms that have no matter. Thomas is not considering such purely spiritual beings in this little work on the principles of physical, material nature.

2 Aristotle, *Physics* 2.2, 194b8–9.

3 Aristotle, *The Generation of Animals* 2.6, 742a19–22.

ality is itself in actuality, and what makes the imperfect perfect is itself perfect. Matter is certainly prior to form in generation and in time, for that which receives is prior to that which is received, but form is prior to matter in perfection, because matter does not have complete being except through form. Likewise, the efficient cause is prior to the final cause in generation and in time, since the efficient cause produces the motion toward the intended goal. The final cause, nevertheless, is prior to the efficient cause, because the action of an efficient cause, which brings about the completion of a substance, can only be completed through the goal or final cause. The material and the efficient causes, therefore, are prior in the process of generation, but the formal and final causes are prior in terms of perfection.

Furthermore, there are two kinds of necessity, absolute necessity and conditional necessity. Absolute necessity is the sort that comes from the causes that are prior in the process of generation, which are the matter and the efficient cause. Death, for example, is necessary because of matter, which is made up of elements with contrary properties. This sort of necessity is called absolute, because there is nothing to block it; it can also be called the necessity of matter. Conditional necessity, however, comes from the causes that are posterior in generation, which are the form and the goal. We say, for example, that conception is necessary if a human person is to be generated, but this is conditional, because it is not necessary that this woman conceive absolutely, but only conditionally—*if* a person is to be generated. This is also called the necessity of the goal.

Three of the causes—the formal, final, and efficient—can be found together in one thing, as is clear in the generation of fire. Fire generates more fire, and therefore fire is the efficient cause insofar as it generates something; but fire is also the form insofar as it is the actualization of what was before in potency. It is also the goal insofar as it is that which is intended by its own agency and as it itself is the product of its own actions.

There are two kinds of goal, the goal of generation and the goal of the thing generated. Consider the making of an artefact such as a knife. The knife itself is the goal of generation, but to cut is the operation of the knife, which is the goal of the thing generated, namely, the knife. The goal of generation can be the same as two of the other causes, that is, when one thing generates something that is the same in species, as, for example, when a human being generates a human being or an olive generates an olive. The same, however, cannot be said about the goal of the thing generated.[1]

Notice, furthermore, that the goal is individually the same as the form, because the form of the thing generated and the goal of generation are individually the same. Since the efficient cause is not individually the same as either the final cause or the formal cause but can be in the same species as those two causes, it is possible that the maker and the thing made be specifically the same, although they cannot be individually the same. When, for example, a human person generates a human person, the generating person and the generated person are individually different but specifically the same. Matter, however, cannot be identified with the other causes, because, since it is being in potency, matter has the nature of what is imperfect, whereas the other causes, since they exist in actuality, have the nature of what is perfect. The perfect and the imperfect cannot be the same thing.

Section 5: The Modes of the Causes

We have established that there are four causes: efficient, material, formal, and final. Each of these can be divided into five modes.

1. A cause can be either *prior* or *posterior*. For example, we say that both skill and the doctor are the cause of health, but skill is the prior cause and the doctor is the posterior cause. The same is also true of the formal cause and of the other causes. Notice that we should always bring our questioning back to the prior cause. If the question is, "why is that man healthy?" it can be answered, "because the doctor has healed him." If, however, the question is, "why is the doctor able to heal?" the answer is, "because of the healing skill that he has."

The term "proximate cause" is the same as "posterior cause," just as "remote cause" is the same as "prior cause." Hence, these two divisions of causes, into prior and posterior and into remote and proximate, signify the same thing. Observe that what is more universal is always called the remote cause and that what is more specific is always called the proximate cause. For example, we say that the proximate form of a human being is the definition, namely, "rational, mortal animal," but "animal" is more remote, and "substance" is still more remote. The higher form is always

---

1 The goal of generation is just the thing itself that has been generated; the goal of the thing generated is always something apart from the thing.

involved in the lower form. Likewise, the proximate matter of the statue is the brass, but the remote matter is "metal," and still more remote is "body."

2. Causes are either *essential* or *accidental*. An essential cause is the cause that is the precise cause of the effect. A builder, for example, is the essential efficient cause of the house and the wood is the essential material cause of the bench. An accidental cause is something that just happens to belong to the essential cause, as, for example, when the builder happens also to be a professor. While it is true that the professor builds a house, the skills of a builder are necessary and the professorial expertise is accidental to the project. The same is true of the other causes.

3. A cause may be either *simple* or *compound*. We indicate a simple cause when we speak of only the essential cause or of only the accidental cause, as, for example, when we say that the builder builds the house or, likewise, when we say that the doctor builds the house. We indicate a compound cause when both essential and accidental causes are indicated. We might, for example, say, "the builder, who is also a doctor, built this house."

A cause can also be simple, as Avicenna explains, when it refers to that which is the cause without the help of any other cause. The bronze of the statue, for example, without the addition of any other matter besides the bronze, is the statue; the doctor causes the patient to regain health; and fire heats. All of these are examples of simple causes. A compound cause, on the other hand, is found when several things are required for the cause to be a cause. No one rower, but rather a whole crew, is the cause of the motion of the ship, and one stone is not the matter of the house, but many are.

4. Also, a cause can be either *actual* or *potential*. An actual cause is that which is actually causing the thing, as the builder while he or she is building, or the bronze of an actual statue. On the other hand, a potential cause is that which, although it does not actually cause the thing, is nevertheless able to cause it, like the builder who is not yet building. It must be noted that when we are talking about actual causes, it is necessary that the cause and the effect be simultaneous, so that if one exists, then so also does the other. If the builder is actually a builder, then he must be building, and if the activity of building is actually going on, then there must be an actual builder. Such is not necessary, however, for merely potential causes.

5. Finally, a cause can be either universal or particular. The universal cause is relative to the universal effect and the particu-

lar cause to the particular effect. We say, for example, that fire is the cause of heat but that *this* fire is the cause of *this* heat.

Section 6: The Predication of Terms

Terms applied to the intrinsic principles, matter and form, may be the same in meaning or may be different in meaning, whether we are talking about the principles of natural things or about the things composed of them. Thus, some terms indicate what is individually the same, such as "Socrates" and "this man" (when Socrates is being pointed at). Other terms indicate what is individually different but the same in species, such as "Socrates" and "Plato," who are both human but differ as individuals. Some terms indicate what is different in species but the same in genus, such as "human being" and "donkey," which are different in species but in the same genus, animal. Still other terms indicate what is different in genus but what is the same only analogously, like "substance" and "quantity," which do not share any genus in common. These two are the same only in that both are beings. Because being is not a genus, and therefore is not predicated univocally but only analogically, the two terms are the same only analogously.

To understand this, we should understand that there are three ways in which the same term can be predicated of more than one: univocally, equivocally, and analogically. A term is predicated *univocally* when it is predicated with the same name and the same meaning or definition, as for instance when "animal" is predicated of a human being and of a donkey. Either one of these is called an animal, and either one is an animate substance capable of sensation, which is the definition of animal. A term is predicated *equivocally* of several things if the same word is predicated but with different meanings, as "dipper" is predicated of a kitchen pot and of a constellation in the sky, which are the same only in the word, but not in the definition or in the signification; the word, of course, signifies the definition, as is said in Book 4 of the *Metaphysics*.[1] A term is predicated *analogically* of many if it is predicated with different meanings but meanings which are all related to some one thing, as "health" is predicated of an animal's body, of urine, and of a drink, but it does not mean exactly the same thing in each case. Health is predicated of urine to indicate a sign of health, of the body to indicate the subject of health, and

---

1 Aristotle, *Metaphysics* 4.16, 1012a22.

of a drink to indicate the cause of health. All of these meanings, however, are related to one goal, which is health.

Sometimes the terms that are the same analogically, that is, through some relation, comparison, or correspondence, are attributed to one goal, as was clear in the example above. Sometimes they are attributed to one agent, as "doctor" is predicated of the one who operates without proper skill, like a quack, or even of the doctor's instruments, but these predications are made with respect to one agent, which is the doctor. Sometimes terms are attributed to one subject, as "being" is said of substance, of quality, of quantity, and of the other categories. The meaning according to which substance is a being is not completely the same as the meaning by which the others are beings, but all are predicated in relation to substance, which is the subject of the others. Thus, being is said primarily of substance and secondarily of the others. Being, therefore, is not a genus for substance and quantity, because any genus is predicated equally of all its constituent species. "Being," thus, is predicated analogically. This confirms what we have said, that substance and quantity are different in genus but the same by analogy.

When terms indicate what is individually the same, the form and matter are also individually the same; for example, "Tully" and "Cicero."[1] When, however, terms indicate what is the same in species but different individually, their matter and form are not the same individually but only in species, as, for example, "Socrates" and "Plato." Similarly, terms that indicate the same genus indicate also principles in the same genus. For example, the form and matter of a donkey and those of a horse differ in species but are the same in genus. Likewise, when terms indicate the same thing only analogically, their principles are the same only analogically or relatively. For example, matter, form, and privation, or potency and act, are principles of substance and also of the other categories, but the matter, form, and privation of substance and those of quantity are different in genus and are the same only relatively; the matter of a substance is related to the substance in the same way in which the matter of a quantity is related to the quantity. Just as substance is the cause of the other categories, so the principles of substance are the principles of all the other categories.

---

1 Cicero's whole name is Marcus Tullius Cicero; hence, "Tully" and "Cicero" are both names of the same man. The matter and form that make up Tully, therefore, are individually the same matter and form that make up Cicero.

Chapter 2: God
Texts from *Summa theologiae* I

A. Theology and Philosophy

Question 1: Theology: Its Nature and Contents

Article 1: Is It Necessary to Have Some Teaching that Goes Beyond Philosophy?

THOMAS'S ANSWER

For our salvation, we must have some divinely revealed teaching beyond philosophy, which is learned through human reason. The primary reason for this is that human beings are ordered to God as a goal that goes beyond the grasp of human reason. This fact is indicated in *Isaiah* 64:4: "No eye, other than your own, has seen the things that you have prepared for those who love you." It is essential that human beings have a prior understanding of their goal, so that they can order their thoughts and actions to this goal. It is, therefore, necessary for their salvation that human beings know certain things through revelation that go beyond human reason.

It is necessary, furthermore, for human beings to be instructed by divine revelation, even in those things that can be known by human reason. This is so because the truth about God that can be known by human reason would only be known by a few people, who would struggle over it for a long time and would get much of it wrong. Because our salvation depends upon our recognition of the truth about God, in order to make salvation easier and more reliable, it has been necessary for certain things to be revealed to us about God.

It is, therefore, necessary to have the revelation of sacred teaching, which goes beyond philosophy known through human reason.

OBJECTION 2

Any real teaching is always about being, because whatever is true is fundamentally true about being. All beings, however, are treated in philosophy, including the being of God. For this reason, a part of philosophy is even called "theology" or "divine science," as Aristotle says.[1] Therefore, it is not necessary to have any teaching beyond philosophy.

REPLY TO OBJECTION 2

Different sciences are distinguished by the different ways in which they make the truth known. An astronomer and a physicist can demonstrate the same truth; for example, they both can demonstrate that the earth is a globe. The astronomer demonstrates this truth by using mathematical reasoning, and mathematics abstracts from what is known about matter and the material elements. The physicist, however, reaches the same conclusion by arguing from what is known about matter and the material elements. Likewise, nothing prevents the same thing from being known about God by philosophy operating under the light of human reason and also by theology operating under the light of divine revelation. Hence, "theology" as something dependent on divine revelation is a different kind of thing from "theology" that is part of philosophy.

Article 2: Is Theology a Science?

THOMAS'S ANSWER

Theology is a science. Note, however, that there are two kinds of science. One kind of science is based on principles that are known by the natural light of the intellect; arithmetic, geometry, and so forth are examples of this sort of science. Another kind of science is based on principles that belong to some higher science, as, for example, the science of optics is based on the principles of mathematics, and music is based on the principles of arithmetic. Theology is a science in this second sense, because it is based on the principles of some higher knowledge, namely, the knowledge possessed by God and by the saints in heaven. Hence, just as music takes for granted the principles known in arithmetic, so theology takes on faith the principles revealed by God.

---

1   Aristotle, *Metaphysics* 6.1, 1026a19.

B. The Existence of God

Question 2: Does God Exist?

Article 1: Is the Existence of God Self-Evident?

THOMAS'S ANSWER

A proposition can be self-evident in two different ways. In one way, a proposition is self-evident in itself but not to us; in another way, a proposition is self-evident in itself and also to us. A proposition of either sort is self-evident if the meaning of the predicate term is included in the meaning of the subject term. For example, "a human being is an animal" is self-evident, because the meaning of "animal" [the predicate] is included in the meaning of "human being" [the subject], because being an animal is a part of what it means to be human. Now, if the meaning of the subject and predicate is known to everyone, then the proposition will be self-evident to everyone, as is the case in the first principles of demonstration, the terms of which are basic, common, and known to everyone. These are terms like "being" and "non-being," "whole" and "part," and so forth. On the other hand, if the terms of a self-evident proposition are not known to everyone, the proposition will still be self-evident in itself, but it will not be self-evident to those who do not know the meanings of the terms. It can thus happen, as Boethius says, that "some terms and propositions are self-evident only to those with specialized knowledge."[1] For example, the proposition, "incorporeal beings do not exist in any place," is self-evident only to those with specialized knowledge.

Accordingly, I say that the proposition, "God exists," is self-evident in itself, because the predicate is identical with the subject, for God is his own being, as will be shown later. However, because we do not know what God is, the proposition "God exists" is not self-evident to us and must be demonstrated to us by means of things that are better known to us, although they are of a lesser nature than God. That is, we must demonstrate the existence of God through the effects that God causes.

---

1 Boethius, *How Substances Are Good in Virtue of Their Existence without Being Substantial Goods (De hebdomadibus)*, Rule 1. On Boethius, see p. 35.

OBJECTION 1

A truth is self-evident if the knowledge of that truth is naturally in us, as is the case with first principles. John of Damascus, in the beginning of his book, says that "the knowledge of the existence of God is naturally implanted in everyone."[1] Therefore, the existence of God is self-evident.

REPLY TO OBJECTION 1

It is true that a general and confused knowledge of God is naturally implanted in everyone. This can be seen in our desire for ultimate happiness, for God is our ultimate happiness, and the fact that we have a natural desire for happiness indicates that we have some natural knowledge of what we desire. Such a natural desire for happiness, however, does not give us any clear knowledge that God exists. If I know, for example, that some person is approaching, that knowledge does not tell me that it is Peter who is approaching, even if in fact it is Peter. Similarly, everyone desires the ultimate human good, but some people think that this good is riches, others think that it is pleasure, and others have other wrong ideas.

OBJECTION 2

A proposition is called self-evident if it is known to be true as soon as the meaning of its terms are known. Aristotle says that the first principles of demonstrations are known to be true in this way.[2] If, for example, you know what a "whole" is and what a "part" is, you immediately know that "any whole is greater than one of its parts." Likewise, if you understand the meaning of the word "God," you immediately know that God exists. The word "God" means "that than which nothing greater can be thought." It is, however, greater to exist both in reality and in the mind than to exist in the mind alone. Hence, when you understand the word "God" and have this meaning in your mind, you immediately know that God also exists in reality. Therefore, the existence of God is self-evident.

---

1 John of Damascus, *An Exposition of the Orthodox Faith* (*De fide orthodoxa*), Bk. I, Ch. 1 & 3. On John of Damascus, see p. 36.

2 Aristotle, *Posterior Analytics* 1.3, 72b18–22.

Reply to Objection 2

It is quite possible that someone who hears the word "God" will not understand it to mean "that than which a greater cannot be thought," because some people think that God is something physical. Still, even if someone should understand the meaning of "God" as "that than which a greater cannot be thought," it does not follow that he or she would understand this to mean that God would exist in reality as something outside of the mind. The real existence of God cannot be shown unless it is granted that "that than which a greater cannot be thought" exists in some way, but this is precisely what atheists deny.

Objection 3

The existence of truth is self-evident, because anyone who attempts to deny the existence of truth must affirm the existence of truth in the process; for if truth did not exist, it would be true that truth did not exist. If anything is true, it is necessary that truth exists. God, however, is Truth Itself, as is written in John 16:6, "I am the way, the truth, and the life." Therefore, the existence of God is self-evident.

Reply to Objection 3

The existence of truth in some general sense is self-evident, but the existence of the First Truth [i.e., God] is not self-evident to us.

Article 2: Is It Possible to Prove the Existence of God?

Thomas's Answer

There are two kinds of proof. One kind of proof is an argument from cause to effect, and this is a proof from what is absolutely prior to what is posterior. The other kind of proof is an argument from effect to cause, and this is an argument from what is prior in our knowledge [to what is posterior in our knowledge]. When an effect is better known to us than its cause, our knowledge proceeds from the effect to the cause of that effect. From any given effect a proof can be given of its proper cause, provided that the effect is better known to us. Since the effect always depends on its cause, for any given effect there must be a pre-existent cause.

Hence, the existence of God, which is not self-evident to us, can be proven through the effects that are known to us.

OBJECTION 1

The existence of God is an article of faith. Whatever belongs to the faith cannot be proven, because proofs or demonstrations produce *knowledge*, but faith is about "the things that cannot be known."[1] Therefore, the existence of God cannot be proven.

REPLY TO OBJECTION 1

The existence of God and other truths of this sort that can be known by natural reason, truths about which Paul was speaking in Romans 1:20,[2] are not articles of faith; rather, they are *preambles* to the articles of faith. This is an indication that faith presupposes natural knowledge, just as grace presupposes nature, and as whatever is brought to perfection presupposes a prior state of imperfection. Furthermore, there is no reason why a truth that can be proven and known could be taken on faith by someone who does not grasp the proof.

OBJECTION 2

In order to give a proof, the nature of the thing to be proven must be known. It is not possible, however, for us to know what God is, for we can only understand what God is not, according to John of Damascus.[3]

REPLY TO OBJECTION 2

When a proof is given from effect to cause, it is necessary to understand about the cause only that it is the cause of the given effect, because the proper definition of the cause cannot be given.

---

1 Hebrews 11:1.
2 "The invisible things of God can be known through those things that have been made by God." Romans 1:20. This verse from St. Paul was generally taken by mediaeval theologians to indicate that we can know God's existence philosophically from a consideration of the world God has made. Thomas uses it thus later in *ST* I, Q. 13, A. 5, pp. 83–86.
3 John of Damascus, *An Exposition of the Orthodox Faith (De fide orthodoxa)*, Bk. 1, Ch. 4.

This is especially so in the case of God. Whenever we prove the existence of something, we can only know what the name of the cause means; we cannot know the real nature of the cause. This is so because the nature of something cannot be discovered until after its existence is known. The names of God are given to God from the effects that he causes, as will be discussed later.[1]

OBJECTION 3

The only way to prove the existence of God is through the effects caused by God. The effects, however, are not proportionate to the cause, because he is infinite and the effects are finite. There can be no proportion between the infinite and the finite. Since a cause cannot be proven through an effect that is not proportionate to it, it seems that it is not possible to prove the existence of God.

REPLY TO OBJECTION 3

From effects that are not proportionate to their cause it is not possible to have a perfect knowledge of the cause, but nevertheless from any effect known to us it is possible to demonstrate the existence of the cause, as I have said. Hence, from the effects caused by God it is possible to demonstrate that God exists, although we are not able to attain a perfect knowledge of God's essence through such effects.

Article 3: Does God Exist?

THOMAS'S ANSWER

The existence of God can be proven in five ways.

The first and most manifest way is through motion. It is a fact and obvious to our senses that some things are moved in this world. Whatever is moved is moved by something else. This is so because nothing is moved unless it is first in a potential state toward the goal to which it is moved. The cause of motion, on the other hand, is in an actual state. For example, fire, which is actually hot, makes wood, which is potentially hot, to be actually so. In this way the fire moves and changes the wood. It is not possible that the same thing can be simultaneously in an actual and in

---

1 *ST* I, Q. 13, A. 1, pp. 79–80.

a potential state in exactly the same way. What is actually hot cannot at the same time be potentially hot but is, rather, potentially cold. It is, therefore, impossible that something be simultaneously, in exactly the same respect, both the mover and the thing moved. In other words, it is impossible that anything can move itself. Therefore, whatever is moved must be moved by something other than itself.

Furthermore, it is not possible to suppose an infinite number of movers, for if there is no first mover, then there are no other movers, either. The other, secondary movers are only movers because they are moved by the primary mover. For example, the stick [secondary mover] is moved by the hand [primary mover]. It is, therefore, necessary to come to some primary mover, which is moved by no other mover, and this everyone understands to be God.

The second way is taken from what it means to be an efficient cause. We find in the things of our experience that there is an order among efficient causes, which means that it is never possible for anything to be the efficient cause of itself. If something were the efficient cause of itself, it would have to be prior to itself, which is impossible.

Furthermore, it is not possible that there be an infinite number of efficient causes. This is so because in all series of coordinated efficient causes, the first is the cause of the intermediate cause, and the intermediate cause is the cause of the last cause. It does not matter how many intermediate causes there are; if the cause is removed, the effect is removed. Therefore, if there is no first efficient cause, neither will there be any intermediate efficient cause or a last efficient cause. Clearly, however, there *are* efficient causes. It is necessary, therefore, to recognize some first efficient cause, which everyone calls God.

The third way is taken from a consideration of what is possible and what is necessary. It goes like this. We find some things that are possible to be or not to be, because some things are generated and destroyed, and such things have the possibility either to be or not to be. It is impossible, however, that anything of this nature can exist forever, because whatever can possibly not exist at some time will not exist. If, therefore, all things could possibly not exist, at some time or other, nothing would exist. This is clearly not the case, for it would mean that now nothing would exist, since something can only come to exist from what already does exist. If there were nothing in existence, it would have been impossible for anything to begin to exist, and thus there would be nothing existing now, which is clearly false. It cannot, therefore, be the case that all beings are merely possible beings; it must be the case that some are necessarily existing. Whatever is necessarily existing either has the cause of its necessity from something else or not.

Again, it is not possible to have an infinite number of causes of necessity, just as we saw above that it is not possible to have an infinite number of efficient causes. It is, therefore, necessary to recognize the existence of something that exists necessarily through itself and does not have the cause of its necessity from outside of itself. This being is the cause of necessity in other things, and everyone calls this God.

The fourth way is taken from the grades of being in things. We find that some things have more goodness, more truth, more nobility, and so forth, than other things. We say "more" or "less" about different things because we recognize a "most." For example, things are more or less hot, because we recognize a maximum in heat.[1] Similarly, there is something that is the maximum in truth, goodness, and nobility, and consequently, the maximum in being, as Aristotle said.[2] Whatever is the maximum in its category is the cause of all the other things in the category. Fire, for example, is the hottest of things and is the cause of heat in all other cases, as Aristotle said in the same place. There is, therefore, something that is the cause of being and goodness in all things, and this we call God.

The fifth way is taken from the order of things. We see that some things that lack knowledge, such as natural bodies, operate for the sake of a goal. This is apparent from the fact that they always or for the most part operate in the same way, and in this way achieve what is best. It is clear that they achieve their goal, not by chance, but by intention. Those things that lack knowledge do not tend toward a goal unless they are so directed by intelligence, as the arrow is directed to the target by the archer. There is, therefore, some intelligent being, by whom all natural things are ordered to a goal, and this we call God.

OBJECTION 1

If one of two contrary things is infinite, the other contrary cannot possibly exist. God, by his very name, is understood to be an infi-

---

1   For Thomas, the maximum in heat would be the element of fire, understood to be something like one of our chemical elements. Any fire he experienced would have been a lesser version of that elemental fire.
2   Aristotle, *Metaphysics* 2.1, 993b22–30.

nitely good being. If, therefore, God does exist, no evil could possibly exist. Evil, however, does exist in the world. Therefore, God does not exist.

REPLY TO OBJECTION 1

As Augustine says, "Since God is supremely good, he would not permit anything of evil to exist in his works, unless he were so omnipotent and good that he would bring good even out of evil."[1] It is characteristic of the infinite goodness of God that he allows evils to exist and that he brings good out of them.

OBJECTION 2

We must not suppose more causes than we need in order to explain effects. It seems, however, that everything that happens in the world can be explained by causes other than God, if we suppose that God does not exist. Natural things can be explained entirely by causes in nature, and artificial things can be explained by human reason and will. There is no need, therefore, to suppose that God exists.

REPLY TO OBJECTION 2

Since nature operates for determinate goals by the direction of a superior cause, it is necessary to recognize that even those things that occur by nature are caused by God as the first cause. Furthermore, as has been shown, it is necessary to find a cause beyond human reason and will, because these things are changeable and can fail. It is necessary that all moveable and possibly failing beings be caused by something that is absolutely immobile and necessary in itself, as has been shown.[2]

---

1 Augustine, *Enchiridion on Faith, Hope, and Charity*, Ch. 3, ¶ 11. On Augustine, see p. 34.
2 In the Five Ways, *ST* I, Q. 2, A. 3, pp. 67–69.

C. Properties of God

Question 3: The Simplicity of God

Article 1: Is God a Body?

THOMAS'S ANSWER

God is certainly not a body; three arguments make this clear.

First, no body causes another body to move unless it itself is moved, as is obvious from our experience. I showed above[1] that God is the first mover and that the first mover is unmoved. From this it is clear that God is not a body.

Second, it is necessary that the First Being be completely actual and not at all in potency. It is true that, among things that change and move, potentiality precedes actuality temporally, but absolutely, actuality is prior to potentiality, because something in a state of potentiality can only be brought into actuality by something that is already actual. I showed above that God is the First Being.[2] It is therefore impossible that there be any potentiality in God. Every body, however, is in potency, because bodies can always be divided and hence are always potentially different. It is impossible, therefore, that God be a body.

Third, God is the most noble of all beings, as I have shown.[3] No body, however, could be the most noble of all beings. Bodies are either living or non-living. Living beings are clearly nobler than non-living bodies. Living bodies, however, are alive because of some non-bodily factor, for otherwise all bodies would be alive. It is necessary, therefore, that whatever is alive is so through something other than the body, as, for example, our bodies are alive through our souls. That non-bodily factor, by which the body becomes alive, is nobler than the body. It is impossible, therefore, that God be a body.

---

1   The First Way of proving the existence of God, *ST* I, Q. 2, A. 3, pp. 67–68.

2   The Third Way of proving the existence of God, *ST* I, Q. 2, A. 3, pp. 68–69.

3   The Fourth Way of proving the existence of God, *ST* I, Q. 2, A.3, p. 69.

Article 3: Is God Identical with His Essence or Nature?

THOMAS'S ANSWER

God is identical with his essence or nature. To help us understand this, we should note that in things that are composed of form and matter, the essence or nature must be different from the individual. The essence or nature includes whatever belongs to the definition of the species; "humanity," for example, includes whatever belongs to the definition of a human being, that is, whatever it is that makes a human being to be human. Individual matter, however, along with all of the individual accidents, does not fall within the definition of the species. *This flesh* or *these bones* do not fall within the definition of a human being, nor does skin colour or anything else of that sort. Hence, *this flesh*, *these bones*, and any *individual accidents peculiar to the individual* do not belong to the definition of humanity. Nevertheless, these things are included in an individual human being. And therefore, to be a human being includes more than the definition of humanity. Hence, "human being" and "humanity" do not mean the same thing, because "humanity" indicates the formal *part* of a human being, since the definition represents the formal part in comparison to the individual matter.

On the other hand, in things that are not composed of matter and form, which are not individuated by individual matter (*this* matter), it is necessary that their forms by themselves simply are individuals.[1] In these kinds of things, there is no difference between the individual and the nature. Since God is not composed of matter and form, as we have shown,[2] it is necessary that God and his nature are one, just as God is his own life, and is whatever else is true about him.

---

1   If something is not composed of matter and form, it must be a form alone without matter. An angel, on Thomas's understanding, would be such a being. Angels are not material beings; they are not composed of matter and form; they simply are existent forms. That is to say, each individual angel is different from every other angel because it is a different form, that is, a different *kind* of being. This means that each angel is its own nature. What is true of angels, Thomas is saying here, is also true of God, because neither angels nor God are composed of matter and form.

2   *ST* I, Q. 3, A. 2 (not included in this volume).

Article 4: Is God Identical with His Being?

THOMAS'S ANSWER

God is not only identical with his own nature, as we have just shown, but also with his own being. This can be shown in a number of ways. First, whatever is outside of the essence of a thing is caused either by the essential principles of the thing (such as the proper accidents that belong to the species; the ability to laugh, for example, is consequent upon being human and is caused by the essential principles of a human being); or it is caused by something outside, as heat is caused in water by fire. If, therefore, the being of a thing is different from its essence, it is necessary that this being be caused either by the essential principles of the thing or by something outside. It is, however, impossible that being be caused by the essential principles of any thing, because no thing can cause itself to exist, if its being has a cause. It is, therefore, true that anything whose being is different from its essence must have that being caused by something else. This, however, cannot be true about God, because God is the first efficient cause [of all being]. It is impossible, therefore, that God's being and his essence be different.

Second, being is the actuality of every form or nature; if we say that goodness or humanity exists in actuality, we mean that it exists in being. If being is different from essence, this means that being is compared to essence as actuality is compared to potentiality. Since it is true that God is not potential in any way, as we have seen,[1] it follows that God's essence cannot be different from his being. Hence, God's essence is his being.

Third, just as that which *has* fire *is not* fire, but is rather something that shares in the nature of fire, so that which *has* being and *is not* being is something that shares in being. God, however, is his own essence, as has been shown.[2] If God were not his own being, he would merely share in being, and he would not have being essentially. God would not, in such a case, be the first being, which is absurd to say. God, therefore, is not only his own essence but also his own being.

---

1 *ST* I, Q. 3, A. 1, p. 71.
2 *ST* I, Q. 3, A. 3, p. 72.

Question 4: The Perfection of God

Article 1: Is God Perfect?

THOMAS'S ANSWER

We learn from Aristotle that ancient philosophers like Pythagoras and Speusippus did not think that the First Principle is the "best and most perfect."[1] These ancient philosophers thought this because they were thinking only about the first *material* principle; it is, of course, true that the first material principle is very imperfect. Since matter by its very nature is in potency, it is necessary that the first material principle be most in potency and, therefore, most imperfect.

God, however, is understood to be, not the first material principle, but the first among all efficient causes. As such, God must be the most perfect. Just as matter by its very nature is in potency, so the efficient or agent cause, by its very nature, is in actuality. For this reason, the first active principle must be completely in actuality and, consequently, the most perfect of all. We call something perfect when it is in actuality, because to be perfect means that nothing is lacking.

OBJECTION 3

It was shown above[2] that the essence of God is his own being, but being itself seems to be very imperfect, since it is common to all things and it receives various added perfections. God, therefore, is imperfect.

REPLY TO OBJECTION 3

Being itself is the most perfect of all things, because it is the actuality of all things. Nothing has actuality unless it exists; being itself is the actuality of all things and even of their forms. It is, therefore, not the *receiver* of other perfections; it is rather that which is received. When we talk about the being of a man or of a horse, "being" is considered to be the formal part that is received, and not the part that is receiving the perfection.

---

1 Aristotle, *Metaphysics* 12.7, 1072b30–34. On Pythagoras, see p. 37; on Speusippus, see p. 37.
2 *ST* I, Q. 3, A. 4, p. 73.

Article 2: Are the Perfections of All Things Found in God?

THOMAS'S ANSWER

The perfections of all things are found in God. God is therefore called completely perfect, because "no good thing in any category is lacking to God," as Averroes says.[1] This can be seen in two ways.

First, any perfection that is found in the effect must also be found in the efficient cause of that effect. This is true either because the perfection is the same in the cause as it is in the effect, if the cause and the effect are of the same nature, as when human beings generate other human beings; or this is true because the perfection in the cause exists in a better way than in the effect, if the cause and effect are different kinds of things, as when the sun contains some likeness of all things that are generated through the power of the sun. It is clear that the effect pre-exists in the power of the efficient cause; to pre-exist in the power of an efficient cause is to pre-exist in a more perfect way, not in a less perfect way. On the other hand, to pre-exist in the power of a material cause is to pre-exist in a less perfect way, because matter, by its very nature, is imperfect, whereas an efficient cause is perfect by its own nature. Since God is the first efficient cause of all things, it is necessary that the perfections of all things pre-exist in God in a better way than they exist in the effects. Dionysius suggests this argument when he says about God, "God is not this, nor is he that; he is rather all things, because he is the cause of all things."[2]

Second, as we showed above,[3] God is in himself subsistent being, which means that God must contain in himself all the perfection of being. It is clear that, if something hot is not *perfectly* or *completely* hot, it does not have all that belongs to the nature of heat. If, however, there were something that is subsistent heat in itself, nothing of the power of heat would be lacking to it. Hence, since God is subsistent being himself, nothing of the perfection of being can be lacking to him. The perfection of being includes the perfections of all things, because, if something is perfect, it

---

1 Averroes, *Commentary on Aristotle's Metaphysics*, Bk. 5, Commentary Text 21 (Aristotle, *Metaphysics* 5.16, 1021b30–1022a3). On Averroes, see p. 34.

2 Dionysius the Areopagite (Pseudo-Dionysius), *On the Divine Names*, Ch. 5, ¶ 8. On Dionysius, see p. 35.

3 *ST* I, Q. 3, A. 4, p. 74.

has being in some way. It follows that God lacks no perfections of any being. Dionysius also suggests this argument, when he says, "God does not exist in some limited way," but rather he has his own being "absolutely and completely in himself."[1] Dionysius then adds, "He is being itself for all existent things."

Question 7: The Infinity of God

Article 1: Is God Infinite?

THOMAS'S ANSWER

Aristotle tells us that "all the ancient philosophers attributed infinity to the first principle, and they were right to do so."[2] They thought that things flowed eternally from the first principle. Some of them, however, fell into error concerning the nature of the first principle, and consequently fell into error about the infinity of the first principle. They thought that the first principle was matter, and as a consequence they attributed a material infinity to the first principle, saying that there was some infinite body that was the first principle of things.

To understand this correctly, we should know that "infinite" is that which is not finite or limited. Matter is limited by form, and form is limited by matter. Matter is limited by form in the sense that matter, before it receives form, is in potency to many forms. But when it receives one form, it is limited to that form. Form, on the other hand, is limited by matter because form, considered in itself, is common to many things. But when form is received in matter, the form becomes determinately singular in that one thing.

Matter is perfected by the form that limits it. For this reason, any infinity attributed to matter is imperfect, because such an infinity is, as it were, matter without form. Form, on the other hand, is not perfected by matter; rather the full extent of form is constrained by matter. For this reason, an infinite on the side of form is not limited by matter and, therefore, is a kind of perfection.

The most formal reality of all is being itself, as I showed above.[3] Since, therefore, the divine being is not being that is

---

1 Dionysius the Areopagite (Pseudo-Dionysius), *On the Divine Names*, Ch. 1, ¶ 5.
2 Aristotle, *Physics* 3.4, 203a1–3.
3 *ST* I, Q. 4, A. 1, Reply to Obj. 3, pp. 74–75.

received in anything, but is rather subsistent being in itself, as we saw above,[1] it is clear that God is infinite and perfect.

Question 8: The Existence of God in Things

Article 1: Does God Exist in All Things?

THOMAS'S ANSWER

God is in all things, not, of course, as a part of their essences, or as an accident, but as an agent is present to that on which it acts. It is necessary that every agent be joined to that on which it immediately acts, and the agent touches its effect through its power. Hence, Aristotle proves that the thing moved and the mover must be together at the same time.[2] Since God is, by his very nature, being itself, it is necessary that created being is the proper effect of God. In the same way, *burning* is the proper effect of fire itself. God causes the effect of *being* in things, not only when things first began to exist, but for as long as they are con-served in being, just as light is caused in the air by the sun for as long as the air is illuminated by the sun. For as long as anything has being, it is necessary that God be present to that thing, causing whatever kind of being the thing has. Being is that which is most intimate and most profound in all things, since it is the formal part with respect to everything in existence, as we have seen.[3] Hence, it is necessary that God be in all things, and most intimately so.

Question 9: The Immutability of God

Article 1: Is God Completely Immutable?

THOMAS'S ANSWER

From what we have already seen, it should be clear that God is completely immutable.

First, we showed above that there is a First Being that we call God[4] and that this First Being must be pure actuality without

---

1 *ST* I, Q. 3, A. 4, p. 73.
2 Aristotle, *Physics* 7.2, 243a3–4.
3 *ST* I, Q. 4, A. 1, Reply to Obj. 3, p. 74.
4 *ST* I, Q. 2, A. 3, pp. 67–70.

any potency mixed in, because potency is absolutely secondary to actuality.[1] Anything, however, that is moved in any way must have some kind of potency in it. This makes it clear that it is impossible for God to be moved in any way.

Second, whatever is moved or changed always remains the same in some respect and also changes in other respects; for example, if something is changed from white to black, it remains substantially the same thing. Hence, it is true that anything that is moved or changed must be composed in some way. It has been shown above, however, that there is no composition at all in God, for he is completely simple.[2] Hence it is clear that God cannot be moved.

Third, whatever is moved must, by its motion, acquire or attain something new that it did not have before. God, however, because he is infinite, includes in his immensity all of the perfections of all beings. As such, God cannot acquire something or attain something that He does not already include. Hence, motion is completely incompatible with the nature of God.

Thus, some of the ancient philosophers, forced by the truth of such considerations, held that the first principle is immutable.[3]

Question 10: The Eternity of God

Article 1: Is God Eternal, that Is, Does He Have the "Complete, Simultaneous, and Perfect Possession of Unending Life"?[4]

THOMAS'S ANSWER

Just as we come to know about simple things by starting with what we know about compound, complex things, so we must come to a knowledge of eternity by starting with a knowledge of time. Time, however, is nothing other than "number applied to motion, respecting what is earlier and later."[5] Since in every motion there is succession, and one part comes after another, we can number what is earlier and later, and thereby recognize time, which is

---

1 *ST* I, Q. 3, A. 1, p. 71.

2 *ST* I, Q. 3, pp. 71–73.

3 Aristotle says this about Parmenides and Melissus, *Physics* 1.2, 184b16–18. On Parmenides, see p. 37; on Melissus, see p. 36.

4 This is the definition of God's eternity that is given by Boethius, *The Consolation of Philosophy*, Bk. 5, Prose 6.

5 Aristotle, *Physics* 4.11, 220a25.

nothing other than the number of what is earlier and later in motion. However, in something that lacks motion and is always the same, there is no "earlier" or "later." Just as the meaning of time consists in the recognition of our numbering of the earlier and the later in motion, so from the recognition of the complete uniformity of that which has no motion we see the meaning of eternity.

Furthermore, "those things are said to be measured by time that have a beginning and an end in time," as Aristotle says.[1] For this reason, we always recognize a beginning and an end in everything that is moved. That which is completely immovable, however, cannot have succession, and likewise, neither a beginning nor an end.

Thus, therefore, these two considerations show the nature of eternity. First, that which exists in eternity has no limits, that is, it lacks a beginning and an end, each of which would be a limit. Second, because eternity lacks succession, it exists entirely, simultaneously, all at once.

D. Analogy: Language about God

Question 13: Using Our Language about God

Article 1: Can Our Words Be Used about God?

THOMAS'S ANSWER

According to Aristotle, words are signs of concepts, and concepts represent things.[2] From this it is clear that words refer to the things they signify by means of intellectual concepts. As long as something can be understood by us, we can express it in words. We showed above,[3] it is true, that God's essence cannot be understood by us in this life, but God can be known by us as the cause of all creatures, provided that we understand that God is excellent beyond any creature and completely lacking in creaturely limitation. We can, therefore, use words about God from what we know about creatures, but the words that signify God do not express the divine essence just as it is. By contrast, the word "human being" does meaningfully express the essence of a human being just as it is; this word signifies the definition, which

---

1 Aristotle, *Physics* 4.12, 221b28–32.
2 Aristotle, *On Interpretation* 1.1, 16a3–6.
3 *ST* I, Q. 12, AA. 11–12 (not included in this volume).

indicates the essence, because the meaning that is signified by the word is the definition.

OBJECTION 2

Every word is used either abstractly or concretely. Words that signify concrete things are inappropriate for God, because God is purely simple [and not composed of form and matter to constitute a concrete thing]. On the other hand, words that signify abstractly are not appropriate for God, because God is perfectly and independently existent. It seems, therefore, that no word can be used about God.

REPLY TO OBJECTION 2

Because we gain our knowledge of God from what we know about creatures, and on this basis we use words about God, the words that we use about God are intended primarily to signify material creatures. It is the knowledge of these material creatures that is most natural to us, as we have said.[1] Because the most perfect and independent of the material creatures are *composed*, the form of such beings is not a complete substance, but is rather just the formal part. Hence, the words that we use to signify a complete substance signify it *concretely*, that is, as composed. On the other hand, when we use words to signify the form alone, the words do not indicate an actually existent thing but rather a formal part; for example, "whiteness" signifies the formal part of a white thing. Since, therefore, God is both completely simple and also independently existent, we use both abstract words to signify God's simplicity and also concrete words to signify his perfect and independent existence. Both kinds of words, however, are really deficient to express the reality of God, because our intellect does not, in this life, understand him just as he is.

Article 2: Can Our Words Signify God *Substantially*?

THOMAS'S ANSWER

Some words are used negatively about God, and others indicate a relation between God and creatures; these terms clearly do not

---

1   *ST* I, Q. 84, A. 7; pp. 125–27. See also *ST* I, Q. 12, A. 4 (not included in this volume).

signify the substance of God at all. They signify, instead, what should *not* be said about God or how creatures are related to God.[1]

There are other words, however, such as "good" or "wise" that are said affirmatively and absolutely about God. There are different opinions about these words. Some people say that words of this sort, although they are used affirmatively about God, nevertheless are intended to deny something about God rather than to affirm something about him. Accordingly, they say that, when we say that God is "living," we really mean that God is not like a non-living thing; and the same would be true of all such words. Rabbi Moses holds this position.[2] Others, however, say that affirmative words are used only to signify how creatures are related to God.[3] For them, when we say that God is "good," the sense would be that God is the cause of goodness in creatures, and the same would hold for other affirmative words.

Both of these positions seem wrong, for three reasons. First, neither of these positions can explain why we use some words about God and not other words. God is the cause of bodies and also of whatever is good. If, therefore, when we say that "God is good," we mean merely that God is the cause of good things, we could equally well say that "God is a body," because he is the cause of bodies. We could further justify calling God a "body" by meaning that we are denying that God is merely in potency, like prime matter. Second, on this erroneous theory, it would follow that all words would be used in a secondary sense about God. For example, the word "health" is used in a primary sense about an animal, but in a secondary sense it is used about medicine, because medicine is the cause of health. The word "health," however, primarily describes an animal. Third, this erroneous view is contrary to what we intend when we speak about God. When we say that God is living, we do not mean to say merely

---

1 Examples of negative words used about God would be "non-temporal" or "immaterial" or "infinite." These terms signify, respectively, that God is not in time, that God is not material, and that God is not finite. Examples of relative words would be "Lord" or "Saviour." To call God the "Lord" is to indicate the relationship of obedience of humans to God; to call him "Saviour" is to say that humanity has been saved by God.

2 Moses Maimonides, *The Guide of the Perplexed*, Bk. 1, Ch. 58. On Maimonides, see p. 36.

3 Alan of Lille, *The Rules of Theology* (*Theologiae Regulae*), Rule 21. On Alan of Lille, see p. 33.

that God is the cause of living things or merely that God is different from non-living things.

My position, therefore, is that words signify the divine substance and are predicated substantially of God, but they are somewhat deficient in representing God. Here is the explanation. Words signify God only to the extent that our intellect can understand God. Since our intellect knows God on the basis of what it knows about creatures, it knows God himself just insofar as creatures can represent God. We saw above that God possesses in himself all of the perfections of creatures, in a completely simple and perfect way.[1] Hence, any creature represents God insofar as the creature is like God and has some perfection. Creatures do not represent God as though God and creatures were in the same category, but they represent him as a transcendent cause, the effects of which have some similarity to their cause, but deficiently so. An example of this is the way in which bodily forms on this earth represent the power of the sun.[2] This has been previously explained on the topic of divine perfection.[3] In a similar way, therefore, affirmative and absolute terms do signify the divine substance, though imperfectly, just as creatures imperfectly represent it.

When, therefore, we say, "God is good," the sense is not "God is the cause of goodness" or "God is not evil"; rather, the sense is that whatever we call good in creatures is found first and in a higher way in God. Hence, the reason that God is good is not because he causes good things, but rather the other way around: because God is good, he causes good things. Augustine supports this when he says, "Insofar as God is good, we exist."[4]

Article 4: Do All Words about God Mean the Same Thing?

THOMAS'S ANSWER

Words used about God are not all synonyms, as we can easily see. Even if it were the case that words about God were only negative

---

1 *ST* I, Q. 4, A. 2, pp. 75–76.
2 The power or energy of the sun can be inferred from the effects it causes on, for example, living organisms, which would not survive without it. A tree, thus, "represents" the power of the sun and is an effect of that power, but it is a very imperfect realization of the sun's vast power.
3 *ST* I, Q. 4, A. 3. (Not included in this volume.)
4 St. Augustine, *On Christian Doctrine*, Bk. I, Ch. 32, ¶ 35.

or were only about the relation of God as cause to his creatures, the words would still have different meanings because they would be negating different things or showing different effects that God caused. It is also clear from what I have said[1] that words about God that signify the divine substance, though imperfectly, also have different meanings. The meaning that the word signifies is a concept in the intellect that points to the thing signified by the name. Our intellect, when it knows God from creatures, forms concepts to understand God that correspond to the perfections caused by God in creatures. Such perfections exist first and as a unity in God, but in creatures they are received separately and in many individuals. Just as for the many different perfections in creatures there is but one, simple cause, which is represented in the many perfections of the creatures, so for the many and different concepts in our intellect there is but one simple principle, imperfectly understood through these concepts. Therefore, although the words used about God signify one thing, nevertheless, because they signify it with different meanings and in different ways, they are not synonyms.

Article 5: Are Words Used *Univocally* when They Are Used about Creatures and about God?

THOMAS'S ANSWER

It is impossible that any word can be predicated of God and of creatures univocally. The reason for this is that any effect that is weaker than its efficient cause will not be like the cause, except in some deficient way. Thus, what is divided and multiple in the effects is one and uniform in the cause; the sun, for example, has one power that produces a variety of different kinds of forms on this earth. Likewise, as we have already shown,[2] all of the perfections that are divided and multiple in creatures exist in a prior and united way in God. When, therefore, some word indicates a creaturely perfection, it signifies that perfection as distinct in its meaning from all other perfections. For example, when the word "wise" is used about a human being, we mean to indicate a perfection that is distinct from the essence, the intellectual power, the existence, and so on, of the human being. When, however, we use this word about God, we do not intend to indicate anything

---

1 *ST* I, Q. 13, A. 2, pp. 80–82.
2 *ST* I, Q. 13, A. 4, pp. 82–83.

distinct from his essence, power, or existence. Hence, when we use the word "wise" about a human being, the word describes adequately the thing it signifies. Such, however, is not the case when the word "wise" is used about God; instead, the word signifies what we do not understand and what goes beyond the meaning of the word. Hence, it is clear that the word "wise" does not have the same meaning when it is used of a human being and when it is used of God. The same will be true for other words. No word, therefore, is predicated univocally of God and of creatures.

On the other hand, words are not predicated of God and of creatures in a purely equivocal way, as some people say.[1] If it were true that words used of God and of creatures were equivocal, nothing could be known or demonstrated about God, for all arguments would be guilty of the fallacy of equivocation. Such a situation is contrary to the position of Aristotle, who proves demonstratively many things about God, and also the position of the Apostle, who says in Romans 1:20, "The invisible things of God can be known through those things that have been made by God."

We must say, therefore, that words of the sort that can be said of God and creatures are said *by analogy*, that is, *by a relationship*. This analogy of words can happen in two ways. In one way, many things have a relationship to some one thing, as, for example, "healthy" is said about medicine and also about urine, because each of these has some order or relationship to the health of the animal (the one is a cause of health, and the other is a sign of health). In another way, there is just one relationship between two things, as, for instance, when "healthy" is said about medicine and about an animal, because medicine is the cause of the health that is in the animal. In this second way, words are said about God and creatures analogously, and not purely equivocally or univocally. We can only use words about God from what we know about creatures, as we saw above.[2] Accordingly, whatever is said about God and creatures is said on the basis of some order of creatures to God, namely, that for creatures God is the source and cause in which all of the perfections of creatures exist in a prior and more excellent way.

This analogous use of language holds a middle place between pure equivocation and simple univocation. In words used analo-

---

1 For example, Moses Maimonides, *The Guide of the Perplexed*, Bk. 1, Ch. 59.
2 *ST* I, Q. 13, A. 1, pp. 79–80.

gously, there is not just one meaning, as there is in univocal words, nor are the meanings completely different, as in equivocal words. Words that can be used in different ways will signify different relationships to some one thing. In this way, "healthy" is said about urine, insofar as it indicates a sign of health in an animal, but it is said about medicine insofar as it indicates the cause of health.

OBJECTION 1

Any equivocal predication is founded on a prior univocal predication, just as all multiplicity is founded on some unity. For example, if the word "dog" is used equivocally about the barking animal and the fish,[1] there must be a univocal use of the word—in this case it is used univocally about barking animals—otherwise there would be no end to the equivocal uses of words. When we are talking about causal agents, some are *univocal* agents, because they are the same in name and in definition as the effects they cause. Human beings, for example, generate other human beings. Other agents, however, are *equivocal*, as the sun, for example, is the cause of heat, although the sun itself is not hot, except in some equivocal sense.[2] It seems, therefore, that the First Agent, which is the basis for all other agents, must be a univocal agent, and hence that whatever is said about God and creatures is said univocally.

REPLY TO OBJECTION 1

It is true that in logical predication, equivocal predication is based on univocal predication. In actions, however, a non-univocal agent must be prior to a univocal agent.[3] The non-univocal

---

1 There is a kind of shark called a dogfish, which Thomas might have intended.
2 In the mediaeval cosmology, the heavenly bodies, including the moon and everything beyond it, did not possess the active qualities of things on earth; that is, they were not hot or cold, wet or dry. They caused effects, however, on earth, including the sun's causing of heat, although the sun itself did not possess the property of being hot.
3 Non-univocal agents are agents that are different in kind from the effects they produce; the sun, for example, is a non-univocal (or equivocal) agent over the effects of life on this earth. A univocal agent is the same in kind as the effect it produces: oak trees generate other oak trees, and they are thus univocal agents.

agent is the universal cause of all of the members of a species, as the sun, for example, is the cause of the generation of all human beings. A univocal agent, on the other hand, is not the universal cause of an entire species, because if it were it would have to be the cause of itself, since the univocal agent is included as a member in the species. The univocal agent, rather, is an individual cause of some other individual that belongs to the species. The universal cause of the entire species, therefore, is not a univocal agent, and the universal cause is prior to the individual cause.

This universal cause, although it is not univocal, is not nevertheless completely equivocal, for if it were it would cause effects that were completely unlike it. It can be called, rather, an *analogous* agent. This is similar to the fact that all univocal predicates must ultimately be founded on one predicate, namely, "being," which is predicated analogically.

Article 6: Are Words Used Primarily about God rather than about Creatures?

THOMAS'S ANSWER

Whenever words are used analogically in a number of contexts, it is necessary that all of these uses be founded on one primary use, and accordingly this primary use must be reflected in all of the other uses. Since "the meaning signified by the word is the definition," as is said in the *Metaphysics*,[1] it is necessary that any word is used first about the primary thing indicated by the definition, and secondarily about other things, which are related to the primary thing more or less closely. "Healthy," for example, which is said primarily about an animal, is included in the definition of "medicine," because medicine is the cause of health in an animal. The definition of "healthy" is also included in the meaning of urine, which is called healthy because it is a sign of the health of an animal.

With this understanding in mind, all words used metaphorically about God are used in a prior way about creatures rather than about God, because when they are used of God they merely indicate some similarity of God to creatures. When we talk about a "smiling meadow," we mean to say that a meadow in bloom has a pleasing appearance, as our faces do when we smile, for there is

---

1 Aristotle, *Metaphysics* 4.7, 1012a23–24.

some similarity in the comparison; in just the same way, if we say that "God is a lion," we mean to say that God is like a lion in that he operates powerfully in his works, as a lion does in his. When such words are said about God, it is therefore clear that whatever signification they have about God is taken from their [prior] use about creatures.

The same reasoning would also apply to non-metaphorical words used about God if we were to hold, as some do, that words used about God only indicate God as a cause. On this [wrong] view, when God is called "good," the meaning is merely that God is the cause of goodness, and consequently when the word "good" is used of God, it really contains in its meaning the goodness that is found in creatures. Hence, on this view, "good" would be used primarily about creatures rather than about God.

We showed above,[1] however, that words of this sort do not merely indicate God as cause but also indicate the essence of God. For when it is said that God is "good" or "wise," we do not mean only that God is the cause of wisdom or goodness, but we also mean that these things exist in a prior and higher way in God.

Given all of this, therefore, we should say that, if we are considering the reality signified by words, non-metaphorical words signify God first and creatures second, because the perfections that they signify flow from God into creatures. On the other hand, if we consider the way in which we learn the meanings of words, we use them first about creatures, which we know first. Hence, such words always signify in a creaturely way as is fitting for the creatures who use them, as we showed above.[2]

---

1   *ST* I, Q. 13, A. 2, pp. 80–82.
2   *ST* I, Q. 13, A. 3 (not included in this volume).

Chapter 3: Human Nature
Texts from *Summa theologiae* I

A. Soul and Body

Question 75: On the Soul Itself

Article 1: Is the Soul a Body?

THOMAS'S ANSWER

To understand the nature of the soul, we must recognize that the soul is the *first principle*[1] *of life* in the living things of our experience. We say that something living is "animate," and we say that "inanimate" things lack life.[2] Life is especially evident to us in two operations: knowledge and self-motion.

The ancient materialist philosophers, however, were not able to understand this principle, because they could not get beyond their imagination. They thought that the soul was some kind of body, because they said that only bodies are real and that, if something is not a body, it is nothing. Hence, they used to say that the soul is a body of some kind.

The falsity of this opinion can be shown in several ways, but I shall make use of only one argument, which in a very general and certain way shows that the soul is not a body. It is clear that not every principle of living operations is the soul, for if that were so the eye would be a soul, because it is a principle of vision, and the same would be true for all of the organs of the body. Instead, the *first* principle of life is called the soul. It is true that something bodily can be a partial principle of life, as the heart, for example, is a principle of life in an animal. Something bodily, however, cannot be the *first* principle of life. This is so because what it means to be a body is not primarily and necessarily to be the

---

1 The Latin word translated as "principle" or "source" is *principium*. This word has a broad range of meanings: "principle," "source," "beginning," "starting-point," "foundation," etc. The problem discussed in this article is to identify the essential feature of living things from which life flows. The English words "principle" and "source" will be used to translate this word.

2 Something "animate" literally has a soul; something "inanimate" lacks a soul.

principle of life or to be alive. If being alive were immediately and essentially what it means to be a body, then all bodies would be alive or would be principles of life. In fact, it is only *certain* bodies that are alive, or are parts of a living organism, and they are alive because they are *different* from other bodies. What makes them different from the others is some primary principle that gives them their *actuality*. The soul, therefore, which is the first principle of life, is not a body but is the actuality of the body. The quality of being hot, for example, which is the principle of heating, is not a body but is a kind of act of a body.[1]

OBJECTION 1

The soul is the mover of the body. But every mover is itself also moved. It seems to be the case that whatever causes motion is itself moved, because whatever gives something to something else can only give what it has. Only a hot thing, for example, can give heat to something else. Another reason that every mover is also moved is that, if there is a mover that is not moved, it could only cause "eternal and constant motion," as Aristotle argues.[2] Animal motion, however, which is caused by the soul, is clearly not of that sort. The soul, therefore, is a mover that is itself moved. But every mover that is moved is a body. The soul, therefore, is a body.

REPLY TO OBJECTION 1

Since anything that is in motion is moved by some other thing, and since there cannot be an actually infinite number of movers, it follows necessarily that not every mover is also moved. Because motion is understood to be a process of going from potency to actuality, the mover gives what it has to the thing moved, that is, it gives a kind of actuality to the thing moved. As Aristotle has shown, this means that "there is one kind of mover that is completely unmoved, that is neither essentially nor accidentally

---

1 This example might seem obscure, but it is not far from what is said about heat today. If something is hot, it gives rise to heat that propagates and affects other things. Being hot is, in this sense, the principle of heating. Being hot, however, is not a sort of body, but it is the *act* of a body, or of many bodies. That is, we would say that it is the *motion* of many molecules.

2 Aristotle, *Physics* 8.10, 267b3.

moved, and such a mover causes eternal and constant motion."[1] There is, however, another kind of mover that is not essentially moved but is moved accidentally, and this sort of mover does not cause eternal and constant motion. The soul is a mover of this sort. There is, further, a third kind of mover that is essentially moved, and this is a bodily mover.

Because the ancient natural philosophers thought that the only real things are bodies, they held that every mover is also moved and that the soul is essentially moved, and hence that the soul is a body.

OBJECTION 2

All knowledge involves some representation, but there can be no representation of a body in a non-bodily thing. If the soul, therefore, were not a body, it could not know bodily things.

REPLY TO OBJECTION 2

It is not necessary that the affinity or mental representation of the thing known exist actually in the nature of the knower. In fact, if the knower goes from potentially knowing to actually knowing, it is necessary that the representation of the thing known *not* exist actually in the nature of the knower; it can only be potentially in the knower. In vision, for example, colour is not actually in the pupil of the eye but is there potentially only. Hence, it is not necessary that there be actual bodily representations in the nature of the knower; rather, such representations must be there only potentially.

Because the ancient natural philosophers did not know enough to distinguish between actuality and potentiality, they thought that, in order to explain how the soul knows all bodies, the soul is itself a body and is made of the same material that is in other bodies.

OBJECTION 3

There must be some contact between the mover and the thing that it moves. Contact, however, always involves bodies. Since the soul moves the body, it seems that the soul must be a body.

---

1 Aristotle, *Physics* 8.5, 258b4–9.

Reply to Objection 3

There are two kinds of contact: the kind that involves quantitative contact and the kind that involves power. In quantitative contact, a body can be touched only by another body. In the second kind of contact, however, a body can be touched by something non-bodily that has the power to cause motion.

Article 2: Is the Human Soul a Subsistent Thing?

Thomas's Answer

It is necessary that the source[1] of intellectual activity, which we call the human soul, is non-bodily and subsistent. For it is clear that the human person, through the intellect, is able to know the natures of all bodies. Whatever is able to know many things cannot have the nature of any of the things that it knows in its own nature. If a body were naturally in the soul, it would block the soul's knowledge of other bodies. For example, we see that, when the tongue of a sick man is infected with some bitter taste, the sick man cannot taste anything sweet, but to him everything tastes bitter. If, therefore, the intellectual source should have some bodily nature in itself, it would not be able to know all other bodies, because each body is an individually determined thing. It is impossible, therefore, that the intellectual principle be a body.

It is likewise impossible that the soul should understand through some bodily organ, because if that were the case, the determinate nature of that bodily organ would make impossible the knowledge of all other bodies. For example, if there should be some determinate colour in the pupil of the eye or in the glass vase, the liquid in the vase would appear to have that same colour.

The intellectual source, therefore, which we call the mind or the intellect, has its own operation that is not shared with the body. Nothing has its own operation, however, unless it also subsists by itself. In order to operate, a thing must be an actually existent being: something operates only to the extent that it exists. For this reason, we do not say that *heat* causes heat but rather that a *hot thing* causes heat. It follows, therefore, that the human soul, which is called the intellect or the mind, is something non-bodily and subsistent.

---

1   Again, the Latin term is *principium*. See p. 89, note 2.

OBJECTION 1

If something is subsistent, it is an independently existing thing. The soul, however, is not an independently existing thing; rather the *composite* of soul and body is an independently existing thing. Therefore, the soul is not a subsistent thing.

REPLY TO OBJECTION 1

An "independently existing thing" can be thought of in two different ways. In one way, an independently existing thing is anything that subsists as opposed to an accident or a form that must belong to matter; in a second way, an independently existing thing is something that is a complete natural substance and not just a part of something else. For example, a hand is an independently existing thing in the first sense but not in the second. Accordingly, the human soul, because it is a part of human nature and therefore only partially subsistent, can be called an "independently existing thing" in the first sense, but not in the second. On the other hand, the *composite* of soul and body is truly an independently existing thing in the second sense.

OBJECTION 2

If something is subsistent, it can operate. The soul, however, does not operate, because, as Aristotle says, "to say that the soul senses or understands is like saying that the soul weaves cloth or builds something."[1] The soul, therefore, is not a subsistent thing.

REPLY TO OBJECTION 2

One might argue that the quoted words of Aristotle do not really reflect Aristotle's own opinion but rather the opinion of those who think that the operation of understanding is something like a kind of motion, as the context of the remarks would make clear.

On the other hand, whatever can operate independently must also exist independently. Sometimes, however, we say that something is independently existing even if it is a part and not a whole, provided that it is not an accident or a material form. Properly, however, something is independently subsisting that does not belong to something else and is not a part. In this proper sense,

---

1 Aristotle, *On the Soul* 1.4, 408b11–12.

neither the eye nor the hand is independently subsistent, and consequently neither of these operates independently. For this reason, the operations of the parts are attributed to the whole *through or with* the parts. We say, for example, that a human person sees *through* his or her eyes and that the person strikes *with* his or her hand. This is different from the way in which we talk about something operating through an accident, because we say that a *hot thing* causes heat; we do not say that "heat" operates by itself. We can say, therefore, that the soul understands in just the same way in which we say that the eye sees, but it is much more correct to say that the whole person understands through the soul.

OBJECTION 3

If the soul were a subsistent thing, it would have an operation without the body. None of its operations, however, can be done without the body, not even the operation of understanding, because there is no understanding without sense images, and sense images require the body. The human soul, therefore, is not a subsistent thing.

REPLY TO OBJECTION 3

The body is required for the action of understanding, not because it is an organ in which the action of understanding takes place, but because the body provides the *object* for the intellect to understand. The sense image is produced by the body and is related to the intellect just as colour is related to vision. The fact that the intellect is dependent upon the body to provide objects to understand does not imply that the intellect is not subsistent. If it did, an animal would not be subsistent because it is dependent on exterior sensible objects in order that it can perceive anything.

Article 3: Are the Souls of Animals Subsistent?

THOMAS'S ANSWER

The ancient, materialist philosophers made no distinction between sensation and understanding; they attributed both to the body, as I have already said.[1] Plato, however, did distinguish

---

1 *ST* I, Q. 75, A. 1, pp. 89–91. Also, *ST* I, Q. 50, A. 1 (not included in this volume).

between sensation and understanding, but he attributed both of these to the incorporeal soul, thinking that both understanding and sensation belong to the soul all by itself. This led him to suppose that even the souls of animals could be subsistent.[1]

Aristotle, however, held that among all the operations rooted in the soul only understanding is performed entirely without a bodily organ. Sensation, on the other hand, and any other operations dependent upon sensation clearly always involve some bodily activity. In vision, for example, the pupil of the eye undergoes bodily change in response to the presence of colour; the same is true for all kinds of sensation. It is therefore clear that a soul capable only of sensation does not have an operation by itself; rather, the operation of such an animal soul is always the operation of the conjunct of soul and body. It follows that, since the souls of animals do not have their own independent operation, they are not subsistent. The principle here is that everything has being in the same way in which it operates.

Article 4: Is the Soul the Human Person?

THOMAS'S ANSWER

To say that "the soul is the human person" could mean one of two things. (1) Some people claim that only the form, and not the matter, belongs to the definition of the species, because matter belongs to individuals and not to the species. In this sense, you would say that the soul is the person in the definition of a human being, but that *this* person, for example, Socrates, is not his soul but is rather a composite of soul and body. This claim, however, cannot be correct because the definition must include whatever pertains to the nature of the species. The definition of natural things does not signify the form alone but both form and matter. Matter is thus a part of the species of natural things, not matter in the sense of *individuating matter*, but matter as *common matter*.[2] Just as the meaning of this individual person is to be composed of *this* soul, *this* flesh, and *these* bones, so also the meaning of

---

1 Thomas seems to be referring to the notion occasionally expressed in Plato's dialogues that human souls could be reincarnated into animal bodies.

2 "Matter" can mean the individual stuff that makes each thing unique, or it can mean commonly what something is made out of. Matter is part of the definition of the human person in the second sense.

human nature in general is to be composed of soul, flesh, and bones. It is necessary that the nature of the species include whatever commonly belongs to all of the individuals included in the species.

In another way (2), it could also be understood that *this* soul is *this* person. This, however, could only be maintained if one supposed that the operations of sensation belonged to the soul without the body. In such a case, all human operations would belong to the soul alone. Any given thing will perform its own operations, and this must be true for the human person: the human person must be able to perform all human operations. It was shown above, however, that sensation is not an operation of the soul alone. Because sensation is one of the essential human operations, even though it is not uniquely human, it is clear that a human person is not a soul alone but is something composed of soul and body. Plato, on the other hand, thinking that sensation belongs to the soul alone, could hold that a human person is a soul "using a body."

OBJECTION 1

In the Bible, Paul says, "Although the outward person undergoes corruption, that which is inward is renewed day after day."[1] The "inward" part of the person is the soul. Therefore, the soul is the inward person.

REPLY TO OBJECTION 1

According to Aristotle, "whatever is most powerful in something is its most important part; for example, what the ruler of the city does is what the whole city seems to do. In the same way, sometimes the most important part of a person is called the human person."[2] If we follow the truth, the most important part of a person is the intellectual part, and this is sometimes called the "inner person." According to some opinions, however, the part of the person capable of sensations and involving the body is thought to be most important; and this is called the "exterior person."

---

1 2 Corinthians 4:16.
2 Aristotle, *Nicomachean Ethics* 9.8, 1168b29–32.

OBJECTION 2

The human soul is subsistent, but it can only be so as an individual substance and not some general abstract thing. It is, therefore, an individual substance and human person. The human soul, therefore, is a human person.

REPLY TO OBJECTION 2

Not every individual substance is a person, but only that which has the complete nature of the species. Hence, neither the hand nor the foot can be called a person. Likewise, neither can the soul be called a person, since it is only a part of the human species.

Article 5: Is the Soul Composed of Matter and Form?

THOMAS'S ANSWER[1]

It is especially clear that the soul cannot be composed of matter and form if we consider the human soul insofar as it is intellectual. This is a general truth: whatever is received in something is received in it according to the manner of the receiver. Furthermore, whatever is known is received in the knower as a form. The intellectual soul, however, knows everything in its nature apart from individuals; for example, it knows a stone as something apart from individual stones. Therefore, the form of the stone, expressing the nature of the stone apart from any individual stone, comes to exist in the intellectual soul. Therefore, the intellectual soul must also be a form apart from matter, and not something composed of matter and form. If the intellectual soul were composed of matter and form, any forms received in it would be received as individuals; and hence it would only know singular things, as is the case with the powers of sensation, which receive the forms of things in corporeal organs. Matter is the principle that individuates forms. It follows, therefore, that the intellectual soul and any intellectual substance that knows forms apart from individuals must lack any composition of matter and form.

---

1 Thomas gives two reasons in this Article; the first has been omitted and the second is given here.

Article 6: Is the Human Soul Destructible?

THOMAS'S ANSWER

It is necessary to say that the human soul, which we call the intellectual principle, is indestructible. Something is destructible for one of two reasons: either it is destructible because of something essential to it or because of something accidental to it. It is, however, impossible that whatever is subsistent be made or destroyed because of something accidental; in other words, a subsistent thing cannot be made or destroyed *because something else is made or destroyed*. A thing is made or destroyed in just the same way that it has its being, because being is acquired whenever a thing is made and lost whenever it is destroyed. Hence, whatever has being in itself cannot be made or destroyed except in itself. On the other hand, whatever is not subsistent, such as an accident or a material form, is made and destroyed because of the making or destroying of the whole composite. It was shown above that the souls of animals do not subsist in themselves and that only human souls do subsist in themselves. Hence, the souls of animals are destroyed whenever their bodies are destroyed, but the human soul cannot be destroyed unless it is destroyed in itself. It is, further, completely impossible for the human soul, or for any subsistent thing that is a form alone, to be destroyed in itself.[1]

It is clear that whatever belongs to a thing in itself is inseparable from it. Being, however, belongs to a form in itself, because form is act. That is why matter acquires being in act only when it acquires form, and matter is destroyed whenever form is separated from it. Since it is impossible that form be separated from itself, it is impossible that a subsistent form cease to exist.

A sign of this truth can be taken from the fact that everything naturally desires being in its own way. Desire, of course, arises from knowledge. The senses only know being in the here and now, but the intellect knows being absolutely and for all time. Hence, whoever has an intellect naturally desires to live forever. A natural desire, however, cannot be in vain. It follows, therefore, that every intellectual substance is indestructible.

---

1 A paragraph on the doctrine of universal hylomorphism (that is, the doctrine that even subsistent forms, like the human soul and angels, are composed of form and matter) is omitted.

OBJECTION 1

If two things have a similar beginning and a similar kind of life, they will have a similar end. If we compare humans and animals, they have the same beginning, for both are generated from physical, earthly elements. Likewise, their kind of life is similar, for "they all breathe and humans have nothing more than the beasts," as is said in Ecclesiastes.[1] Therefore, as is concluded in the same book, "All go to one place; all are from the dust, and all turn to dust again."[2] The souls of brute animals are destructible; therefore, also, the human soul is destructible.

REPLY TO OBJECTION 1

Solomon[3] gave that opinion, not as his own, but as representing the opinion of the foolish. The fact that humans and the animals have the same beginning of their existence is true about the body, because all animals are made out of physical, earthly elements. It is not, however, true about the soul, because although the animal soul is produced by a bodily process, the human soul is produced by God. To indicate this, in Genesis it is said about the animals, "Let the earth bring forth the living spirit;"[4] but about the first human person it is said, "He breathed into his face the breath of life."[5] [...] The process of life is similar for humans and beasts with respect to the body, but it is not similar with respect to the soul, because humans understand and beasts do not. It is therefore false to say that humans have nothing more than beasts. Again, there is a similar death for humans and beasts as to the body, but not as to the soul.

OBJECTION 2

Whatever is from nothing will also return to nothing, because the end should reflect the beginning. As is said in the Book of Wisdom,[6] however, "we were born from nothing"; this is true not only of the body but also of the soul. Therefore, as is concluded

---

1 Ecclesiastes 3:19.
2 Ecclesiastes 3:20.
3 Thomas understood Solomon to have been the author of Ecclesiastes.
4 Genesis 1:24.
5 Genesis 2:7.
6 Wisdom 2:2.

in the same book, "we will be after this life as though we never had been." This is true even for the soul.

REPLY TO OBJECTION 2

Just as the possibility of being created does not indicate some kind of potency in the creature, but only an active power in the Creator who makes things out of nothing, so also the possibility of being annihilated does not imply some kind of potency in the creature to non-being, but only the power of the Creator who could stop causing being. If we say, however, that something is "destructible" this must be because there is some real potency in the thing for non-being, but there is no such potency in the human soul.

OBJECTION 3

Nothing can exist without its proper operation. The proper operation of the soul, which is to understand from sense images, cannot take place without the body. Without sense images, the soul understands nothing; and "sense images cannot exist without the body," as Aristotle says.[1] Therefore, the soul cannot remain after the destruction of the body.

REPLY TO OBJECTION 3

Understanding with sense images is the proper operation of the soul so long as it is united to the body, as it is in this life. When, however, it is separated from the body it will have a different way of understanding that is similar to that of the angels, as will appear more clearly later.[2]

Question 76: On the Union of Soul and Body

Article 1: Is the Intellect United to the Body as Its Form?

THOMAS'S ANSWER

It is necessary to say that the intellect, which is the source of our intellectual operation, is the form of the human body. The fundamental reality for anything to operate is the form of that thing.

---

1 Aristotle, *On the Soul* 1.1, 403a9.
2 *ST* I, Q. 89, A. 1 (not included in this volume).

For example, if a body becomes healthy, the fundamental reality is health itself; if the soul knows, the fundamental reality is knowledge. In these cases, health is a form of the body, and knowledge is a form of the soul. The explanation for this is that nothing acts unless it is in actuality. The fundamental reality that makes something actual also makes it able to act. It is clear that the fundamental reality whereby a body is alive is the soul. Since life is manifest in different operations in different kinds of beings, that which is fundamental to each of the operations we perform is the soul. The soul is the fundamental reality by which we are able to nourish ourselves, to sense, to move, and to understand. This reality, which is fundamental to our understanding, whether it is called the intellect or the intellective soul, is the form of the body. This is Aristotle's argument in *On the Soul*.[1]

Whoever should wish to say that the intellectual soul is not the form of the body would have to find some way to explain how the action of understanding is the action of any individual person. We all know that it is we ourselves who understand. Action is attributed to an agent in one of three ways, as Aristotle points out.[2] "An agent causes motion or action either because it acts as a whole (for example, a doctor causes health), or because it acts through a part (for example, an animal sees through its eyes), or because it acts in some accidental way (for example, a white person builds—if the builder happens to be white)." Accordingly, when we say that Socrates or Plato understands, clearly we do not mean that understanding is accidental to them; we mean, rather, that understanding is something they do because they are human beings, because it is essential to them. What remains, therefore, is either that Socrates understands because he does this *as a whole* (which Plato thought to be the case, thinking that the human person is an intellective soul), or that the intellect is *a part* of Socrates. This first option, however, is impossible, because it is the very same person who recognizes that he or she understands and senses. Sensation, of course, cannot occur without a body, and hence the body must be an essential part of the human person. The other option therefore remains, namely, that the intellect by which Socrates understands is some part of Socrates, such that the intellect is united in some way to the body of Socrates.[3]

---

1 Aristotle, *On the Soul* 2.2, 414a4–28.
2 Aristotle, *Physics* 5.1, 224a31–33.
3 A paragraph on Averroes's position is omitted.

Some people wish to say that the intellect is united to the body as a mover. On this view, soul and body are thought to be one because in some way the same action is attributed to them both. This position, however, is weak for several reasons. First, because the intellect only moves the body through appetite, the motion of which presupposes the operation of the intellect. Socrates does not understand because he is moved by his intellect; rather, because Socrates understands, he is therefore moved by his intellect. Second, this position is weak because, given that Socrates is an individual with a nature that is composed of matter and form, if the intellect were not his form, it would follow that his intellect would be something outside of his essence. As such, as something outside of the essence, it would be related to the whole of Socrates as a mover is related to the thing moved. The activity of understanding, however, is something that remains in the agent; it is not an action like heating that transfers its action onto something else. We cannot, therefore, attribute the action of understanding to Socrates as though Socrates were moved by his intellect. Third, this position is weak because the action of a mover is only attributed to the thing moved if the thing moved is an instrument. For example, the action of a carpenter is attributed to his or her saw because the saw is his or her instrument. If, then, the action of understanding is attributed, not to Socrates, but to the mover of Socrates, it follows that it is attributed to him only because he is an instrument of understanding. Aristotle, however, denies that the action of understanding can be attributed to any bodily instrument.[1] Fourth, this position is weak because, although the action of the part may be attributed to the whole, as the action of the eye is attributed to the whole person, the action of one part is never attributed to some other part, except possibly in some accidental sense. We do not say that the hand can see because the eye can see. If the intellect and Socrates are united without distinction, then the activity of understanding cannot be attributed to Socrates. On the other hand, if Socrates is a whole composed of the union of the intellect and of whatever else belongs to Socrates, and if nevertheless the intellect is united to the rest of Socrates as nothing but a mover, then it would follow that Socrates is not one unified thing nor a complete being. A thing is a complete being only if it is unified as one.

Aristotle's position is the only one remaining: namely, the position that an individual person understands because the intel-

---

1 Aristotle, *On the Soul* 3.4, 429a17–30.

lectual part is the human form. Hence, from the very operation of the intellect, it is clear that the intellectual part is united to the body as form.

The same conclusion can be reached from a consideration of human nature. The nature of each thing is shown from its operation. The proper operation of the human person as such is the activity of understanding; in this, the human person transcends all other animals. For this reason, Aristotle says in his *Ethics* that the ultimate human happiness consists in the operation of reason, which is the proper operation of the human person.[1] It is necessary that the human person be classified according to human nature, which is the source of human characteristic operation. Each thing is classified according to its nature, which is shown in its form. It remains, therefore, that the intellectual principle is the proper form of the human person.

Here is a general consideration about matter and form. To the extent that a form is more noble, to that extent it dominates more over matter, it is less immersed in matter, and its operation and power goes beyond matter. To start with what is less noble, we see that the form of a chemical compound has properties not found in the properties of the elements out of which it is composed. As we proceed up the scale, the more noble the form the more its ability goes beyond its elemental matter. Thus, for example, the plant soul has more abilities than the form of a metal, and the soul of an animal has more abilities than the soul of a plant. The human soul is the ultimate in the nobility of forms. The abilities of this human form so exceed their bodily matter that it has an operation and an ability that goes completely beyond bodily matter. This ability is called the intellect.[2]

OBJECTION 1

Aristotle says that "the intellect is separate"[3] and that it is the actuality of no body. It is not, therefore, united to the body as its form.

---

1 Aristotle, *Nicomachean Ethics* 1.7, 1098a7–18.
2 A paragraph following on universal hylomorphism (see p. 98, note 1) is omitted.
3 Aristotle, *On the Soul* 3.4, 429b5.

REPLY TO OBJECTION 1

Aristotle tells us in the *Physics* that the ultimate of all natural forms, which is the highest consideration of the student of nature, is the human soul, "which is both separate [from matter] and nevertheless in matter. [...]"[1] It is separate in its intellectual operation, because the intellectual ability is not the operation of any bodily organ, in the way that vision is the operation of the eye. The operation of understanding, in fact, is an activity that cannot be exercised through a bodily organ, unlike the operation of vision. On the other hand, the soul is in matter insofar as it is the power and form of the body and the goal of human generation. In this light, Aristotle says that "the intellect is separate" because it is not the ability of any bodily organ.

OBJECTION 4

Ability and action belong to the same thing; that is, what is able to act and what acts are the same thing. Intellectual activity, however, is not the activity of any body, as has been shown. Therefore, the intellectual ability is not the ability of any body. The ability or the potency cannot be more immaterial or more abstract than the nature to which it belongs. Therefore, an intellectual substance cannot be the form of a body.

REPLY TO OBJECTION 4

The human soul, because of its perfection, is not a form immersed in or completely involved in bodily matter. Therefore, there is no inconsistency if some ability of the soul is not the act of a body even though the soul is essentially the form of a body.

OBJECTION 5

That which has being by itself is not united to the body as form, because form is that which makes something to be. It follows that the being of form is not something that belongs to form by itself. The intellectual part, however, does have being by itself and it is subsistent, as was shown above.[2] It is not, therefore, united to the body as its form.

---

1 Aristotle, *Physics* 2.2, 194b12.
2 *ST* I, Q. 75, A. 6, "Thomas's Answer," p. 98.

REPLY TO OBJECTION 5

The human soul shares its own subsistent being with bodily matter, with which the intellectual soul is united as one. The being that belongs to the whole composite is also the being of the soul itself. This, however, is quite different from other forms, which are not subsistent. For this reason, the human soul retains its own being after the body has been destroyed, but this is not the case for other forms.

OBJECTION 6

That which belongs to anything essentially is always in that thing. A form, however, is essentially united to matter, for it is not accidental but the very essence of form that it is the actuality of matter. If this were not so, form and matter would not unite to compose one thing essentially but only accidentally. Form, therefore, cannot exist without its own proper matter. The intellectual part, because it is indestructible, as was shown above, remains in existence apart from the body after the body is destroyed. The intellectual part is not, therefore, united to the body as its form.

REPLY TO OBJECTION 6

It is essential to the soul to be united to a body, as it is essential to a heavy body to fall downward. Just as a heavy body remains heavy even when it is removed from its natural place, and it retains its inclination and tendency to return to that natural, downward place, so the human soul, when it is separate from the body, retains its inclination and tendency to its natural union with the body.

B. Will and Choice

Question 82: The Will

Article 1: Does the Will Desire Anything Necessarily?

THOMAS'S ANSWER

Whatever is necessary is that which cannot be otherwise, but there are different senses of this. What is necessary might be so because of what is intrinsic to something's nature: either because of its make-up (as when we say whatever is made up out of contrary elements will necessarily decompose) or because of its formal structure (as when we say that it is necessary that a triangle have interior angles equivalent to 180 degrees). This sort of intrinsic necessity is natural and absolute. In another way, necessity belongs to a thing because of what is extrinsic to the thing, either because of its goal or because of an outside agent. Necessity comes from the goal when some goal cannot be achieved or achieved well without something else. For example, food is necessary for life, and a horse is necessary for a trip. This is called the necessity of the goal; it is a practical necessity. Necessity comes from an outside agent when something is forced by an outside agent; for example, a person forced by an outside agent cannot do anything different from what he or she is forced to do. This necessity is called coercion.

This last sort of necessity—coercion, necessity caused by the outside agent—is completely repugnant to the will. Whatever is opposed to the inclination of a thing is violent. The movement of the will is a kind of inclination toward something. Just as whatever is natural is in accord with the natural inclination, so whatever is voluntary is in accord with the inclination of the will. It is impossible that something be both violent and natural at the same time. It is therefore impossible that the will be at the same time both violently coerced and also voluntary.

Necessity of the goal, however, is not repugnant to the will, as in the case when the goal can only be reached in one way. For example, if one wills to cross the sea, it is necessary that one choose to sail on a ship. Similarly, natural necessity is also not repugnant to the will. In fact, just as the intellect necessarily accepts the first principles of knowledge, so also the will necessarily desires the ultimate goal, which is happiness. The goal plays the role in practical action that first principles play in knowledge, as Aristotle says.[1] Whatever is natural and fixed in a thing is the foundation and source of everything else, because the nature of a thing is primary in each thing, and all motion proceeds from something given that is fixed.

Objection 1

Augustine says that if something is necessary it is not voluntary.[2] Everything, however, that the will desires is voluntary. Therefore, the will desires nothing necessarily.

---

1 Aristotle, *Physics* 2.9, 200a20–29.

2 Augustine, *City of God* Bk. 5, Ch. 10.

Reply to Objection 1

Augustine is speaking in this passage about the necessity that comes from coercion. Natural necessity, however, does not remove the liberty of the will, as Augustine himself says in the same book.[1]

Objection 2

According to Aristotle, "rational powers extend to opposite objects."[2] The will is a rational power, because, as Aristotle says, "the will is a part of reason."[3] Therefore, the will extends to opposite objects. It is, therefore, not determined necessarily.

Reply to Objection 2

If we think about the will as it naturally desires something, it is more like the intellect in its grasp of its fundamental principles than like reason, which extends to opposing objects. In this regard, the will is an intellectual rather than a rational power.

Objection 3

Because of the will, we are in control of our own actions. We do not, however, control whatever happens necessarily. Therefore, no act of the will can happen necessarily.

Reply to Objection 3

We are in control of our actions insofar as we can choose this or that. Choice, however, is not about the goal but about the way to get to the goal, as Aristotle says.[4] Hence the desire of the ultimate goal is not an act of which we are in control.

---

1 Augustine, *City of God* Bk. 5, Ch. 10.
2 Aristotle, *Metaphysics* 9.1, 1046b4–6.
3 Aristotle, *On the Soul* 3.9, 432b5–8.
4 Aristotle, *Nicomachean Ethics* 3.2, 1111b27.

Article 2: Do We Will Necessarily Everything that We Will?

THOMAS'S ANSWER

The will does not will everything necessarily. To make this clear, consider that, just as the intellect naturally and necessarily agrees to first principles, so the will desires the ultimate goal—happiness, as was said.[1] There are, however, some truths that do not have a necessary connection to first principles, because they are contingently, or not necessarily, true; and these can be denied without denying the first principles. The intellect does not assent to these truths necessarily. Other propositions, however, are necessary because they have a necessary connection with the first principles; demonstrated conclusions, for example, are necessary in that they cannot be denied without also denying the first principles. To these propositions, the intellect must necessarily assent, provided that it knows the demonstration that gives the necessary connection of these to the first principles. Before the intellect knows the demonstration, however, it does not assent to these propositions necessarily.

The same is true in the case of the will. There are certain individual good things that do not have a necessary connection to ultimate happiness, because one can be happy without them. The will does not desire any of these things necessarily. There are other goods that do have a necessary connection to happiness, by which, for example, we would be brought to God in whom is our true happiness. Even so, before we have the necessary demonstration that will come in the vision of God of how these goods are related to God, the will does not necessarily desire God or the things that will lead to him. The will, however, of the person seeing the essence of God will necessarily desire God, just as now we necessarily will to be happy. It is clear, therefore, that the will does not will necessarily whatever it wills.

OBJECTION 1

Dionysius says that "evil is not willed."[2] Therefore, the will tends necessarily to any good that it finds.

---

1   *ST* I, Q. 82, A. 1, pp. 105–07.
2   Dionysius the Areopagite (Pseudo-Dionysius), *On the Divine Names*, Ch. 4, ¶ 32.

REPLY TO OBJECTION 1

The will cannot intend anything unless it recognizes it as good. Because there are many and varied good things, however, the will is not necessarily determined to any one of them.

OBJECTION 2

The object of the will is like the mover of some movable thing. Motion, however, in the movable thing is necessarily caused by the mover. It seems, therefore, that the object of the will moves it necessarily.

REPLY TO OBJECTION 2

The mover causes motion necessarily in the movable thing whenever the power of the mover exceeds the movable thing, so that its possible movements are completely subject to the mover. Since the possible choices of the will concern whatever in general is good, its possible choices are not completely directed to any one particular good. Therefore, it is not moved necessarily by any one particular good.

OBJECTION 3

Just as the good that we sense is the object of the sense appetite, so the good that we understand is the object of the intellectual appetite, which is the will. The good that we sense moves the sense appetite necessarily; for Augustine says that "animals are moved by what they see."[1] Therefore, what we understand to be good necessarily moves the will.

REPLY TO OBJECTION 3

The sense abilities are not able to compare diverse and opposing goods as reason can, but they simply grasp whatever individual thing is presented to them. Hence, one individual thing can determinately move the sense appetite. Reason, however, is able to compare many things; and thus the intellectual appetite or the will is able to be moved by many things and not just by one necessarily.

---

1 Augustine, *Literal Commentary on Genesis*, Bk. 9, Ch. 14, ¶ 24.

Article 4: Does the Will Move the Intellect?

THOMAS'S ANSWER

A mover causes motion in two different ways. In one way, a goal causes motion, because the goal moves the mover. In this way, the intellect moves the will, because the good that is understood is the object of the will and moves the will as a goal.

In another way, an agent, or efficient cause, causes motion, as the pusher moves the thing pushed. In this way, the will moves the intellect and all the abilities of the soul, as Anselm says.[1] The reason for this is that, when there are a number of coordinated active abilities, the ability that is oriented to the general goal moves all of the abilities oriented to particular goals. We can see this in natural causes and also in government. In natural causes, the sun, for example, which sustains everything on our earth, moves or affects all bodies on earth, but still each of these earthly bodies also acts to help conserve and sustain the various species and individuals on earth.[2] In government, the king, who intends the good of the whole kingdom, gives commands to individual subordinates, who in turn extend his rule into the individual cities entrusted to their care. Likewise, the object of the will is in general what is good as a goal. Each other human ability is ordered to the proper good that is suitable for it, just as vision is ordered to the perception of colours and the intellect to the knowledge of the truth. The will, therefore, moves as an efficient cause all the powers of the soul to their acts, except for the abilities of the non-sensitive parts of the soul, which are not subject to our will.

OBJECTION 3

We can will nothing unless we first understand what is good. If, therefore, the will moves the intellect by willing the act of under-

---

1   Anselm, *Similitudes* (*Liber de similitudinibus*), Ch. 3. This is an anonymous collection of Anselm's sayings; a version of this can be found in J.-P. Migne, *Patrologia Latina* (PL 159, 605–708). The comments on the will are in Ch. 3 (PL 159, 605–06). On Anselm, see p. 34.
2   In mediaeval cosmology, the heavenly bodies above our atmosphere played a causal role in conserving all life and natural order on this earth. This was understood by Thomas to be a general causality, affecting everything on earth, but it did not take away the causality exercised by all of the things on earth.

standing, it will be necessary that that act of the will is preceded by another act of the intellect, and so on infinitely, which is impossible. Therefore, the will does not move the intellect.

REPLY TO OBJECTION 3

There is no need to go on infinitely, because the beginning of the decision-making process is in the intellect. It is necessary that some apprehension of what is good precede every motion of the will, but it is not necessary that a motion of the will precede every apprehension.

Question 83: Free Choice

Article 1: Do Human Persons Have Free Choice?

THOMAS'S ANSWER

Human persons have free choice, otherwise advice, encouragements, instructions, prohibitions, rewards, and punishments would be in vain. To see the truth about this, we should consider that there are some things in nature that simply act and do so without any judgement at all. A rock, for example, falls down without making any judgement, and anything in nature that lacks knowledge is of this sort. Other things, however, such as animals do have judgement, but not a *free* judgement. When the sheep sees the fox it knows that it should flee, but its judgement is natural and not free, because it makes this judgement from a natural instinct and not from a comparison of various options. All animals operate by instinct and not from reason.

Human persons, however, decide what should or should not be done on the basis of a judgement that comes from human knowledge. This judgement does not come from an instinct that determines us to do some one thing but rather from reason, with which we can compare various possible goods. Because of this free judgement, the human person is able to act in different and novel ways. Reason can reach different and opposing conclusions when it is dealing with matters of opinion that have no necessity about them. Likewise, individual choices that we make have no necessity about them, and when we reason about them we can reach different conclusions and not always the same conclusion. From the fact that human persons have reason, it is necessary that they have free choice.

OBJECTION 1

Whoever has free choice does what he or she wishes. Human persons, however, do not do what they wish, because, as is written in Scripture, "I do not do the good that I wish; but I do the evil that I hate."[1] Human persons, therefore, do not have free choice.

REPLY TO OBJECTION 1

The sensitive appetite does obey reason but it can also fight against reason, by desiring what reason has rejected. This is the sort of thing that was indicated in Objection 1, namely, that our senses desire against reason. In fact, the "good that I wish," but do not do, is that the sense desires should not fight against reason, as Augustine says.[2]

OBJECTION 3

"To be free is to be self-caused," as Aristotle says.[3] Whatever is caused by something else is not free. God, however, moves our wills, for it is said, "the heart of the king is in the hand of God and he will turn it wherever he wishes."[4] Also, "God works in us, willing and accomplishing his will in us."[5] Human persons, therefore, do not have free will.

REPLY TO OBJECTION 3

Free choice is the source of motion, which means that human persons by free choice move themselves to act. Freedom, however, does not require that whatever has free choice be the first cause absolutely. In general, something can be a cause, even if it is not the *first* cause. God, of course, is the first cause who causes all natural and voluntary agents below him. Just as God does not take away the actions of the natural agents when he moves them, so also when he moves voluntary agents, he does not

---

1 Romans 7:15.
2 Augustine, from the *Glossa ordinaria* on Romans 7:19 and 7:23 (texts can be found in J.-P. Migne, *Patrologia Latina* 114, 493–94).
3 Aristotle, *Metaphysics* 1.2, 982b26.
4 Proverbs 21:1.
5 Philippians 2:13.

take away their voluntary actions; in fact, God supports this voluntary activity in them. God always operates in each thing by using what is proper to each thing's nature.

OBJECTION 5

Aristotle says, "the kind of person you are determines what seems good to you."[1] We have no control, however, over the kind of person we are, because we are what we are by nature. We will pursue, therefore, whatever seems naturally to be good to us, and not do so from free choice.

REPLY TO OBJECTION 5

You are "the kind of person you are" either because of nature or because of practice. By nature, we have dispositions or inclinations, either because of our intellect or because of our body. Because of our intellect, we naturally want what is ultimately good for us, which is happiness. This natural inclination that we have to happiness is not subject to choice, as we have said.[2] On the other hand, because of the body and bodily capacities, we as individuals are subject to various influences that affect us physically but not intellectually. These influences give us differing inclinations and dispositions, such that what is physically appealing to one person is not so to someone else. These inclinations are subject to reason, because they are inclinations of our lower appetites. Hence, these inclinations do not take away free choice.

Dispositions that we acquire by practice come from the habits we develop in our emotional lives. From such habits, one person is more inclined one way, and another in another way. Nevertheless, even these inclinations are subject to the judgement of reason, because it is within our control to acquire or to lose these inclinations by developing or by breaking our habits. Hence, nothing in these inclinations or dispositions is repugnant to free choice.

---

1 Aristotle, *Nicomachean Ethics* 3.5, 1114a32–33.
2 *ST* I, Q. 82, AA. 1–2, pp. 105–09.

C. Knowledge

Question 84: How the Soul While Joined to the Body Understands Bodily Things

Article 1: Does the Soul Understand Bodies Through the Intellect?

THOMAS'S ANSWER

[Some history of philosophy will help] to clarify this question. The early philosophers, who studied the natures of things, thought that nothing existed except bodies. Because they saw that all bodies were changing, they thought that bodies were in a continual state of flux, and they judged that no certain knowledge was possible for us about the truth of things. Whatever is continually flowing cannot be grasped with any certainty, because it will always flow away before the mind can make any judgement. Heraclitus said that "it is not possible to touch a flowing river twice," as Aristotle reports.[1]

Plato surpassed these early philosophers. In order to guarantee the certain knowledge of truth that our intellect can have, he supposed that, beyond all these bodily things, there are beings of another sort, completely separate from matter and motion. He called these separate beings "Forms" or "Ideas," and he thought that every individual sensible thing, such as a human being or a horse, is what it is by participating in these Forms. Accordingly, he said that sciences, definitions, and whatever the intellect knows, are not about these sensible bodies, but are rather about those immaterial and separate Forms. On Plato's account, the soul does not understand these bodily things but rather it understands the separate Forms of these bodily things.

Plato's position, however, is false for two reasons. First, since those Forms are immaterial and immobile, any knowledge of motion or of matter would be excluded from the sciences. The whole purpose, however, of natural science is to give us causal demonstrations of moving and natural things. Second, it seems ridiculous, when we are trying to gain knowledge about things that are manifestly before us, to introduce, as a means to our knowledge, other entities that are completely different from them in substance and in being. Even if we did get a knowledge of

---

1 Aristotle, *Metaphysics* 4.5, 1010a14.

those separate Forms, it would give us no knowledge of the sensible things that we are trying to make judgements about.

Plato seems to have strayed from the truth because he thought that, since all knowledge requires some kind of mental representation, the form of the thing known must necessarily be in the knower in the same way in which it exists in the thing known. Plato recognized that the form of the thing understood exists in the intellect in a universal, immaterial, and immobile way. This fact is apparent from the very operation of the intellect, which understands whatever it understands in a universal and necessary way. The way that the intellect operates indicates the way its form must be. Plato concluded that the things we understand must exist in themselves in just the same way in which they are understood, that is, immaterially and immovably.

There is, however, no necessity for this conclusion. Even in sensation we can see that the same form can exist in one way in one thing and in another way in another thing. For example, the colour white can be more intense in one thing and less intense in another thing; or, in one case a white thing might be sweet, while in another case a thing of the same colour is not sweet. Similarly, the form of a sensible thing exists in one way in the thing outside of the soul and in another way in the activity of sensation, which receives the forms of sensible things apart from the matter in which they exist; we can sense the colour gold apart from the matter of gold. In the same way, the intellect derives concepts that are immaterial and immobile from bodies that are material and in motion, because they exist in the intellect in a way appropriate to the intellect. The principle is that whatever is received is in the receiver in the way appropriate to the receiver. We may conclude, therefore, that the soul through the intellect knows bodies with a knowledge that is immaterial, universal, and necessary.

OBJECTION 1

Augustine says "the intellect cannot understand bodies, and only the senses can see bodily things."[1] He also says that intellectual vision reports the things that are essentially in the soul,[2] but these are not bodies. The soul, therefore, does not understand bodies through the intellect.

---

1 Augustine, *Soliloquies*, Bk. 2, Ch. 4.
2 Augustine, *Literal Commentary on Genesis*, Bk. 12, Ch. 24, ¶ 50.

REPLY TO OBJECTION 1

Augustine's words are meant to be understood, not about the objects that we understand, but about the means of understanding those objects. We know bodies *by understanding*, that is, not by means of bodies or through material or bodily likenesses, but through immaterial and intellectual *concepts*, which by their nature can exist in the soul.

OBJECTION 2

The senses are related to their objects, and not to the objects of the intellect, just as the intellect is related to its objects, and not to the objects of the senses. We cannot, however, know spiritual or intellectual things through the senses. Therefore, by parity of reasoning, the intellect has no ability to know bodies, which are sensible.

REPLY TO OBJECTION 2

As Augustine says, we should *not* say that, because the senses know only bodily things, so the intellect knows only spiritual things, for if that were so it would follow that neither God nor the angels could know bodily things, but obviously they can. The explanation for the difference between intellectual and sense knowledge is that the lower power cannot extend itself to do what the higher can do, but the higher power can, in a more excellent way, do what the lower power can do.

OBJECTION 3

The intellect knows things that are necessary and always remain the same. All bodies, however, are changing and do not remain the same. The soul, therefore, cannot know bodies through the intellect.

REPLY TO OBJECTION 3

All change presupposes something that does not change. When, for example, something changes in a quality such as colour, the substance remains unchanged; and when the substance itself is destroyed, the underlying matter remains unchanged. Further, there are unchanging conditions of changing things; for example, even if Socrates is not always sitting, it is unchangeably true that, whenever he does sit, he is sitting in some one place. Given these considerations, nothing prevents us from having unchanging knowledge about changing things.

Article 2: Does the Soul Understand Bodies because It Is Essentially the Same as the Bodies It Understands?

THOMAS'S ANSWER

The ancient materialist philosophers held that the soul knew bodies by being essentially like them. The common opinion among them was that "like is known by like." They thought that the form of the thing known was in the knower in the same way in which it was in the thing known. The Platonists, although they agreed with the common opinion, drew the opposite conclusion. Because Plato saw that the intellectual soul was immaterial and that it knew in an immaterial way, he supposed that the forms of things known existed in an immaterial way. The early materialists, however, because they recognized that the things known were bodily and material, supposed that even in the knowing soul the things known must exist materially. Therefore, since they thought that the soul could know all things, they supposed that the soul had a nature in common with all material things. Since they thought that everything was made up of certain basic elements, they thought that the soul, too, must be made of the same elements. Thus, if they thought that the primary element was fire,[1] then they thought that the soul, too, was composed of fire. The same was true if they though the primary element was air[2] or water.[3] Empedocles, however, who thought that there were four primary elements and two moving causes,[4] said that the soul was made up out of these elements. So it was that, since they thought that everything existed materially in the soul, they also thought that the knowing process was a material process, and they made no distinction between understanding and sensation.

This position, however, can be disproven. First, the material elements, about which they spoke, do not contain other things

---

1 On Heraclitus, see pp. 35–36.
2 On Anaximenes, see p. 34.
3 On Thales, see pp. 37–38.
4 On Empedocles, see p. 35; Aristotle gives this version of Empedocles: *On Generation and Corruption* 1.1, 314a16.

except potentially. Whenever something is known, however, it is known, not as something potential, but as something actual, as Aristotle points out.[1] Hence the potency of these elements could only be known as something else that is actual. Therefore, it would not be enough to say that the soul was composed of these elements to account for the knowledge of all things; one would have to go further and suppose that the nature of all knowable things, bones, flesh, etc., were also in the soul. This is the argument of Aristotle against Empedocles.[2] Second, if we suppose that the known thing must exist materially in the knower, there would be no reason why other things which also exist materially but outside the soul should lack knowledge. Thus, for example, if the soul can know fire because it is fire, then it should follow that the fire outside of the soul can also know fire.

The conclusion of all of this is that material things when they are known must be in the knower, not materially, but immaterially. The reason for this is that the act of knowing extends itself to things that are outside of the knower: we know things that are outside of us. Through matter, however, a form is determined to be just one thing. It is clear, therefore, that the power of knowledge increases as the materiality of the knower decreases. Hence, those things that can only receive forms materially are not able to know in any way, such as plants, for example, as is said in *On the Soul*.[3] To the extent that something has the form of the thing known more immaterially, to that extent it knows more perfectly. Hence, the intellect, which abstracts the form not only from matter but even from the individuating material conditions, knows more perfectly than the senses, which receive the form of the thing known without matter but always subject to material conditions. Among the senses, vision is superior because it is less material, as was shown above;[4] among intellects, those that are more immaterial know better than those that are more material.[5]

From all of this it follows that if there is some intellect that essentially knows all things, it would have to possess all things in

---

1 Aristotle, *Metaphysics* 9.9, 1051a29–31.
2 Aristotle, *De anima* 1.5, 409b23–410a9.
3 Aristotle, *On the Soul* 2.12, 424a32–424b3.
4 *ST* I, Q. 78, A. 3 (not included in this volume).
5 That is, the angel's intellect is more immaterial than the human intellect, because angels are completely immaterial beings. The human intellect is more material, because the intellect is a part of the soul that is the form of the human body.

itself immaterially (just as the ancient materialists thought that the essence of the soul must be actually composed of the elements of all things in order to know them). This, however, is proper to God alone, namely, that he include all things in his essence insofar as all effects, which are caused by God, are present in God as cause. Only God, therefore, understands all things through his very essence; neither the human soul nor the angel can do so.

OBJECTION 2

Aristotle says that the "soul is all things in a certain way."[1] Since what is like is known by what is like, it seems that the soul knows bodily things by being like them.

REPLY TO OBJECTION 2

Aristotle did not suppose that the soul is actually composed of all things, as the ancient materialists thought. Rather, he said "that the soul is all things *in a certain way.*" That is, the soul can *potentially* know all things. Through the senses it can potentially know all sensible things, and through the intellect it can potentially know all intelligible things.

Article 3: Does the Soul Understand All Things through Innate Ideas?

THOMAS'S ANSWER

Form is the principle of action. If something is going to be able to act, it must have the appropriate form, which is the principle or source of that action. For example, if a body is potentially hot, it can only potentially give off heat; when the body is actually hot, it can actually give off heat.[2] In the case of knowledge, we observe that the human person is sometimes only a potential knower, and this is true both about sensation and also about understanding. The person goes from potential to actual knowing: in sensation this happens when sense objects affect the sense organs; in understanding this happens through study and discovery. Hence,

---

1   Aristotle, *On the Soul* 3.8, 431b21.
2   The difference between potentiality and actuality in this case is the *form* of heat; form makes something actual.

we must say that the knowing soul is in potency both to the sense images, which are the principles of sensation, and to the concepts, which are the principles of understanding. For this reason Aristotle held that the intellect, by which the soul understands, does not have any innate ideas but is, rather, from the beginning in potency to receive all ideas.

Because, however, something that has a form for acting might still be prevented from acting because of some impediment (for example, something actually light might be prevented from rising by a barrier), Plato supposed that the human intellect is naturally filled with all intelligible ideas but is prevented from actually using them because of the impediment caused by the union with the body. This position, however, is wrong for two reasons.

First, if the soul has a naturally innate knowledge of all things, it does not seem possible that it would have forgotten this knowledge so completely so that it would not even be aware that it had such knowledge. In fact, no one forgets the things we naturally know; for example, no one forgets that a whole is greater than one of its parts, and other truths of this sort. This position seems especially wrong if we recognize, as I have argued above,[1] that the union of soul and body is natural. It seems wrong to say that the natural operation of something is blocked by whatever naturally belongs to it.

Second, the falsity of this position clearly appears from the fact that, when one sense is lacking, all of the knowledge that comes through that sense is also lacking. For example, a person born blind cannot have any knowledge of colours. This, however, should not be the case if it were true that the human intellect were naturally supplied with all innate ideas. We should, therefore, conclude that the human soul does not know bodily things through innate ideas.

OBJECTION 3

No one can give a true answer unless he or she knows the answer. Even an uneducated person, however, who does not have scientific knowledge, will give true answers to questions, if asked in an orderly fashion, as is shown in Plato's *Meno*. Therefore, even before we have learned a science, we have knowledge of certain things. We could not, however, have such knowledge if we did not already have innate ideas. The soul, therefore, understands bodily things by means of innate ideas.

---

1 *ST* I, Q. 76, A. 1, pp. 100–05.

REPLY TO OBJECTION 3

When a teacher puts questions in an orderly fashion, the questions start with commonly held principles and take the student to conclusions that are more specific. By such a process, knowledge is caused in the soul of the learner. Hence, the student responds truly to the questions, not because he or she already knew the truth, but because the student is learning it for the first time. It does not make a difference whether the teacher teaches by asking questions or by lecturing, provided that the teacher proceeds from commonly held truths to conclusions. In either way, the student will be made certain of the conclusions on the basis of the common principles.

Article 4: Do Our Intellectual Concepts Come into Our Soul from Separate, Platonic Forms?

THOMAS'S ANSWER

Some have held that the intelligible concepts in our intellects come from some Forms or Separate Substances. They explain this in two ways. Plato, as has been said,[1] held that the Forms of sensible things exist by themselves without matter, such as the Form of human person, which he called Human Person Itself, and the Form or Idea of Horse, which he called the Horse Itself, and so forth. He held that both our souls and the material things participate in these separate Forms: our souls participate in them for knowledge, and material things participate in them in order to exist. Just as a material body participates in the Idea of Stone and thereby becomes a stone, so also our intellect participates in the Idea of Stone and thereby understands what a stone is. Participation in the Idea means that whatever participates in the Idea does so through some likeness of the Idea, just as any copy participates in its model. Plato held that the sensible forms in corporeal matter flowed from the Ideas as likenesses of them, and in a similar way he held that the intelligible concepts in our intellects are likenesses of the Ideas that flow from them. On this account, as has been said,[2] sciences and definitions would be about the Ideas.

It is, however, contrary to the nature of sensible things that their forms should subsist without matter, as Aristotle often

---

1 *ST* I, Q. 84, A. 1, pp. 114–17.
2 *ST* I, Q. 84, A. 1, pp. 114–17.

argues.[1] For this reason, Avicenna,[2] separating himself on this point, held that the intelligible concepts of all sensible things do not exist by themselves without matter but rather exist immaterially in Separate Intellects. From the first of these Intellects the concepts are given to subsequent Intellects until eventually they are given to the Last Separate Intellect, which Avicenna called the Agent Intellect. From this Agent Intellect the concepts flow into our intellects, and material forms flow into corporeal matter. Hence, Avicenna agrees with Plato in holding that the intellectual concepts in our intellects flow from some Separate Forms, but Plato thought that these Forms subsist by themselves, whereas Avicenna held that they were in the Agent Intellect. A difference between the two is that Avicenna held that the intellectual concepts do not remain in our intellects after we cease to understand them actually; rather our intellects must repeatedly receive these concepts afresh. He did not, therefore, hold that we have innate knowledge, as Plato did, who held that the participations of the Ideas remain permanently in our souls.

The problem with this Platonic position is that, if it is true, no sufficient reason can be given to explain why the soul is united to the body. It is wrong to say that the intellectual soul is united to the body for the sake of the body, because form does not exist for the sake of matter, nor does the mover exist for the sake of the thing moved, but rather the other way around. The body seems to be especially necessary for the intellectual soul in its proper operation of understanding because the soul does not depend upon the body for its being. If it were true that the soul could naturally receive intellectual concepts from the influence of the Separate Forms alone, and not from the senses, there would be no need of the body for understanding. If that were so, the union of soul to body would be in vain.

Some might say that the soul uses the senses for understanding in that the senses rouse the intellect to pay attention to the intellectual concepts that it receives from the Separate Forms. This, however, is insufficient also. This sort of rousing would only

---

1 Aristotle, *Metaphysics* 7.14, 1039a24–b19.
2 Avicenna held a version of the Platonic theory of separated Forms. In Avicenna's version, the Forms do not exist by themselves but exist rather as concepts or ideas in the mind of an intelligent being, an angel, the Separate Agent Intellect. On this view, we receive concepts from this Separate Agent Intellect, a sort of cosmic radio broadcaster who sends out ideas to anyone who "tunes in." On Avicenna, see pp. 34–35.

be needed for a soul that has "fallen asleep" or "become forgetful," as the Platonists would say, because of the soul's union with the body. On this account the senses would not benefit the intellectual soul except by removing an impediment arising from the union with the body that prevents knowledge. This position would provide no explanation for the union of the soul to the body.

If it should be said, as did Avicenna, that the senses are necessary to the soul to turn the soul to the Separate Agent Intellect from which it receives concepts, this, too, is insufficient. If the soul can naturally understand concepts derived from a Separate Agent Intellect, it would follow that the soul could obtain concepts from this Separate Agent Intellect whenever it wished to do so. It should be able to do so even if one sense would rouse it to receive the sense images from a different sense. Thus, for example, a person born blind should be able to get the knowledge of colours, which is manifestly false. Hence, we should say that the concepts by which the soul understands are not derived from separate Forms.

Article 6: Does Our Intellectual Knowledge Come from the Things We Sense?

THOMAS'S ANSWER

On this question there are three philosophical positions. First, Democritus[1] held that "our knowledge is entirely caused by our sensation of bodies, when physical images enter into our souls," as Augustine reports.[2] Also, Aristotle says that Democritus held that knowledge is created by "the influence of physical images."[3] The reason for this position is that neither Democritus nor the other ancient materialists distinguished between the intellect and the senses, as Aristotle points out.[4] Since the senses are affected by sense objects, they thought that all of our knowledge is reduced to nothing more than sense experience. Democritus thought that this sense experience is brought about by physical images that flow from the sense object into our souls.

---

1 On Democritus, see p. 33.
2 Augustine, *Letters*, 118 [To Dioscorus].
3 Aristotle, *On Prophecy in Sleep* 2, 464a5.
4 Aristotle, *On the Soul* 3.3, 427a17–21.

[Second] Plato, on the other hand, held that the intellect is distinct from the senses, and he thought that the intellect is an immaterial power that does not use a bodily organ in its operation. Since a non-bodily thing cannot be affected by a body, he held that intellectual knowledge does not require that the intellect be affected by sense objects; instead, intellectual knowledge arises from the soul's participation in certain separate Forms, as we have explained.[1] Further, he thought that the senses are powers that operate by themselves, apart from bodily organs. Hence not even the senses, which are spiritual powers, are affected by sense objects; instead, when the sense organs are affected by sense objects, this experience in some way rouses the sense powers to form sense images. Augustine expresses this position when he says, "the body does not sense but the soul senses through the body, just as a messenger forms a message within but uses the body to announce the message outside."[2] According to Plato, therefore, neither is intellectual knowledge derived from sensation, nor is sensation completely derived from sense objects; rather the sense objects rouse the soul to sensation, and similarly the senses rouse the intellectual soul to understanding.

[Third] Aristotle, however, took a middle position. He agreed with Plato that the intellect is distinct from the senses. He did not think, however, as Plato did, that the senses have their own operation apart from the operation of the body; that is, he did not think that "sensation is an act of the soul alone," but is rather an operation of the *union* of soul and body.[3] In fact, he said the same about all the operations of the sensitive part of the human person. Because there is no reason why sense objects that exist outside the soul cannot affect the union of soul and body, Aristotle agreed with Democritus that the operations of the sensitive part of a human person are caused by the influence of sense objects. Aristotle did not think, however, that the influence was the flowing of physical images, as Democritus held. Democritus, of course, thought that all action is caused by the movements of atoms, as is clear in *On Generation and Corruption*.[4] On the other hand, Aristotle held that the intellect has an operation apart from the body. Because nothing bodily can have an influence on something non-bodily, Aristotle thought that the influence of bodily

---

1 *ST* I, Q. 84, AA. 3–4, pp. 119–23.
2 Augustine, *Literal Commentary on Genesis*, Bk. 12, Ch. 24, ¶ 51.
3 Aristotle, *On Sleep and Waking* 1, 454a7–12.
4 Aristotle, *On Generation & Corruption*, Ch. 8, 324b25–425a2.

sense images was insufficient for intellectual knowing; intellectual knowing requires something higher because "the active part is higher than the passive part."[1] This does not mean, as Plato thought, that the intellectual operation is caused entirely by the influence of the separate Forms. Rather "the higher or more noble" active part, which Aristotle calls the "active intellect," makes the sense images taken from sense objects to be actually understood through a process of abstraction. We have spoken about this elsewhere.[2]

Therefore, it is true that the intellectual operation necessarily requires the sense images caused by the senses. The sense images, however, are insufficient to bring the potential capacity for understanding to actual understanding. This requires the operation of the active intellect and we can therefore say that sense knowledge is not the complete cause of intellectual knowledge; it provides rather the raw material so to speak of intellectual knowing.

OBJECTION 3

An effect cannot be greater than the power that causes it. Intellectual knowledge, however, extends farther than sense knowledge, for we understand some things that cannot be perceived by the senses. Intellectual knowledge, therefore, is not derived from the things we sense.

REPLY TO OBJECTION 3

Sense knowledge is not the total cause of intellectual knowledge. It is not, therefore, surprising that intellectual knowledge extends farther than sense knowledge.

Article 7: Can the Intellect, Using Its Own Concepts, Understand without Using Sense Images?

THOMAS'S ANSWER

While in the present life where we are united to a passive body, it is impossible for our intellect to understand actually without

---

1 Aristotle, *On the Soul* 3.5, 430a14–19.
2 *ST* I, Q. 79, AA. 3–4 (not included in this volume). Abstraction will also be discussed below, *ST* I, A. 85, A. 1, pp. 128–33.

using sense images. There are two indications of this truth. First, since the intellect is an ability that operates without a bodily organ, its operation would never be interrupted when bodily organs are harmed, if the activity of bodily organs were not required for its operation. Clearly, the senses, the imagination, and other such sense abilities do use bodily organs. In order that the intellect actually understand, both in acquiring new knowledge and also in remembering what is already known, our intellect requires the imagination and other sense abilities. We see, for example, that when the imagination is hampered because of some damage to bodily organs, as happens in the case of someone delirious, or when the memory is blocked as it is in some handicapped people, a person is prevented from actually knowing what he or she otherwise would know.

Second, we can all experience in ourselves that, whenever we try to understand something, we form images as examples to aid us in our efforts to understand. Similarly, when we try to explain something, we offer examples to our listeners, from which they can form sense images to help them understand.

The underlying principle of all of this is that any knowing ability must be adequate to its object. For example, an angel's intellect, which is completely separated from any body, understands intellectual, immaterial substances; and, on the basis of these, the angel can understand material things. On the other hand, the proper object of the human intellect, which is united to a body, is the nature or essence that exists in bodily matter. From a consideration of the natures of visible things, it ascends to some knowledge even of invisible things. The sort of nature that is known by the human intellect primarily exists in individual and bodily matter. The nature of a rock is something that exists in this individual rock, the nature of a horse exists in this individual horse, and so forth. Hence, the nature of a rock, or of any material thing, cannot be known completely and truly unless it is known as existing in some individual thing. We know the individual through our senses and imagination. In order that the intellect know its proper object, it is therefore necessary that the intellect use sense images, for its proper object is to know the universal nature that exists in individual things. If the proper object of our intellect were to know immaterial things, or if the forms of sensible things existed separately from matter (as the Platonists thought), our intellect would not always need sense images for understanding.

OBJECTION 1

The intellect is activated by intellectual concepts that it forms. An activated intellect is, in fact, an intellect that actually understands. The intellectual concepts, therefore, are sufficient for the intellect to understand actually, without using sense images.

REPLY TO OBJECTION 1

The concepts that are stored in the intellect remain passively there when we are not actively using them. It is not enough, therefore, for actual understanding that the concepts merely *be* in the intellect; it is necessary further that we *use* them about the things they represent, which are known by sensation.

OBJECTION 3

There are no sense images of non-bodily things, because sensation is always restricted to what is in time and space. If, therefore, our intellect always requires sense images to understand, it would follow that it could not understand anything that is non-bodily. This conclusion is false, however, because we understand such things as truth, God, and the angels.

REPLY TO OBJECTION 3

Non-bodily things, of which there are no sense images, are known by us by comparing them to sensible bodies, of which there are sense images. We understand truth, for example, by considering the thing about which the truth is known. We know God by thinking of him as a cause or as something that transcends and is different from the things we do know, as Dionysius says.[1] The other non-bodily substances that we know in this life we only know in a negative way or by some comparison to bodily things. It is, therefore, necessary that, when we know something about these things of which there are no sense images, we make use of the sense images of bodies.

---

1   Dionysius the Areopagite (Pseudo-Dionysius), *On the Divine Names*, Ch. 1, ¶ 5.

Question 85: The Manner and the Order of Human Understanding

Article 1: Does Our Intellect Understand Bodily and Material Things through Abstraction from Sense Images?

THOMAS'S ANSWER

As we have already said,[1] the knowable object is proportioned to the knowing ability. There are, however, three levels of knowing abilities. One kind of knowing ability is the operation of a bodily organ, and this power is sensation. Hence, the object of any of the senses is the form as it exists in bodily matter. Since matter of this sort is the principle of individuation, any of the senses can know only individual things. Another kind of knowing ability is neither the operation of a bodily organ nor is it joined in any way to bodily matter; this ability is the intellect of an angel. The object of this kind of knowing ability is the form that exists without matter. If such a knowing power does know material things, it will only understand them through the immaterial things that it knows, whether this knowledge is natural to the angel or God-given.

The human intellect—the third kind of knowing ability—occupies a middle position between the first two. It is not the operation of any bodily organ, but nevertheless it is the ability of a *soul*, which is the form of a body, as we have explained.[2] Accordingly, the proper object of the human intellect is to know the form that exists in individual bodily matter, but to know it not *as* it exists in such matter. To know that which exists in individual matter but not as it exists in such matter is to abstract the form from individual matter, which is represented by the sense images. We must, therefore, say that our intellect understands material things by abstracting from sense images. After due consideration is given to material things, we do eventually come to some knowledge of immaterial things, just as, contrariwise, angels proceed from a knowledge of immaterial things to a knowledge of material things. Plato, however, paying attention only to the immateriality of the human intellect and not to the fact that it is united in some way to the body, thought that the object of the intellect is the separate Forms. He did not think that we understood *by abstracting*, but rather *by receiving* the forms that are already abstract, as we have said.[3]

---

1 *ST* I, Q. 84, A. 7, pp. 125–27.
2 *ST* I, Q. 76, A. 1, pp. 100–05.
3 *ST* I, Q. 84, A. 1, pp. 114–17.

OBJECTION 1

Any intellect that understands something otherwise than as it is understands falsely. The forms of material things do not exist abstracted from the individuals, which are represented by sense images. If, therefore, we understand material things by abstracting concepts of them from sense images, the intellect will be false, because it will have separated the universal concept from the sense image of the individual.

REPLY TO OBJECTION 1

"Abstraction" can be taken in two different ways. In one way, it indicates composing or dividing; in this way, we understand that one thing is abstract from another when it is not in the other or is separate from it. In another way, it indicates a way of simplifying things; for example, we can understand one thing, while not considering something else. With this distinction in mind, if abstraction means that the intellect understands what is abstract to be in fact separate, as in the first way, then this understanding is false. In the second way, however, to abstract one thing from another that is not really separate involves no falsity. An example of this can be seen in sensation. If we say that colour does not exist in the coloured body or that it is separate from it, we will say or think what is false. If, however, we *consider* the colour and its properties, and if we do not consider the apple in which it is found, there is no falsity in what we understand or say. The meaning of an apple is different from the meaning of a colour; there is, therefore, nothing to prevent us from understanding the colour, while not thinking about the apple, although the colour does exist in the apple. In the same way, whatever belongs to the nature of any material thing, whether a stone, a person, or a horse, can be considered without the individual characteristics, which are not part of the nature of the thing. This is to abstract the universal from the individual or the intellectual concept from the sense images; that is, to consider the nature of the species without considering the individual characteristics, which are represented by the sense images.

When it is said, in Objection 1, that the intellect is false if it understands a thing otherwise than as it is, this remark is true if the "otherwise" refers to the *thing* that is understood. In that case, the intellect is false if it understands a thing to be otherwise than as it is. Accordingly, an intellect would be false if it understood the nature of the rock to be abstract from matter, meaning that it existed separately from matter, as Plato thought. On the other hand, the remark is not true, if the "otherwise" refers to the act of understanding. There is no falsity in the fact that the way in which something is understood is *otherwise* than the way in which the thing exists, because what is understood is in the intellect immaterially (in an intellectual way), not materially (in the way that material things exist).

OBJECTION 2

Material things are natural things, and matter is included in their definitions. A thing cannot be understood without whatever is included in the definition. Therefore, material things cannot be understood without matter. Matter, however, is the principle of individuation. Therefore, material things cannot be understood by abstracting universal concepts from individuals, which is what happens when intellectual concepts are abstracted from sense images.

REPLY TO OBJECTION 2

Some have thought that the species of a natural thing is the form alone and that matter is not part of the species. On this view, matter would not be part of the definition of a natural thing, which is false. We should say, therefore, that there are two ways to consider matter: as common and as individual. Common matter is, for example, flesh and bones; individual matter is *this* flesh and *these* bones. With this distinction in mind, the intellect abstracts the concept of a natural thing from individual sensible matter, but not from common sensible matter. Thus, for example, the concept of the human person is abstracted from this flesh and these bones, which are not in the meaning of the species but are parts of the individual, as is said in the *Metaphysics*;[1] thus the concept of human person can be considered without these. The concept of human person cannot, however, be intellectually abstracted from common flesh and bones.

Mathematical concepts, on the other hand, can be abstracted by the intellect, not only from individual sensible matter but even from common matter; they cannot, however, be abstracted from intelligible common matter, but only from individual matter.

1 Aristotle, *Metaphysics* 7.10, 1035b28–32.

Sensible matter is called bodily insofar as it is subject to sensible qualities, like hot/cold, hard/soft, and so forth. Intelligible matter is the substance insofar as it is subject to quantity. It is clear that quantity belongs to a substance first before sensible qualities. For this reason, quantities, such as numbers, dimensions, and shapes, can be considered without a consideration of sensible qualities; and this is to abstract them from sensible matter. These quantities cannot be considered, however, without an understanding of a substance that is subject to quantity; that is, they cannot be abstracted from intelligible matter. Quantities can also be considered without considering this or that substance; that is, they can be abstracted from individual intelligible matter.

Some things, however, can be abstracted even from common intelligible matter, such as the concepts of being, one, potency/actuality, and things of this sort. These realities can even exist without matter, as is the case in immaterial substances.[1]

Because Plato did not make the distinction that we have made between the two kinds of abstraction,[2] he thought that all of the things are abstracted in reality that we have said are abstracted only intellectually.

OBJECTION 3

Aristotle says that "sense images are related to the intellectual soul just as colours are related to vision."[3] Vision, however, does not occur when images are *abstracted* from colours but rather when colours are *received* in vision. Therefore, understanding does not occur when something is abstracted from sense images but rather when sense images are received in the intellect.

REPLY TO OBJECTION 3

Colours have the same individual way of existing when they are in bodily matter and when they are in the power of vision; hence, they can impress their own image on vision. The sense images, since they are the representations of individuals and since they exist in organs of the body, do not have the same way of existing that the human intellect has, as is clear from what we

---

1 An immaterial substance would be, according to Thomas, an angel, God, or the human soul apart from the body.
2 *ST* I, Q. 85, A. 1, Reply to Obj. 1, pp. 129–30.
3 Aristotle, *On the Soul* 3.7, 431a14–19.

have said.[1] Hence, the sense images cannot impress themselves by their own power on the passive intellect. The power of the active intellect causes a representation in the passive intellect that the active intellect takes from the sense images. These are representations of what the sense images also represent, but they represent only the nature of the species. In this way the intellectual concept is abstracted from the sense images, not as though some one, single form that first existed in the sense images was transferred later into the passive intellect, as though it were a body being carried from one place to another.[2]

OBJECTION 4

Aristotle says that in the intellectual soul there are two parts: the passive intellect and the active intellect.[3] Abstracting intellectual concepts from sense images does not pertain to the passive intellect, because its job is to receive abstracted concepts. Nor does it pertain to the active intellect, because it treats sense images the way that light treats colours: light does not abstract from colours but rather shines on them. Therefore, we do not understand by abstracting from sense images.

REPLY TO OBJECTION 4

The active intellect both illuminates the sense images and also abstracts intellectual concepts from them. The sense images are illuminated in that, because the sensitive part is strengthened by its union with the intellect, the sense images are rendered apt for understanding by the active intellect. The active intellect abstracts intellectual concepts from the sense images in that, by the power of the active intellect, we are able to consider the natures of the species without individuating conditions, and this consideration informs the passive intellect.

---

1 *ST* I, Q. 85, A. 1, "Thomas's Answer," p. 128.
2 The active intellect abstracts the universal form from the individual sense images. This does not mean that it so to speak carries the form from the sense images to the passive intellect; rather, it *considers* what is common and leaves out of consideration whatever is individual.
3 Aristotle, *On the Soul* 3.5, 430a14–19.

OBJECTION 5

Aristotle says that "the intellect understands its concepts *in* the sense images.[1] It does not, therefore, understand the concepts by abstracting *from* the sense images.

REPLY TO OBJECTION 5

Our intellect both abstracts intellectual concepts from sense images, insofar as it considers the natures of things as universals, and it also understands these natures in the sense images, because it is not able to understand the natures except by making use of the sense images, as we have said.

Article 2: Are the Intellectual Concepts *That Which* We Understand or *That By Which* We Understand?

THOMAS'S ANSWER

Some philosophers think that our knowing abilities know only their own representations. For example, the senses, on this view, would know only the sense images produced by the sense organs. Also on this view, the intellect would know only the intellectual concepts that it has received, and hence the concept would be *that which* we understand.

This opinion, however, is clearly false for two reasons. First, the objects of our understanding are also the objects of the sciences. If it is true that we understand only that which is in the soul, it would follow that all of the sciences are not about things outside of the soul but are about only what is in the soul. This is like the position of the Platonists, who held that all of the sciences are about the Ideas which are in the intellect.

Second, if this position were true, these ancient errors would also be true: "whatever seems to be true is true" and "contradictories are true at the same time." If the knowing power knows only its own ideas, it can judge only about them. Whatever the knowing power produces is what seems to be true; and the knowing power will always know about what it judges, namely, about its own ideas. As such, every judgement will be true. For example, if the sense of taste judges only about its own ideas, whoever has a healthy taste will judge truly that honey is sweet.

---

1 Aristotle, *On the Soul* 3.7, 431b2.

Someone, however, with a sick sense of taste will judge honey to be bitter, and this, too, will be a true judgement. Each person will judge according to what his or her own tastes will show, and it follows that each opinion will be equally true. Thus, whatever anyone claims will be true.

We should say, therefore, that the intellectual concept is *that by which* the intellect understands. Here is the explanation. There are two sorts of action, as Aristotle says,[1] one that remains in the agent, like the action of seeing or of understanding, and the other that acts upon some exterior thing, like the action of heating or cutting. Action of either sort involves some form. Just as the form of the action that acts on an exterior object is the image of the object of the action (the heat in the heater is like the heat in the exterior object), so also the form according to which action remains in the agent is the image of its object. Hence, the image of the visible object, the sense image, is that by which vision sees; and the image of the understood thing, which is the intellectual concept, is the form by which the intellect understands.

Because, however, the intellect reflects upon itself, it understands from this reflection both its own act of understanding and also the concept by which it understands. So it is that the understood concept is secondarily that which is understood. Primarily, however, that which is understood is the thing, of which the intellectual concept is the image.

OBJECTION 2

Actual understanding must exist somewhere, otherwise it would be nothing at all. It is not, however, in the thing that is outside of the soul, because the thing outside of the soul is material and no such thing can be actual understanding. It remains, therefore, that actual understanding occurs in the intellect, which is nothing other than the intellectual concept.

REPLY TO OBJECTION 2

Actual understanding involves two things: the thing that is understood and the act of understanding. Likewise, when we talk about an abstract universal, two things are understood: the nature of the thing and the abstraction or universality. The nature itself, about which there is understanding or abstraction or the intention of

---

1   Aristotle, *Metaphysics* 8.8, 1050a23–29.

universality, exists only in individual things. On the other hand, the understanding, abstracting, or intention of universality exists in the intellect. We can understand this by a comparison with vision. Vision sees the colour of the apple without its smell. If it should be asked where the colour exists that is seen without the smell, it is clear that the colour that is seen exists only in the apple. That it is perceived, however, without smell is attributable to vision, because in vision there is a likeness of colour but not of smell. Likewise, the humanity that is understood exists only in this or that human person; the fact, however, that humanity is grasped without individual characteristics, that is, the act of abstracting with the resultant intention of universality, this is attributable to the cognition in the intellect, in which there is a likeness of the nature of the species without individual characteristics.

universality, exist only in individual things. On the other hand, the understanding, assuming, or intention of universality exists in the intellect. We can understand this by a comparison with vision. Vision sees the colour of the apple without its smell. If it should be asked where the colour exists that is seen without the smell, it is clear that the colour that is seen exists only in the apple. That it is perceived, however, without smell is attributable to vision, because in vision there is a likeness of colour but not of smell. Likewise, the humanity that is understood exists only in this or that human person; the fact, however, that humanity is grasped without individual characteristics, that is, the act of abstracting with the resultant intention of universality, this is attributable to the cognition in the intellect, in which there is a likeness of the nature of the species without individual characteristics.

Chapter 4: Ethics
Texts from *Summa theologiae* I–II

A. The Goal: Happiness

Question 1: The Ultimate Goal for Human Beings

Article 1: Do Human Beings Act for the Sake of a Goal?

THOMAS'S ANSWER

Among the actions that human beings do, only the actions that are proper to us as human beings are properly human. Human beings are different from non-rational creatures because we have control over our own actions. Hence, only the actions over which we have control are properly *human* actions. Human beings control their actions through the use of reason and will, and hence free choice is called "the power of will and reason."[1] Properly human actions, therefore, are those that proceed from deliberate acts of the will. By contrast, other actions that humans do can be called actions *of* a human being, but they are not properly *human* because they are not proper to us as human beings. It is furthermore clear that all actions that proceed from some power are caused by that power for the sake of a suitable object. Since the object of the will is the goal that is good, it follows that all properly human actions are done for the sake of a goal.

OBJECTION 3

Human beings seem to act for a goal only when they act deliberately. Many actions, however, that we do seem to involve no deliberation, especially when they are done with no thought. We might, for example, move a foot or a hand, while intending something else, or we might scratch our beard unintentionally. Not everything we do, therefore, is for the sake of a goal.

---

1 Peter Lombard, *The Sentences* (*Sententiae*), Bk. 2, Dist. 24, Ch. 3. On Peter Lombard, see p. 36.

Reply to Objection 3

Actions of this sort are not properly human, because they do not proceed from the deliberation of reason, which is the proper principle of human actions. Such actions have, therefore, a goal for the sake of some bodily need but not a goal that has been established by reason.

Article 4: Is There Some Ultimate Goal of Human Life?

Thomas's Answer

If we are speaking about essential goals, it is impossible that there be an infinite series of goals, at either end of the series. This is so because, whenever there is an essential order among several things, if the first is removed, whatever is related to the first is necessarily lost. For this reason, Aristotle argues in the *Physics* that "it is not possible in the causes of motion to proceed to infinity,"[1] for if there were no first mover, other things would not be able to move, since they move because they are moved by the first mover. Goals, however, are ordered in two different ways: the order of what we intend and the order of what we do. In either sort of order, it is necessary that some goal be first. That which is first in what we intend is, so to speak, the first mover of our desires, which means that, if the first is taken away, there is nothing to move the desire. That which is first in what we do is the starting point of our action. If there were no starting point, we would never begin to do anything. The first thing in our intentions is the ultimate goal, and the first in what we do is the first thing that leads to that goal. It is, therefore, impossible that there be an infinite series in either direction, because, if there were no ultimate goal, nothing would be desired, no action would ever end, and no intention in acting would ever be satisfied. Likewise, if there were no first step that led to the goal, no one would ever begin to do anything, and no deliberation would ever come to an end, for it would go on forever.

On the other hand, where there is no essential order, but only an accidental ordering of things, nothing prevents there being an infinity, for accidentally ordered causes have no determinate order. In this sense, there can be an infinite series of accidental goals and of means to the goals.

---

1 Aristotle, *Physics* 8.5, 256a17–20.

Article 5: Can One Human Being Have More than One Ultimate Goal?

It is impossible that the will of one human being have as its object more than one thing as the ultimate goal. There are three reasons why this is so.

First, since everything seeks its own perfection, a person seeks the highest good that is the most perfect and fulfilling of him or herself. Augustine says, "When we speak of the goal for human beings, we do not mean a good that is consumed and lost, but rather a good that is brought to perfection and fulfilment."[1] It is, therefore, necessary that the ultimate goal so fulfil the whole human desire that nothing be left over to be desired. This would not be possible if something in addition to the ultimate goal is required for perfection. It is, therefore, impossible that human desire should tend toward two things, as though each were the good that perfects the person.

Second, just as in the working of reason the starting point is what is naturally known, so in the working of the rational appetite, which is the will, it is necessary that there be a starting point that is naturally desired. It is further necessary that this be one, because any natural thing is determined in one way. The starting point in the working of the rational appetite is the ultimate goal. It is, therefore, necessary that that which the will intends as the ultimate goal be one.

Third, since voluntary actions are categorized specifically on account of their goals, as we said above,[2] it follows that the will is generically categorized according to the ultimate goal, which is common to all actions. In the same way, any natural thing is categorized generically on account of the formal nature that is common to many species. Since everything that is desirable by the will, insofar as it is simply desirable, is of the same generic kind, it follows that the ultimate goal is one. This is especially so since in any generic category there is one first principle, and the ultimate end has the nature of a first principle, as we have said.

The ultimate goal of human beings as such is related to all of mankind, just as the ultimate goal of any one human being is related to that one person. It accordingly follows that, just as

---

1 Augustine, *The City of God*, Bk. 19, Ch. 1.
2 *ST* I-II, Q.1, A. 3 (not included in this volume).

there is naturally one ultimate goal for all human beings, so the will of any individual human being is rooted in one ultimate goal.

Article 7: Is There One Ultimate Goal for All Human Beings?

THOMAS'S ANSWER

We can talk about the ultimate goal in two different ways. In one way, we talk about the nature of the ultimate goal; in another way, we talk about the object in which this nature is found. As to the nature of the ultimate goal, everyone agrees about the desire for the ultimate goal, for everyone desires to achieve his or her perfection, which is the nature of the ultimate end, as we have said above.[1] As to the object in which this nature is found, not everyone agrees about the ultimate goal. Some, for example, desire riches as the highest good, others desire pleasure, and others other things.

A comparison could be drawn with taste: everyone might agree that what is sweet tastes good, but to some the most desirable sweet thing is the sweetness of wine, whereas to others it might be the sweetness of honey, or some other thing. Nevertheless, the more truly desirable sweet thing is the one that is desired by the person who has good taste; and similarly, the most fulfilling good thing is the one that is desired by the person whose desires are well ordered.

Question 2: The Constituents of Human Happiness

Article 1: Can Wealth Make Us Happy?

THOMAS'S ANSWER

It is impossible that human happiness consist in wealth. There are two types of wealth, as Aristotle says,[2] natural and artificial. Natural wealth is used by human beings to remove natural deficiencies; examples of such wealth are food, drink, clothing, vehicles, houses, and so forth. Artificial wealth, such as money, is not in itself naturally useful. Human ingenuity has created money in order to facilitate exchanges, so that the value of goods can be measured.

---

1   *ST* I-II, Q. 1, A. 5, pp. 139–40.
2   Aristotle, *Politics* 1.9, 1256b40–1258a18.

It is clear that human happiness cannot be found in natural wealth, for such wealth is ordered to sustaining human life, and for this reason it cannot be the ultimate goal but is properly used, rather, as a means to the goal. So it is that in the order of nature all things of this sort are below humans and are made for their sake. Accordingly the Psalmist says, "You have put all things under his foot."[1]

Artificial wealth is sought only for the sake of natural wealth, for it would not be sought except to buy those things that are needed for the necessities of life. Such wealth, hence, is even less connected with the ultimate goal. It is impossible, therefore, that happiness, which is the ultimate goal of human beings, consist in wealth.

Article 2: Can Honour Make Us Happy?

THOMAS'S ANSWER

It is impossible that happiness consist in honour. Honour is shown to someone because of some excellence in that person; it is, thus, a sign or a witness of the excellence that is in the person honoured. The excellence of a human being is especially relevant to happiness, which is the perfect good of a human being; it also belongs to a part of happiness, that is, to the goods that form a part of happiness. Hence, honour can be a consequence of happiness, but happiness cannot principally consist in it.

Article 4: Can Power Make Us Happy?

THOMAS'S ANSWER

It is impossible that happiness consist in power, for two reasons. The first reason is that power has the nature of a starting point, as is clear in the *Metaphysics*,[2] but happiness has the nature of the ultimate goal. The second reason is that power is related to both good and evil, but happiness is the proper and perfect good of a human being. For this reason, some happiness might consist in the good use of human power, which comes about through virtue, but not in the power itself.

---

1 Psalms 8:6.

2 Aristotle, *Metaphysics* 5.12, 1019a15–20.

Four general reasons can be given to show that human happiness consists in none of the exterior goods just discussed.[1] The first reason is that, since happiness is the highest human good, nothing evil can be mixed with it. All of the previously discussed goods can be found in both good and evil people. The second reason is that, since the nature of happiness is that it be "sufficient of itself," as is said in the *Ethics*,[2] it is necessary that, once happiness is acquired, no needed good be lacking to the human person. When, however, any of the individual goods of this sort have been obtained, many goods necessary to human beings can still be lacking, such as wisdom, bodily health, and so forth. Third, since happiness is a perfect good, no evil can come from that happiness to afflict someone. Such, however, is certainly not the case with these exterior goods, for it is said in Ecclesiastes that wealth is sometimes "kept for the evil of its possessor."[3] The same is true for the other exterior goods. The fourth reason is that human beings are ordained to happiness, and they are so ordained naturally by the interior principles of human nature. The previously discussed goods, however, come rather from exterior causes, and they are especially dependent upon fortune; they are called, in fact, goods of fortune. It is clear that happiness in no way consists in such goods.

OBJECTION 3

Since happiness is the most desirable thing, it is opposed to that which is the most shunned. Human beings shun slavery most of all, and slavery is opposed to power. Happiness, therefore, consists in power.

REPLY TO OBJECTION 3

Slavery is a failure of the good use of power, for which reason human beings naturally shun it, and not because power is the highest human good.

---

1   That is, happiness does not consist in money, honour, fame, or power. The article on fame (A. 3) is not included in this volume.
2   Aristotle, *Nicomachean Ethics* 1.7, 1097b8–13.
3   Ecclesiastes 5:13.

Article 5: Will Bodily Health Make Us Happy?

It is impossible that human happiness consist in a good of the body, for two reasons. First, whatever is ordered to something else as its goal cannot have its own preservation in existence as its ultimate goal. For example, the ship captain does not intend, as the ultimate goal, the preservation of the ship that has been entrusted to him; this is so because the ship is ordered to something else, namely, to transporting passengers or goods. Just as the ship is entrusted to the captain to be commanded, so the human being has been entrusted to the command of will and reason. As is said in Ecclesiasticus, "God from the beginning made humans and left them in the power of their own counsel."[1] It is clear, moreover, that human beings are ordained to something that is their goal, for human beings are not the highest good. It is, therefore, impossible that the ultimate goal of human reason and will be the preservation of human existence.

Second, even if it were true that the goal of human reason and will were the preservation of human existence, nevertheless it would not be true that the human goal is some good of the body. The reason is that human existence is composed of soul and body, and although the existence of the body depends upon the soul, nevertheless the existence of the human soul does not depend upon the body, as has been shown.[2] The body itself exists for the sake of the soul, just as matter exists for the sake of form, and instruments exist for the sake of the mover, which uses them to achieve its actions. All goods of the body, therefore, are ordained to the goods of the soul as the goal. Hence, it is impossible that happiness, which is the ultimate goal, consist in goods of the body.

Article 6: Will Pleasure Make Us Happy?

THOMAS'S ANSWER

"Because bodily delights are known to everyone, they are taken to be pleasures," as is said in the *Ethics*.[3] They, however, are not

---

1 Ecclesiasticus or Book of Sirach 15:14.
2 *ST* I, Q. 75, A. 2 & 6, Ch. 3, pp. 92–94, 98–100.
3 Aristotle, *Nicomachean Ethics* 7.13, 1153b33–35.

what happiness principally consists of. In everything, we should distinguish between what is essential and what is a proper accident. In human beings, for example, there is a difference between being a rational, mortal animal [the human essence] and having the ability to laugh [a proper accident of that essence]. We should note that every delight is a sort of proper accident and consequent of happiness, or it is some part of happiness. We take delight from the fact that we have something appropriately good for us, whether in actual fact, in expectation, or at least in memory. The appropriate good, however, if it is the perfect good, is the very happiness of human beings; if, however, it is imperfect, it is a partial happiness, whether greater, lesser, or merely apparent. It is, therefore, clear that the delight that follows from the perfect good is not the essence of happiness but is, rather, a certain consequence of happiness or a proper accident of it.

Bodily pleasure, however, cannot be a consequence of the perfect good in the way just described. Bodily pleasure is a consequence of the good that is perceived by the senses, which are powers of soul operating through the body. The good that pertains to the body, which is perceived by the senses, cannot be the perfect human good. Since the power of the rational soul exceeds the capacity of bodily matter, the part of the soul that operates apart from any bodily organ has a certain infinity in comparison to the body and to the parts of the soul that are connected to the body. Just as immaterial things are in a way infinite in comparison to material things, because form is in some way constrained and limited by matter, so, as a result, form that is freed from matter is infinite in a qualified way. For this reason, the senses, which are bodily powers, know only individuals, which are determined by matter; the intellect, however, which is a power that is free from matter, knows the universal, which is abstracted from matter and which contains under it an infinite number of individuals. It is clear, therefore, that the good appropriate to the body, which causes bodily delight through sense perception, is not the perfect human good, but is rather a very small good in comparison to the good of the soul. Accordingly it is said in the Book of Wisdom that "all gold, in comparison to wisdom, is but paltry wealth."[1] Therefore, bodily pleasure is not happiness itself, nor is it a proper accident of happiness.

---

1   Book of Wisdom 7:9.

Article 7: Can Some Good of the Soul Make Us Happy?

THOMAS'S ANSWER

The goal, as we have said, can be understood in two ways: it could be the very thing that we are trying to obtain; or, it could be the enjoyment, gaining, or possessing of that thing. If we are talking about the ultimate human goal as the thing that we are trying to obtain, it is impossible that the ultimate human goal be the human soul or anything belonging to it. The reason is that the soul, just in itself, exists in a kind of potential state, for it goes from potentially knowing to actually knowing, and from potentially being virtuous to being actually so. Since potency exists for the sake of actuality, as its completion, it is impossible that that which by nature is in potency have the nature of the ultimate goal. It is, therefore, impossible that the soul itself be its own ultimate goal.

Likewise, also, no part of the soul could be the ultimate goal, whether the part is a power, a habit, or an act. The good that is the ultimate goal is the good that perfectly fulfils the soul's appetite for good. The *human* appetite, however, which is the will, is an appetite for the universal good. Any good, however, that belongs to the soul itself is a partial good, and consequently limited. It is, therefore, impossible that any such good be the ultimate human goal.

If, however, we talk about the ultimate human goal with respect to gaining or possessing that goal, or about some enjoyment of that which is sought as the goal, in this sense the human soul does belong to the ultimate goal, because a human being attains happiness through the soul. The thing itself, therefore, which is sought as the goal is that in which happiness consists and which makes us happy, but the gaining of this thing is called happiness. In this sense, we should say that happiness is something belonging to the soul, but that in which happiness consists is something outside of the soul.

Article 8: Can *Any* Created Good Make Us Happy?

THOMAS'S ANSWER

It is impossible that human happiness be found in any created good. Happiness is the perfect good that completely satisfies the human appetite, and it would not be the ultimate goal, if something remained still to be desired after it. The object of the will, which is the human appetite, is universal good, just as the object of the intellect is universal truth. From this it follows that nothing can satisfy the human will except the universal good. This, however, cannot be found in any created good, but only in God, because every creature has only a partial or shared goodness. Only God, therefore, can fulfil the human will; as the Psalmist says, "He is the one who satisfies the desire of the good."[1] Human happiness, therefore, is found in God alone.

Question 3: What Happiness Is

Article 8: Is Human Happiness Found in the Vision of God?

THOMAS'S ANSWER

The ultimate and perfect human happiness can only be found in the vision of the divine essence. To show this, two things should be considered. First, a human being is not perfectly happy so long as something remains that could be desired or sought. Second, the perfection of any power is found in the nature of the object of that power. "The object of the intellect is [to know] what something is, that is, the essence of a thing," as is said in *On the Soul*.[2] Hence, the perfection of the intellect is achieved to the extent that it knows the essence of anything. If, therefore, an intellect should know the essence of some effect, through which it could not know the essence of the cause or what the cause really is, such an intellect could not be said to know the cause, even though it would know through the effect that there was a cause. Although the human intellect, operating on the natural level, knows effects and knows that they have a cause, there remains nevertheless the desire for humans to know what the cause really is. That desire, as is said in the *Metaphysics*, comes from wonder and gives rise to a search.[3] For example, if someone should know that an eclipse occurred and should wonder what caused the eclipse to occur, he or she would wonder about the cause that is unknown, and this wonder would cause him or her to enquire. This enquiry would not come to an end until he or she should come to know the essence of the cause.

---

1 Psalms 102:5.
2 Aristotle, *On the Soul* 3.6, 430b27.
3 Aristotle, *Metaphysics* 1.2, 983b12–20.

If, therefore, the human intellect, while knowing the essence of some created effect, only knows about God that he exists, the perfection of that intellect in knowing the first cause has not yet been achieved, and there remains for it still the natural desire of enquiring into the cause. It is, therefore, not yet perfectly happy. For perfect happiness, therefore, it is necessary that the human person grasp the very essence of the First Cause. It will achieve its happiness, therefore, through a union with God as its object, in whom alone human happiness consists, as we have said.

Question 5: Acquiring Happiness

Article 3: Can Anyone Be Happy in this Life?

THOMAS'S ANSWER

Some partial happiness can be found in this life, but true and perfect happiness cannot be found in this life. We can see this in two ways. First, this can be seen from the general nature of happiness. Happiness, since it is the perfect and sufficient good, excludes all evil and satisfies every desire. In this life, however, it is impossible to exclude every evil. The present life, as we know, is subject to many evils that cannot be avoided: such as ignorance on the part of the intellect, disordered desire on the part of the appetite, and the many infirmities on the part of the body, as Augustine thoroughly enumerates in *The City of God*.[1] Likewise also, the desire for good in this life can never be satisfied, because human beings naturally desire the permanence of any good that they have. The good things, however, in this present life are transitory, and life itself is transitory, even though we naturally desire it and wish it to remain forever, as we naturally shun death. It is, therefore, impossible that true happiness be obtained in this life.

Second, we can see that happiness is impossible in this life, if we consider that in which human happiness especially consists, namely, in the vision of the divine essence, which cannot be given to human beings in this life. From all of this it is perfectly clear that no one in this life can attain true and perfect happiness.

---

1 Augustine, *The City of God*, Bk. 19, Ch. 4.

Article 5: Can Human Beings with Their Own Natural Abilities Acquire Happiness?

THOMAS'S ANSWER

The imperfect happiness which can be found in this life can be acquired by human beings through their own natural powers, just as they can acquire virtue on their own, by the practice of which they can be imperfectly happy, as will be shown below.[1] Perfect human happiness, however, as we have shown,[2] consists in the vision of the divine essence. To see God's essence, however, is beyond the nature not only of a human being but of any creature, as has been shown.[3] The reason is that the natural knowledge of any creature is proportionate to the kind of substance it is. The intellect, as is said in the *Book of Causes*,[4] knows things that are above its nature and below its nature, but knows these things according to its own nature. All knowledge at the level of any created substance will fail to reach the vision of the divine essence, which infinitely goes beyond any created substance. Hence, neither human beings nor any creature can attain the ultimate happiness by their own natural powers.

OBJECTION 1

Natural things never lack what is necessary to them. Nothing, however, is more necessary to human beings than what brings them to their ultimate goal. This, therefore, cannot be lacking to human nature, and human beings can by their own natural powers attain happiness.

REPLY TO OBJECTION 1

Even though nature has not given to human beings weapons and armour, as it has to other animals, nevertheless nature has not failed to provide what is necessary for human beings, because it has given them reason and human hands, by which they can acquire what they need. In the same way, nature has not failed to provide what is necessary to human beings, even though it has

---

1 *ST* I-II, Q. 63 (not included in this volume).
2 *ST* I-II, Q. 3, A. 8, pp. 146–47.
3 *ST* I, Q. 12, A. 4 (not included in this volume).
4 *Book of Causes* (*Liber de causis*), Prop. 8.

not given them a self-sufficient means of attaining happiness, for to do so would be impossible. It has, however, given them free choice, by which humans might turn to God, who would make them happy. "What we are able to accomplish with the help of our friends, we are able to accomplish to some extent by ourselves," as is said in the *Ethics*.[1]

B. Voluntary Actions

Question 6: Human Acts as Voluntary and as Involuntary

Article 1: Are Human Acts Voluntary?

THOMAS'S ANSWER

It is necessary that human acts be voluntary. As evidence for this, we should consider that the source of some acts or motions is within the agent or the moving thing; the source, however, of other acts or motions is outside. When, for example, a stone is moved upward, the source of this motion is outside of the stone, but when the stone falls down, the source of this motion is in the stone itself. Among the things that move by an intrinsic source, some move themselves and others do not. Because any agent or moving thing has a goal, as we have shown,[2] a thing moves itself intrinsically in the most perfect sense if it both has the source of its motion but also moves *for the sake of* a goal. In order, however, that there be motion for the sake of a goal, there must be some knowledge of the goal. Whatever, therefore, acts or moves because it has a knowledge of the goal, has within itself the source not only of action but of action for the sake of the goal. On the other hand, whatever has no knowledge of the goal, even if the source of action or motion is within it, nevertheless does not have within it the source of acting or moving for the sake of the goal; instead, the source of motion for the sake of a goal is imposed on it by something outside of it. Thus, things of this sort do not move themselves but are, rather, moved by something else. On the other hand, whatever does have a knowledge of the goal moves itself, because it has within itself both the source of its action and the source of its action for the sake of a goal. Since the source both of acting and of acting for the sake of a goal is intrin-

---

1 Aristotle, *Nicomachean Ethics* 3.3, 1113b27.
2 *ST* I-II, Q. 1, A. 2 (not included in this volume).

sic, any actions or motions from such an agent are voluntary. In fact, the meaning of the word "voluntary" is just that the motion or action of an agent comes from its own proper inclination. For this reason, the definition of voluntary action given by Aristotle,[1] Gregory of Nyssa,[2] and John of Damascus[3] is not only that "its source is within" but also that it requires in addition "knowledge." Consequently, since human beings recognize fully the goal of their actions, and since they move themselves, their actions are fully voluntary.

Article 2: Do Non-Rational Animals Act Voluntarily?

THOMAS'S ANSWER

Voluntary actions require that the source of the action be within the agent and that there be some knowledge of the goal, as I have said.[4] There are two different ways of knowing the goal: a perfect way and an imperfect way. We have perfect knowledge of the goal when we know not only the object that is our goal but also the meaning of the goal and how our actions lead to it. Such knowledge, of course, belongs only to rational beings. On the other hand, there is an imperfect knowledge of the goal when one knows only the goal and not the meaning of the goal nor how actions are related to it. Such knowledge is found in non-rational animals, which act through sensation and natural judgement.

When, therefore, there is perfect knowledge of the goal, actions are perfectly voluntary, because when we know the goal we can deliberate about it and about actions that lead to it, and we can decide to act or not to act. When there is imperfect knowledge of the goal, actions are voluntary only in the diminished sense that an animal recognizes a goal but does not deliberate about it; it simply acts immediately. Hence perfectly voluntary actions are found only in rational beings; in a diminished sense, however, voluntary actions are found even in non-rational animals.

---

1 Aristotle, *Nicomachean Ethics* 3.1, 1111a23.
2 The author was really Nemesius, *On the Nature of Man*, Ch. 32. On Nemesius, see p. 37.
3 John of Damascus, *On the Orthodox Faith*, Bk. 2, Ch. 24.
4 *ST* I, Q. 6, A. 1, pp. 149–50.

Article 3: Can *Inaction* Be Voluntary?

We call something voluntary because it comes from the will. "To come *from* something," however, can mean two different things. In one way, something comes from something else *directly*, because it proceeds from something that actively causes it, as heat comes from fire. In another way, something comes from something else *indirectly*, as a result of something not acting. For example, we say that the sinking of the ship came from the captain, because he stopped piloting the ship. Note, however, that what results from a lack of action is not always attributable to the fact that some agent did not act; it is only attributable to the agent that could and should act. If, for example, the captain was not able to pilot the ship, or if the command of the ship had not been entrusted to him, the sinking of the ship, which resulted from a lack of command, would not be attributed to him.

Hence, because by willing or by acting the will is able to do the opposite of not willing or not acting, and the will ought to have such control, the non-willing or non-acting is attributable to it as what comes from it. In this way, something voluntary can come about without any act; sometimes this occurs without any exterior act, though with an interior act, but at other times this occurs even without an interior act, as when someone simply refrains from willing.

Article 4: Can the Will Be Coerced by Force?

THOMAS'S ANSWER

There are two ways to consider the act of the will. One way is the will's immediate action, caused immediately by itself, namely, the very act of willing. The other way is the act that is commanded by the will but exercised through the mediation of some other power; for example, walking or talking, which are commanded by the will through other bodily powers. Acts commanded by the will in this second sense can be coerced by violence, because exterior parts of the body can be impeded by violence so that they cannot follow the command of the will. The immediate act of the will, however, cannot be coerced by violence.

The reason for this is that the act of the will is nothing other than a sort of inclination that proceeds from an interior source of knowledge, just as the natural appetite is a sort of inclination that proceeds from an interior source but without knowledge. Whatever is coerced or forced is caused by an external source. Hence, it is contrary to the very meaning of the act of the will that it be coerced or forced, just as it is contrary to the natural inclination or motion of a stone that it be moved upward. A stone can indeed be moved upward by force, but it is impossible that that forced motion come from its natural inclination. In the same way also human beings can be moved by force, but to be moved by force is repugnant to the very meaning of the will.

Article 6: Does Fear Make Our Actions Absolutely Involuntary?

THOMAS'S ANSWER

As Aristotle[1] and Gregory of Nyssa[2] say, actions that are done out of fear are a mixture of the voluntary and the involuntary, for that which is done through fear is, in itself, not voluntary, although it is accidentally voluntary, insofar as we are avoiding the evil that we fear. If we rightly consider this, however, actions of this sort are really more voluntary than involuntary. They are, in fact, absolutely voluntary and only involuntary in some restricted sense. We say that something exists absolutely if it is in actuality; if something exists only in the mind, it does not exist absolutely but only in a restricted sense. Whatever is done through fear exists in actuality as an action, and since actions exist as individual entities, and individuals as such exist in the here and now, any actual action exists in the here and now under individual conditions. Thus, whatever is done through fear is voluntary, that is, as an action in the here and now it is in this particular situation an avoidance of a greater evil that is feared. For example, when a sea-faring merchant throws his merchandise overboard into the sea, this action is voluntary at the time of a storm because of the fear of danger. Hence, it is clear that such an action is absolutely voluntary and what we mean by voluntary describes this action, because the source of the action is intrinsic.

On the other hand, if we consider what is done through fear apart from the individual case and as something repugnant to the will, this is merely a hypothetical consideration. In this restricted

---

1 Aristotle, *Nicomachean Ethics* 3.1, 1110a11–13.
2 The author was really Nemesius, *On the Nature of Man*, Ch. 30.

sense, the action is involuntary, but only so when it is considered apart from the individual case.

Article 7: Does Physical Desire Cause Our Actions to Be Involuntary?

THOMAS'S ANSWER

Physical desire does not cause our actions to be involuntary but rather makes them to be voluntary. We call something voluntary because the will tends toward it. Through physical desire the will is inclined to will that which it desires. Physical desire, therefore, makes what we will more voluntary rather than involuntary.

OBJECTION 3

Voluntary actions require knowledge, but physical desire destroys knowledge, for Aristotle says that pleasure or the desire for pleasure destroys the judgement of prudence.[1] Physical desire, therefore, makes our actions involuntary.

REPLY TO OBJECTION 3

If physical desire completely removed knowledge, as happens in those who are demented through such desire, it would follow that physical desire would make our actions not voluntary. However, such actions would not properly speaking be involuntary, for if there is no use of reason, the actions are neither voluntary nor involuntary. There are, however, times when actions done through physical desire are not done completely without knowledge, because the power of knowing remains, but the actual recognition of the particular situation is lacking. Nevertheless, even in these situations the actions are voluntary, because what is voluntary is in the power of the will, and to act or not to act, or to consider or not to consider, still remains. The will is able to resist passion, as will be shown.[2]

---

1 Aristotle, *Nicomachean Ethics* 6.5, 1140b12–16.
2 *ST* I-II, Q. 10, A. 3; I–II, Q.77, A. 7 (not included in this volume).

Article 8: Does Ignorance Cause Our Actions to Be Involuntary?

Ignorance causes actions to be involuntary insofar as ignorance negates knowledge that is a condition for voluntary action, as we have said.[1] Not every sort of ignorance, however, negates the sort of knowledge required. To see this we should know that ignorance is related to the act of the will in three different ways: in one way it is concomitant with the will; in a second way it is consequent upon the will; in a third way it is antecedent to the will.

Ignorance concomitant with the will occurs when there is ignorance about what is being done such that if it were known it would still be done. In this case, ignorance does not cause one to will an action, but the ignorance occurs simultaneously with the action. An example of this is the case of someone who wishes to kill his enemy and does so in ignorance, thinking that he is killing a deer. Such ignorance does not make the action involuntary, as Aristotle says,[2] because it does not cause something to occur that is repugnant to the will. Rather, it makes the action non-voluntary, because an action of which one is actually ignorant cannot be willed.

Ignorance consequent upon the will occurs when the ignorance itself is voluntary. This occurs in two ways, according to the two ways in which actions are voluntary, as we noted above.[3] In one way, the act of the will [directly] produces ignorance, when someone wills not to know, either in order to have an excuse for sinning or in order not to be restrained from sinning, as is said in Job 21:14: "We have refused the knowledge of your ways." This is called self-caused ignorance. In another way, ignorance is called [indirectly] voluntary of that which one is able to know and ought to know. In this sense, not acting and not willing are voluntary, as we have said.[4] Ignorance in this sense occurs either when someone actually does not consider what he can and ought to consider (this is called the ignorance of a bad choice, resulting

---

1 *ST* I-II, Q. 6, A. 1, pp. 149–50.
2 Aristotle, *Nicomachean Ethics* 3.1, 1110b19–21.
3 *ST* I-II, Q. 6, A. 3, p. 151. This is the distinction between what we will directly, by actually willing something, and what we will indirectly, by not willing something.
4 *ST* I-II, Q. 6, A. 3, p. 151.

from passion or a bad habit), or when someone does not bother to acquire the knowledge that one ought to have. In this way, an ignorance of universal moral laws, which anyone ought to know, is called voluntary, because it proceeds from negligence. Since this sort of ignorance, in either of these ways, is voluntary, it cannot cause our actions to be absolutely involuntary. It does, however, cause them to be accidentally involuntary, insofar as it precedes the action of the will to do something, which would not happen if knowledge were present.

Ignorance is antecedent to the will when it is not voluntary and is nevertheless the cause of willing what one would otherwise not will. This sort of ignorance is found when we do not know some circumstance of our action that we are not morally required to know and when we would not have done the action if we had known otherwise. For example, someone who has done due diligence might be ignorant of someone crossing the road and shoot an arrow that kills the walker. Such ignorance does cause actions to be involuntary absolutely.

Question 13: Choice, the Act of Will or Reason

Article 1: Is Choice an Act of the Will or of Reason?

THOMAS'S ANSWER

The word "choice" indicates something pertaining to reason or intellect and also something pertaining to the will. Aristotle, in fact, says "choice is an appetitive intellect or an intellectual appetite."[1] Sometimes two things come together to constitute one thing, one of which is formal with respect to the other. Accordingly, Gregory of Nyssa says that "choice is neither appetite by itself nor intellectual reasoning by itself but is something composed out of both. Just as we say that an animal is composed of soul and body, and is not merely a soul by itself nor a body by itself, but is both together—so also with choice."[2]

In acts of the soul, however, we should note that an act that belongs essentially to one power or habit can receive its form or character from a higher power or habit, insofar as the lower thing is ordered by the higher. If, for example, someone performs an act of courage out of love for God, that act is *materially* an act of

---

1   Aristotle, *Nicomachean Ethics* 6.2, 1139b4.
2   The author was really Nemesius, *On the Nature of Man*, Ch. 33.

courage, but it is *formally* an act of charity. It is furthermore clear that reason in some way precedes the will and orders the act of the will, in that the will intends its object only insofar as it is ordered by reason, because the cognitive power displays the object to the appetitive power.

So it is, therefore, that any act intended by the will as something shown to be good, because it has been ordered by reason to a goal that is good, is *materially* an act of the will but *formally* an act of reason. The essence, however, of such an act is found in the act materially considered, though in relation to the order that is imposed by the higher power. Choice, therefore, is essentially not an act of reason but of the will, for choice is realized in an action of the soul toward the good that is chosen. Choice, thus, is clearly an act of the appetitive power.

Article 3: Do We Choose Only the Means to the Goal or also the Goal?

THOMAS'S ANSWER

Choice, as we have said,[1] follows upon reasoned opinion or judgement, which is the conclusion of practical arguments. Hence, what we choose is the conclusion of a practical argument. The goal in practical matters is rather the premise of an argument than the conclusion, as Aristotle says.[2] Hence, the goal as such is not a matter for choice.

In scientific reasoning, there is nothing to prevent that which is a principle in one science or demonstration from being a conclusion in another science or demonstration. Of course, the very first principle cannot be the conclusion of any science or demonstration. In just the same way, also, it can be the case that what is a goal in one activity is a means in another; in this way, a goal can be a matter of choice. For example, in the work of the doctor, health is taken as a goal; it is not a matter of choice for the doctor but is presupposed as a principle. The health of the body, however, is ordered to the good of the soul, and thus for the one who cares for the health of the soul, bodily health or illness can be a matter of choice. The Apostle, in fact, says in II Corinthians

---

1   *ST* I-II, Q. 13, A. 1, Reply to Obj. 2 (not included in this volume).
2   Aristotle, *Physics* 2.9, 200a20–22. The goal, as a premise in the argument, would be *assumed* rather than proven.

12:10: "When I am weak, then I am strong." The ultimate goal, however, is in no way a matter of choice.

Article 6: Do Human Beings Choose Freely or Out of Necessity?

THOMAS'S ANSWER

Human beings do not choose out of necessity. The reason for this is that whatever might possibly not exist does not exist necessarily. The fact that it is possible to choose or not to choose can be seen from the two-fold power of human beings. A human person can will or not will, act or not act; a person can also will this or that. The reason for this can be seen in the very power of reasoning. The will can intend whatever reason can recognize as good. Reason can recognize as good, not only what it wills or does, but also what it does not will and does not do. Furthermore, in all individual good things, reason can consider what makes one thing good, or the lack of goodness that makes something else bad. In this way, reason can recognize in each individual good thing what should be chosen and what should be rejected. The only exception, however, is the perfect good, or happiness, in which reason cannot recognize anything bad or any defect. In that case, therefore, human beings out of necessity will happiness, and it is not possible to will not to be happy or to be miserable. Choice, however, since it is not about the goal but rather about the means to the goal, as we have said,[1] does not concern the perfect good, which is happiness, but is rather about other, limited goods. Therefore, human beings do not choose out of necessity but do so freely.

C. The Moral Goodness of Human Acts

Question 18: The Goodness and Evil of Human Actions, Generally

Article 1: Is Every Human Action Good, or Are Some Bad?

THOMAS'S ANSWER

We should talk about what is good and bad in human actions in the same way that we talk about what is good and bad in things,

---

1   *ST* I-II, Q. 13, A. 3, pp. 156–57.

because things produce actions that are like themselves. Each thing has as much goodness as it has being, because "good" and "being" are convertible, as we explained.[1] Now, only God has the complete fullness of his being in a united and simple way. In contrast, every other thing has a fullness of being appropriate to its own nature but in some restricted way. So it is that some things have being in some respect but they still lack the fullness of being that they should have. For example, to have the fullness of being a human person must be composed of soul and body and must have all of the powers and organs needed for cognition and activity; if, therefore, one of these powers or organs should be defective in someone, such a person would be lacking the fullness of his being. As much as anyone has being, therefore, he or she also has goodness; on the other hand, as much as someone lacks the fullness of being, to that extent he or she lacks goodness, and this is bad. A blind man, for example, has the goodness of being alive, but he lacks vision, which is bad. If, however, something had no being or goodness at all, we could not call it either good or bad. Since, in fact, the fullness of being expresses what it means to be "good," if something lacks the fullness of being that it should have, we will not call it good absolutely but only good in some limited way, insofar as it has being. It will, nevertheless, be possible to call something a being substantially but also a non-being in some qualified way, as was said.[2]

We can therefore say that every action, insofar as it has something of being, also has something of goodness; but insofar as it lacks the fullness of being that ought to belong to a human action, it also lacks goodness, and thus is called bad. For example, an otherwise good action might be deficient in that it is done too little or too much, or because it is done in the wrong place, or something of this sort.

Article 2: Are Human Actions Good or Bad *Objectively*?

THOMAS'S ANSWER

As we have just said,[3] what is good or bad in actions, as in other things, is found in the fullness of being or in the lack of it. In the first place, what pertains to the fullness of being is what makes

---

1 *ST* I, Q. 5, A. 1 (not included in this volume).
2 *ST* I, Q. 5, A. 1, Reply to Obj. 1 (not included in this volume).
3 *ST* I-II, Q. 18, A. 1, pp. 157–58.

anything to be the kind of thing that it is. Just as any natural thing is determined in its species by its form, so actions are different in kind because of the *objects* of the actions, as also motions are differentiated by their end points. Therefore, just as the primary goodness of a natural thing is found in its form, which determines the thing in its species, so also the primary goodness of a moral act is found in the object produced by the act. Some call this sort of good the generic good of the act; for example, using one's own property is generically good. Just as in natural things the primary evil occurs when something generated fails to reach its specific form, as when human generation produces something other than a human being, so the primary evil in moral actions is found in the object. Taking what belongs to another, for example, is evil in this way. This sort of act is called generically evil, although "generically" is taken to indicate the "kind" or "species," as when we say that what is "generally" true of humans indicates what is true of the human species.

OBJECTION 1

The object of an action is an exterior thing. In exterior things, however, there is no evil, other than in their use by sinners, as Augustine says.[1] Human action, therefore, does not have its goodness or badness in its object.

REPLY TO OBJECTION 1

Although it is true that exterior things are in themselves good, nevertheless they do not always have the proper relationship to this or that action. Therefore, insofar as exterior things are considered as the objects of bad actions, they do not have the full meaning of what is good.

Article 3: Do Circumstances Make Human Actions Good or Bad?

THOMAS'S ANSWER

The complete fullness of perfection that should belong to natural things does not come from the substantial form, which determines the species of the thing. In fact, much is added to the sub-

---

1 Augustine, *On Christian Doctrine*, Bk. 3, Ch. 12, ¶ 19.

stance from the subsequent accidents; for example, much is added to a human being because of shape, colour, and other such accidents. If a human being is deficient in some such way, the result is something bad. The same is true about action, for its complete goodness does not consist merely in the kind of act that it is, but something is added to the act from those things that are like accidents of it; these are the circumstances of the act. If something is lacking in the circumstances that ought to belong to the action, the action will be evil.

Article 4: Are Human Actions Good or Bad because of the Intended Goal?

THOMAS'S ANSWER

We talk about the goodness and the being of things in the same ways. The being of some things does not depend on what is outside, and for them it is sufficient to consider their being just by itself. The being of other things, however, does depend on outside things, and for them it is necessary to consider the cause upon which they depend. Just as the being of a thing depends upon its causal agent and its form, so the goodness of a thing depends on the intended goal. Thus, for example, the Divine Persons of the Trinity, who have no dependence on anything outside of themselves, do not have their goodness from some goal outside of them. Human actions, however, and any goodness that is dependent on something outside of them, have their goodness from the intended goal, upon which they depend, beyond the simple goodness of the action itself.

Accordingly, therefore, we can consider the goodness of human actions in four ways. One goodness is generic, in that any action has as much goodness as it has being, as we have said.[1] A second goodness is specific, which belongs to an action according to the objective character of the act. A third goodness is from the circumstances of the action, which amount to accidents, as it were, of the action. The fourth goodness is from the intended end, which comes from the relation of the action to the cause of its goodness.

---

1 *ST* I-II, Q. 18, A. 1, pp. 157–58.

OBJECTION 3

It can happen that a good action is ordered to a bad end, as when someone gives alms in order to be praised; and, in the opposite case, a bad action can be ordered to a good end, as when someone steals in order to give to the poor. Human actions, therefore, are not good or bad because of the intended end.

REPLY TO OBJECTION 3

There is no reason why an action that is good in some of the senses noted above cannot be lacking goodness in some other sense. Accordingly, it happens that an action that is good in its objective kind or done in the right circumstances is ordered to a bad end, or vice versa. A human action, however, is not completely good unless it is good in all of the four senses, because "any defect of one kind of goodness causes the action to be evil, and an action is made good by its goodness as a whole," as Dionysius says.[1]

Article 6: Does the Intended Goal Determine the Moral Character of the Act?

THOMAS'S ANSWER

Acts are called human because they are voluntary, as we have said.[2] A voluntary act, however, includes two acts: an interior act of the will and an exterior act, and both of these have an object. The intended goal is the proper object of the interior voluntary act; what the act accomplishes is the object of the exterior act. Just as the exterior act is the kind of act that it is because of the object that it accomplishes, so also the interior act is the kind of act that it is from the intended goal, which is its proper object.

Now, the part of the act that comes from the will is *formal* with respect to the part that comes from the exterior act, because the will uses the members of the body for acting as its instruments. Furthermore, exterior acts would not be moral at all, if they were not voluntary. Therefore, a human act is determined *formally* in its kind by the intended goal, but it is determined *materially* by

---

1 Dionysius the Areopagite (Pseudo-Dionysius), *The Divine Names*, Ch. 4, ¶ 30.

2 *ST* I-II, Q. 1, A. 1, pp. 137–38.

the object of the exterior act. For this reason, Aristotle says that "he who steals in order to commit adultery is properly speaking more an adulterer than a thief."[1]

Article 8: Are Some Kinds of Human Acts Morally Indifferent?

THOMAS'S ANSWER

Every act is determined in its kind by its object, as we have said.[2] A human act, which is a moral act, is determined in its kind by the object seen in relation to the source of human acts, which is reason. If, therefore, the object of an act includes something that accords with the order of reason, the act will be a good kind of act; giving alms to a needy person, for example, is a good act. On the other hand, if the object of the act includes something that is repugnant to the order of reason, the act will be an evil kind of act; taking what belongs to another, for example, is stealing and is wrong. It can happen, however, that the object of an act has no inherent connection to the order of reason; lifting some straw from the ground, for example, or going into the country, and acts of this kind are morally indifferent.

Article 9: Is Any Individual Act Morally Indifferent?

THOMAS'S ANSWER

An act that is morally indifferent in its kind, nevertheless, can be good or bad when considered as an individual, concrete act. This is so because the moral act, as we have said, not only has its goodness from its object, from which it is determined in its kind, but also from the circumstances, which are as it were the accidents of the act. In the same way, what may be true for one individual, because of individual accidents, will not be true for human beings taken as a species. It is necessary that any individual act has some circumstance that makes the act either good or bad, at least on the part of the goal that has been intended. Since it is the function of reason to order things, if an act that is chosen by deliberative reason is not ordered to the proper end, such an act is, for this very reason, repugnant to reason and has a bad character. If, on the other hand, the act is ordered to its proper goal, it agrees

---

1 Aristotle, *Nicomachean Ethics* 5.2, 1130a24–25.
2 *ST* I-II, Q.18, A. 2, pp. 158–59.

with the order of reason and has, therefore, a good character. It is, however, necessary that an act is either ordered to the proper goal or not so ordered. It is, therefore, necessary that every human act that is chosen by deliberative reason, considered in its individual circumstances, is either good or evil.

Of course, if an act is not chosen by deliberative reason, but comes instead from some stimulus, as when someone scratches a beard or inadvertently moves a hand or a stone, such an act is not properly speaking moral or human, since the act occurs without reason. Such an act will be indifferent, insofar as it is outside of the category of moral acts.

Question 19: The Goodness and Evil of the Interior Act of the Will

Article 5: Is the Will Bad if It Refuses to Follow Mistaken Reason?

THOMAS'S ANSWER

Conscience is the command of reason, or, as we have said,[1] it is an application of knowledge to action. For this reason, it is the same thing to ask whether the will is bad if it refuses to follow mistaken reason as to ask whether a mistaken conscience is morally binding.

On this matter, some theologians have distinguished three kinds of acts: acts that are good in kind, acts that are indifferent, and acts that are bad. They say that if reason or conscience should order something to be done that is good in kind, there is no error. Likewise, if it should order something not to be done that is bad in kind, there is again no error. It is, of course, by the same reason that good things are ordered and bad things forbidden. If reason or conscience, however, should tell someone that he or she is bound to do what is bad in itself, or if it should say that he or she is forbidden from doing what is in itself good, reason or conscience will be mistaken in either case. Likewise, if reason or conscience should tell someone that what is in itself indifferent (such as lifting straw from the field) is either ordered or forbidden, reason or conscience will again be mistaken. They say, therefore, that mistaken reason or conscience about morally indifferent actions, whether in ordering or in forbidding action, does morally bind us, so that if the will refuses to follow such mis-

---

1 *ST* I, Q. 79, A. 15 (not included in this volume).

taken reason it will be bad and sinful. On the other hand, when mistaken reason or conscience either orders us to do what is bad in itself or forbids us from doing what is good in itself, it is not morally binding. Hence, in such cases the will that refuses to follow mistaken reason or conscience is not bad.

This sort of reasoning, however, is irrational. In the case of indifferent acts, the will that refuses to follow mistaken reason or conscience is bad. The reason it is bad has to do in some way with the object, on which the goodness or evil of the will depends. The concern here is not with the proper object of the will in its own true nature, but rather with the object accidentally understood by reason, as something bad to be done or avoided. Because the object of the will is something proposed to it by reason, as we have said,[1] the very fact that something is proposed to the will as bad means that the will, in responding to the object, accepts it as having a bad character. This is the case, moreover, not only in indifferent acts but also in those that are good or bad in themselves. This is so because the will can accept the accidental character of good or bad, not only for an indifferent act, but it can also accept that a good act has a bad character, or that a bad act has a good character, if reason apprehends it so. For example, refraining from fornication is a good thing, but the will is not inclined to this good unless it is proposed as good by reason. If, therefore, it should be proposed to the will as something bad by mistaken reason, the will would be inclined to something that it accepts as bad. In such a case the will is bad, because it wants what is bad; it does not want what is in itself bad but it wants that which is accidentally bad insofar as it is so grasped by reason. Likewise, believing in Christ is good in itself and necessary for salvation, but the will is only inclined to this insofar as it is proposed to the will by reason. Hence, if reason should propose this as something bad, the will would be inclined to this as something bad, not because it is in itself bad but because it is accidentally bad as it is grasped by reason. Hence, Aristotle says[2] that "properly speaking, the immoderate person is the one who does not follow right reason; accidentally, however, such a person does not even follow false reason." Hence we can say simply that any will that refuses to follow reason, whether it is right or mistaken, is always wrong.

---

1   *ST* I-II, Q. 19, A. 3 (not included in this volume).

2   Aristotle, *Nicomachean Ethics* 7.9, 1151a33.

Article 6: Is the Will Good if It Follows Mistaken Reason?

Just as the previous question is the same question as whether a mistaken conscience is morally binding, so this question is the same as whether a mistaken conscience provides a moral excuse. This question, however, depends upon what was said above about ignorance.[1] We said that ignorance sometimes causes an action to be involuntary, but sometimes it does not. Since morally good and bad actions are those that are voluntary, as we have said,[2] it is clear that the ignorance that makes an action involuntary takes away the character of moral good or evil. On the other hand, the ignorance that does not make an action involuntary does not take away the character of moral good or evil. We have said above[3] that ignorance that is in some way voluntary, whether directly or indirectly, does not cause involuntary action. By "directly" voluntary ignorance I mean ignorance that is willed by an act of the will; "indirectly" willed ignorance results from negligence, from the fact that someone does not wish to know what he or she ought to know. If, therefore, reason or conscience is mistaken because of voluntary error, whether directly or through negligence, since in either case the error is about something one ought to know, then such an error of reason or of conscience does not provide a moral excuse such that the will that follows mistaken reason or conscience is not bad. For example, if mistaken reason should say that a man should have sexual relations with another man's wife, the will following this mistaken reason is bad, because this sort of error comes from an ignorance of the law of God, which one ought to know. If, however, reason is mistaken in that a man believes that the woman in his bed is his wife, and so has sexual relations with her, his will is excused and as a result is not bad. The error in this case comes from an ignorance of the circumstances, which causes the action to be involuntary and excuses the man morally.

---

1   *ST* I-II, Q. 6, A. 8, pp. 154–55.
2   *ST* I-II, Q. 19, A. 2 (not included in this volume).
3   *ST* I-II, Q.6, A. 8, pp. 154–55.

D. Habits and Virtues

Question 49: Human Habits in General

Article 4: Are Habits Necessary?

THOMAS'S ANSWER

As I have said,[1] a habit is a kind of readiness to act in a natural thing that has operations and goals; it is a readiness to act either well or badly. If something needs to be made ready to act, three conditions are required. First, that which is made ready to act must be different from the action it is made ready for, that is, the thing made ready to act is in potency to some act. Hence, if there should be some being whose nature is not composed of potency and actuality, whose substance is its very operation, and whose existence is for its own sake, in such a being there would be no place for habits or being made ready to act; this is the case for God.

The second requirement is that that which is in potency to something else can be determined to different goals and in different ways. Hence, if something is in potency to something else but it is in potency to only one thing, there is no place there for being made ready to act and habit. Such a subject has by its very nature a fixed relationship to a given goal. If, for example, heavenly bodies are composed of matter and form, since that matter has no potency to any other form, as was said,[2] there is no place there for being made ready to act or for habit to another form or even to another operation, because the nature of the heavenly body is in potency to only one determined motion.

The third requirement is that the many things that come together to make the subject ready to be or to act in one way rather than another are so coordinated as to make the subject well or badly disposed in being or in operating. Hence, the simple qualities of elements, which belong to the elements in fixed ways, are not called "ready to act" or habits; they are simply qualities. On the other hand, readiness to be or to act, or habits, are things

---

1 *ST* I-II, Q. 49, AA. 1 & 2 (not included in this volume).
2 *ST* I, Q. 66, A. 2 (not included in this volume). Thomas, following Aristotle, thought that the matter of the heavenly bodies was different from the matter of earthly bodies. The matter of the heavens—ether—had a potency for one thing only, the regular motion of the heavenly body.

like health, beauty, and so forth, which involve a coordination of several things in various ways. For this reason, as I have pointed out,[1] Aristotle says that "habit is a readiness to act," and "a readiness to act is an order in something that has parts, in relation to place, power, or species."[2] Since, therefore, there are many kinds of beings that require a coordination of things in their nature and operations, and this can be done in different ways, habits are necessary.

Question 51: The Cause of Habits—How They Are Generated

Article 2: Are Some Habits Caused by Actions?

THOMAS'S ANSWER

In some agents there is only an active source of action, as, for example, in fire there is only the active source of heat. In such an agent no habit can be caused from its own action, and generally no natural thing can develop a habit or lose one, as Aristotle says.[3] On the other hand, there are other agents in which there is both an active and a passive source of action, as is the case in human actions. Actions from desire, for example, arise because the desire is passively moved by some desirable object that is apprehended; in addition, the intellect, as it reasons about what should be done, provides a self-evident judgement that is an active incentive to action. Hence, from actions of this sort, some habits can be caused in the agents, not in the primary active source of action, but in the source of the action that is itself moved in causing motion. The reason is that whatever is affected and moved by something else is thereby made ready to act by such action; hence, from repeated actions a certain quality is generated in the power that is passively moved, and this quality is called a habit. Just as the moral virtues are caused in the powers of desire, as these are moved by reason, so also the scientific disciplines are caused in the intellect, as these are moved by the first principles of science.

---

1 *ST* I-II, Q. 49, A. 1 (not included in this volume).
2 Aristotle, *Metaphysics* 5.20, 1022b10–14.
3 Aristotle, *Nicomachean Ethics* 2.1, 1103a19–20.

OBJECTION 1

It seems that a habit is not caused from actions, because a habit is a kind of quality, as we have said.[1] Every quality, however, is caused to exist in a subject insofar as the subject is *receptive* of something. Since, therefore, an agent as something that *acts* does not *receive* anything but rather *emits* something, it seems that it is not possible for any habit to be formed in an agent from its own actions.

REPLY TO OBJECTION 1

It is true that an agent just as an agent does not receive anything. However, insofar as an agent is moved by something else, it does receive something from whatever moves it, and in this way a habit is formed.

Article 3: Can a Habit Be Generated by One Action?

THOMAS'S ANSWER

As we have said, habits are generated by action insofar as a passive power is moved by some active power. In order that a quality be caused in the passive power, it is necessary that the active power completely overcome the passive. We see, for example, that fire does not all at once overcome the combustible matter, because it does not immediately cause it all to burn but, instead, it spreads itself slowly, overcoming resistant parts gradually, until it completely overwhelms the matter, making it all like itself. It is furthermore clear that the active power of reason cannot completely overcome the desiring power with one action, because the desiring power is in an indeterminate relation to many things. Reason, however, judges that one thing should be sought in certain determinate circumstances and for certain determinate reasons. From just one action the desiring power is not completely overcome so that it will consistently do the same thing most of the time, as though it were natural to do so, which is the mark of a virtuous habit. A virtuous habit, therefore, cannot be caused through just one action; many actions are required.

In the cognitive powers, however, note that there are two different kinds of passive power. One is the receptive intellect itself; the other is the intellect that Aristotle calls "passive," which is the

---

1 Just above in Thomas's Answer.

power to reason about individual sense experiences and hence to retain them in memory and imagination.[1] Concerning the receptive intellect, an active power can completely overcome the passive power with one action. This happens, for example, when one self-evident truth convinces the intellect to assent firmly to a conclusion; a merely probable truth could not do this. Hence, creating the habit of an opinion requires many acts from reason and even from the receptive intellect, but a scientific habit can be caused by one act of reason on the receptive intellect.

If we consider, however, the lower cognitive powers, it is necessary that the same actions be repeated numerous times in order that something be retained firmly in memory. Hence, Aristotle says that "repetition strengthens the memory."[2]

Finally, bodily habits can be caused by one action, if the active power is very powerful, as, for example, strong medicine can cause health immediately.

Question 55: The Essentials of Virtue

Article 1: Is Human Virtue a Habit?

THOMAS'S ANSWER

The word "virtue" indicates some sort of perfection of a power. Now, the perfection of anything can be found especially in relation to its goal, and the goal of a power is an action. Hence, a power is called perfect when it is determined toward its action. There are some powers that all by themselves are determined to their actions, as is the case in purely natural active powers. For this reason, natural powers of this sort can be considered "virtues" just in themselves. Rational powers, however, which are peculiar to human beings, are not determined to just one action but are indeterminately able to do many different things. Human powers, however, are determined to actions by habits, as has been said.[3] Human virtues, therefore, are habits.

---

1 Thomas, following Aristotle, thought that there were the five obvious external senses, but he also thought that there were a number of important internal senses, powers that humans and higher animals have of comparing, retaining, and even reasoning about our sense experiences. For Thomas's explanation of the interior senses, see *ST* I, Q. 78, A. 4 (not included in this volume).

2 Aristotle, *Memory and Recollection* 1, 451a12–14.

3 *ST* I-II, Q. 49, A. 4, pp. 166–67.

Question 61: The Cardinal Virtues

Article 2: Are There Four Cardinal Virtues?

THOMAS'S ANSWER

When we are trying to count something, we can consider either the formal principles of what we are trying to count or the subjects in which what we are counting are found; in either way, we will find that there are four cardinal virtues.

The formal principle of the virtue about which we are now speaking is *the good of reason*. This, in turn, can be considered in two ways. In one way, the good of reason is found in the consideration of reason itself. In this sense, there is one principal virtue, and this is called *prudence*. In another way, the good of reason is found wherever some order of reason is found. Such an order of reason may be found in human actions, where the virtue is *justice*, or in human emotions, where there are two virtues. For we must recognize an order of reason in emotions that may run contrary to reason. Such order may be found in two ways. In one way, emotion impels us to something that is contrary to reason, and such an emotion needs to be restrained; and for this the virtue is called *temperance*. In another way, emotion draws us away from what reason shows us to do, as does, for example, a fear of danger or of work. In this case it is necessary that we be strengthened so that we do not run away from what reason requires; and for this the virtue is called *courage*.

Likewise, if we consider the subjects of the virtues, we will get the same number, for there are four different subjects of the virtue about which we are now speaking. There is the power that is reason itself, and *prudence* perfects this. There are also the three powers that are rational by sharing in reason: the will, which is the subject of *justice*; the concupiscible power, which is the subject of *temperance*; and the irascible power, which is the subject of *courage*.

Article 3: Are Other Moral Virtues More Fundamental than the Cardinal Virtues?

THOMAS'S ANSWER

As was said above,[1] the cardinal virtues are understood on the basis of the four formal reasons of the moral virtue about which

---

1 *ST* I-II, Q. 61, A. 2, p. 170.

we are speaking, and these are fundamental in human actions and emotions. (1) The good that belongs to reason itself is found primarily in the command of reason, and not in mere rational deliberation or rational judgement, as was said above.[1] (2) Likewise, the good of reason in human actions about what is right and what is owed is primarily found in the exchanges and distributions that occur among people who are equals. (3) The good of restraining emotions is found primarily in the emotions that are especially difficult to control, that is, in the pleasures of touch. (4) The good of standing firm to uphold the good of reason against the force of emotions is found primarily in the fear of death, against which it is hardest to stand.

With this in mind, we can consider the four virtues in two different ways. First, we can consider the four virtues in comparison to the four formal reasons; these are principles that are common to all virtues. Every virtue, for example, that brings about good in the use of reason may be called prudence; every virtue that makes what is right and owed in human actions may be called justice; every virtue that restrains and subdues the emotions may be called temperance; and every virtue that makes the soul strong against any emotions may be called courage. Many speak about these virtues in this way, both theologians and philosophers.

Second, these virtues can be understood from what is primary in the peculiar matter of each virtue. In this sense, each virtue is specific and not common, but each virtue is said to be primary in comparison to the other virtues in regard to its own peculiar matter. Thus, prudence is the virtue that issues commands; justice is the virtue concerning actions that ought to occur among equals; temperance is the virtue that restrains the desires for the pleasures of touch; and courage is the virtue that strengthens us against the fears of death.

E. Law and Natural Law

Question 90: Laws

Article 1: Is Law a Product of Reason?

THOMAS'S ANSWER

Law is a kind of rule and measure of actions, according to which human beings are either required to do something or forbidden

---

1 *ST* I-II, Q. 57, A. 6 (not included in this volume).

from doing something. The word "law" [*lex*] is taken from a word that means "binding" [*ligandum*], because law binds us in our actions. Now, the rule and measure of human action is reason, which is the first principle of human actions, as we have said.[1] It belongs to reason to order things to the goal, "which is the first principle in human actions," according to Aristotle.[2] Moreover, in any category, that which is first is the rule and measure of the whole category, as unity is the rule and measure in the category of number and the primary motion is first in the category of motions. It follows, therefore, that law is something that belongs to reason.

OBJECTION 3

The law moves those who are subject to the law to act correctly. To move someone to act, however, properly belongs to the will, as has been said.[3] The law, therefore, does not belong to reason but rather to the will, as the Jurist also says, "Whatever is pleasing to the prince has the force of law."[4]

REPLY TO OBJECTION 3

It is true that reason's power of causing motion comes from the will, as I said above, because first someone wills the goal, and then reason commands what is needed to reach the goal.[5] The will, on the other hand, cannot command with the force of law unless it is first ruled by reason. Only in this way can the will of the prince have the force of law, for otherwise the will of the prince would not be law but would be unjust.

Article 2: Is Law Always Directed to the Common Good?

THOMAS'S ANSWER

Law, as we have said,[6] is found in the very beginning of human actions, because it is their rule and measure. Just as reason is the

---

1 *ST* I-II, Q. 1, A. 1, Reply to Obj. 3, p. 138.
2 Aristotle, *Physics* 2.9, 200a22–24.
3 *ST* I-II, Q. 9, A. 1 (not included in this volume).
4 *The Body of Civil Law* (*Corpus iuris civilis*), *Digesta*, Bk. I, Title 4, Law 1.
5 *ST* I-II, Q. 17, A.1 (not included in this volume).
6 *ST* I-II, Q. 90, A. 1, pp. 171–72.

principle of human actions, so also in reason itself there is something that is prior to everything else. To this prior thing law primarily and especially belongs. The first principle in actions, about which we exercise practical reason, is the ultimate goal. The ultimate goal of human life is happiness or blessedness, as has been shown.[1] It is necessary, therefore, that law especially shows the way to blessedness. Furthermore, since every part is ordered to the whole, as everything imperfect is ordered to what is perfect, and since any individual person is a part of a whole community, it is necessary that the law shows the way to the common happiness.

So it is that Aristotle, when defining the law as we have seen, includes both happiness and political association. He says in the *Ethics* that "we call legal justice that which makes and preserves the happiness of the individuals sharing in political association."[2] The perfect community is the city, as he said in the *Politics*.[3] Now, in any category, that which is recognized to be the greatest is the principle of the other things in the category, and these other things are understood insofar as they are ordered to that principle. Fire, for example, which is the hottest of things, is the cause of heat in all bodies made up of various elements; these bodies are hot to the extent that they are composed of fire. It is, therefore, necessary that, since law in its greatest sense shows the way to the common good, any other particular rule has the force of law only because it is ordered to the common good. Hence, every law is ordered to the common good.

Article 3: Can Anyone Make a Law?

THOMAS'S ANSWER

Law properly and primarily shows the way to the common good. The task of ordering something to the common good belongs either to the whole population or to someone having authority over the whole population. Establishing the law, therefore, belongs either to the whole population or to the public person who has the care of the whole population. The same is true in all other cases: the task of ordering to the goal belongs to the one who is properly responsible for the goal.

---

1   *ST* I-II, Q. 2, A. 7, p. 145.
2   Aristotle, *Nicomachean Ethics* 5.1, 1129b17–19.
3   Aristotle, *Politics* 1.1, 1252a5.

OBJECTION 2

As Aristotle says in the *Ethics*, "the intention of the law-maker is to lead human beings to virtue."[1] Any individual person, however, can lead another one to virtue. The reason, therefore, of any individual can make a law.

REPLY TO OBJECTION 2

A private person cannot effectively lead another to virtue. Such a person can only make an effort to do so, but if this effort is not received, a private person has no power to coerce behaviour, which the law must have if it is to be able to lead human beings *effectively* to virtue, as Aristotle notes in the *Ethics*.[2] This coercive power belongs to the whole population or to the public person to whom the power to inflict punishment belongs, as will be explained below.[3]

Article 4: Must Law Be Promulgated?

THOMAS'S ANSWER

Law, as we have said,[4] is imposed on others as a rule and a measure. A rule and measure, however, is imposed insofar as it is applied to those who are ruled and measured. Hence, in order that law have its binding power, which is essential to the law, it is necessary that it be applied to human beings who should be ruled by it. Such an application occurs, however, when human beings are brought to a knowledge of the law through its promulgation. Accordingly, promulgation is necessary in order that law have its power.

From these four articles we can now grasp the definition of law, which is nothing other than an ordinance of reason for the sake of the common good, promulgated by the one who has the care of the community.

---

1 Aristotle, *Nicomachean Ethics* 2.1, 1103b3–4.
2 Aristotle, *Nicomachean Ethics* 10.9, 1180a20–22.
3 *ST* I-II, Q. 92, A. 2, Reply to Obj. 3; *ST* II-II, Q. 64, A. 3 (not included in this volume).
4 *ST* I-II, Q. 90, A. 1, pp. 171–72.

Question 94: Natural Law

Article 1: Is the Natural Law a Habit?

THOMAS'S ANSWER

We can call something a habit in two ways. In one way, something is a habit in the proper and essential meaning of the term. In this way, natural law is not a habit. We said above[1] that natural law is something established through reason, just as a proposition is a product of reason. There is, furthermore, a difference between *what* someone does and the *means* by which it is done, as, for example, someone produces a beautiful speech through the habit of good grammar. Since, therefore, a habit is the means by which someone acts, it is not possible that any law be a habit in the proper and essential meaning of the word.[2]

In a second way, we can call a habit that about which the habit is concerned, as faith [the doctrine] is what faith [as a habit] is concerned about. In this way, because the precepts of natural law are sometimes actually considered by our reason, but other times are only in our reason as a habit, natural law can be considered to be a habit. Another example of this is the first, indemonstrable principles of all knowledge; these principles are not the habit of using the principles, but are the principles about which there is a habit.

OBJECTION 2

Basil says that "conscience or synderesis is the law of our intellect,"[3] which must be a reference to the natural law. Synderesis, however, is a habit, as we have said above.[4] Natural law, therefore, is a habit.

---

1   *ST* I-II, Q. 90, A. 1, pp. 171–72. Thomas spoke there of law, in general, not specifically of natural law.

2   This is so because law is the product of reason, not the means by which reason produces the law.

3   St. Basil, *Homilies on Hexaemeron*, Homily 7; a better expression of this can be found in John of Damascus, *On the Orthodox Faith* (*De fide orthodoxa*), Bk. 4, Ch. 22.

4   *ST* I, Q. 79, A. 12 (not included in this volume). Thomas explains that synderesis is a naturally occurring habit of knowing the first principles of moral behaviour or of natural law.

Synderesis is called the law of our intellect, because it is the habit containing the precepts of natural law, which are the first principles of human actions.

Article 2: Does Natural Law Contain Many Precepts or Just One?

THOMAS'S ANSWER

As was said above,[1] the precepts of natural law are related to practical reason in the same way that the first principles of demonstration are related to speculative reason: there are self-evident principles in both sorts of reasoning. Something is called "self-evident" in two different ways: in one way, a proposition is self-evident *in itself*, in another way, a proposition is self-evident *to us*. Any proposition is self-evident in itself, provided that its predicate is included in the meaning of its subject. It may happen, however, that such a proposition will not be self-evident to someone who does not know the meaning of the subject. For example, the proposition, "A human being is rational," is self-evident by its own nature, because the word "human being" includes in its meaning "rational." Nevertheless, to someone who did not know what it means to be a human being, this proposition would not be self-evident. For this reason, Boethius tells us that fundamental truths or self-evident propositions are known commonly by all.[2] The terms of such propositions are known to everyone; for example, "Every whole is greater than one of its parts," and "Two things that are both equal to some third thing are also equal to each other." On the other hand, some propositions are self-evident, but only to those with specialized knowledge who know what the terms of the proposition mean. For example, to someone who understands that an angel is not a body, it is self-evident that an angel cannot be located in a place. This, however, is not self-evident to the uneducated who would not understand this.

Things come into human understanding according to a certain order. The very first thing that comes into human understanding is *being*, the meaning of which is included in anything

---

1   *ST* I-II, Q. 91, A. 1 (not included in this volume).
2   Boethius, *How Substances Are Good in Virtue of Their Existence without Being Substantial Goods* (*De Hebdomadibus*), Proposition 1.

else that someone understands. For this reason, the first indemonstrable principle, on which all knowledge is founded, is that one cannot simultaneously affirm and deny, which is founded on the meaning of *being* and *non-being*, as Aristotle says.[1] Just as *being* is first in the understanding of everything in general, so is *good* the first thing in the understanding of practical reasoning, which is directed to action. Every agent acts for the sake of a goal, which is something good. For this reason the first principle in practical reasoning is founded on the meaning of *good*. This principle is, *the good is what all things seek*. This, therefore, is the first precept of law: *that good should be done and sought, and evil should be avoided*. On this precept all of the other precepts of natural law are founded, with the result that everything that should be done or avoided is contained within the precepts of natural law. Practical reason naturally understands whatever should be done as a human good.

Because any good thing includes the idea of a goal, and evil has the opposite meaning, it is therefore true that all of the things toward which human beings have natural inclinations are naturally understood as good, and consequently as things that should be sought; on the other hand, the contrary sort of things are understood as bad and should be avoided. The order of the precepts of natural law, therefore, follows the order of our natural inclinations. There is, first, in human beings a natural inclination to the good that is shared with all other substances, namely, that any substance seeks the conservation of its own being in its own nature. From this inclination follow all of the precepts of the natural law that pertain to conserving human life and to avoiding the contrary. Second, there is an inclination in human beings to more specialized goods, insofar as we share a nature in common with other animals. In this sense, those precepts belong to the natural law "that nature has taught all animals." These concern the union of man and woman, the education of children, and so forth. Third, there is an inclination in human beings to the good of our rational nature, which is proper to us. In this sense, human beings have a natural inclination to know the truth about God and to live in society with others. Accordingly, those precepts belong to the natural law that help us to realize this inclination: for example, that human beings avoid ignorance, that they do not offend others with whom they must live, and that they do other such things.

---

1 *Metaphysics* 4.3, 1005b19–29.

Article 3: Are All the Acts of Virtue Contained in the Natural Law?

THOMAS'S ANSWER

We can talk about virtuous acts in two different ways. In one way, we talk about acts insofar as they are virtuous in general; in another way, specific acts of virtue can be considered. If we are talking about virtuous acts in general, then all acts of virtue belong to the natural law. We have already explained that whatever human beings are inclined to from their very nature belongs to the natural law.[1] It is furthermore true that everything is naturally inclined to the operation that is appropriate to its form, as fire is inclined to produce heat. Therefore, since the rational soul is the proper form of a human being, the natural inclination for every human being is to act according to reason; and this means to act according to virtue. This shows that all acts of virtue belong to the natural law, because our own reason naturally commands each and every one of us to act virtuously.

On the other hand, if we should speak about individual virtuous acts, in their own specific kinds, in this sense, not all acts of virtue belong to the natural law. In fact, there are many virtuous acts to which nature does not immediately incline, but which human beings have discovered, through an investigation of reason, to be most useful for living well.

Article 4: Is There One Natural Law for All People?

THOMAS'S ANSWER

Natural law, as we said above,[2] concerns those things to which human beings are naturally inclined; among these it is specifically proper to human beings to be inclined to act according to reason. Reason operates by proceeding from what is common to what is proper or individual, as is clear in the *Physics*.[3] Scientific reasoning, however, operates differently in this regard from practical reasoning. Since scientific reasoning deals mainly with necessary truths, which cannot be other than they are, the truth in the proper conclusions of such reasoning is no less deficient than it is

---

1   *ST* I-II, Q. 94, A. 2, pp. 176–77.
2   *ST* I-II, Q. 94, AA. 2–3, pp. 176–78.
3   Aristotle, *Physics* 1.1, 184a16.

in the common scientific principles. On the other hand, practical reasoning deals with contingent matters, which are the matters of human action; accordingly, if there is some necessity in the common principles of practical reasoning, this necessity diminishes the more we descend to proper conclusions. In scientific reasoning, therefore, there is the same truth for all people both in the principles and in the conclusions, although not everyone will know the truth of the conclusions as well as they know the principles, which are said to be "common conceptions of the mind."[1] In practical action, however, all people find the same truth or rightness in the principles, but not in the conclusions. Further, even when there is the same rightness in the proper conclusions as in the principles, it will not be equally known to all people.

The clear conclusion, therefore, is that everyone recognizes the same truth or rightness in the common principles of reason, whether in science or in practical reasoning, and these principles are equally known to all. On the other hand, the truth of proper scientific conclusions is the same for everyone, although it might not be known by everyone. It is true, for example, for everyone that a triangle has three interior angles equivalent to 180°, although this may not be known to everyone. The proper conclusions of practical reason, however, do not have the same truth or rightness for all people and, even among those for whom it is the same, it is not known by all. For example, everyone knows that it is true and right that we should act according to reason. From this principle, it follows, as a proper conclusion, that what has been borrowed ought to be returned. Such a conclusion is certainly true in most cases, but it can happen in some individual case that returning what has been borrowed would be injurious and consequently unreasonable, as in the case of someone who would intend to use the returned goods to commit a crime. The truth of practical conclusions is more deficient the more we descend to individual conclusions, as when we say that what has been borrowed should be returned with certain restrictions or in a certain way. The more particular conditions we put on such conclusions, the more the conclusions can be deficient in different ways, with the result that either returning or not returning borrowed goods may be wrong.

We should say, therefore, that, concerning the first common principles, the natural law is the same for all people, both in its

---

1 Boethius, *How Substances Are Good in Virtue of Their Existence without Being Substantial Goods* (*De Hebdomadibus*), Proposition 1.

rightness and in its being known to all. Concerning, however, more specific matters, which are as it were conclusions of the common principles, the natural law is in most cases the same for all people, insofar as it is both right and known to all. In a few cases, however, the natural law can be deficient: both because the rightness of the conclusion can be blocked by certain individual impediments, as it is also the case in nature that, in some few cases because of impediments, naturally generated things are deficient; and also because of being not known, as when someone's reason is ruined because of excessive emotion or because of a bad habit. It was said, for example, about the Germans, that they once did not regard piracy as wrong, although it is expressly against the natural law.[1]

OBJECTION 3

The natural law concerns whatever human beings are naturally inclined to, as was said above.[2] Different people, however, are naturally inclined to different things: some are inclined to physical pleasures, others to honours, and others to other things. There is not, therefore, one natural law for all people.

REPLY TO OBJECTION 3

Just as reason rules in human beings and commands the various human powers, so it is necessary that all of the natural inclinations found in the various powers be ordered according to reason. This, therefore, everyone recognizes to be right: that all human inclinations should be directed according to reason.

Article 5: Can the Natural Law Be Changed?

THOMAS'S ANSWER

The natural law can be changed in two ways. In one way, it can be changed by adding to it, and this is fitting, for many things are added to the natural law that are useful for human life, both in religious law and in human laws. In another way, the natural law can be changed by subtracting from it, as when something ceases to belong to the natural law that had previously belonged to it.

---

1 Julius Caesar, *The Gallic War* (*De bello Gallico*), Bk. 6, Ch. 23.
2 *ST* I-II, Q. 94, AA. 2–3, pp. 176–78.

This will not apply to the first principles of natural law, which are completely immutable. The secondary principles as well, which we call proper or particular conclusions drawn from the first principles, are not changed in most cases, because the natural law is right and does not usually change. In some individual cases, however, natural law may rarely be changed, because there may be some unusual circumstances that will block the observation of the normal precepts of natural law, as we have said above.[1]

OBJECTION 2

Killing an innocent person is against the natural law, and so is adultery and stealing. All of these acts, however, have been ordered by God: for example, God told Abraham to kill his innocent son;[2] he told the Jews to take and steal the vessels of the Egyptians;[3] and he told Hosea to take a wife in fornication.[4] The natural law, therefore, can be changed.

REPLY TO OBJECTION 2

All human beings without exception die, whether they are guilty or innocent, because death is our natural lot. This natural death, however, is imposed by God's power because of original sin; 1 Kings 2:6: "The Lord gives death and life." Therefore, God's command can inflict death on any human being whatsoever, without any injustice, whether the person is guilty or innocent. Similarly, adultery is sleeping with another man's wife, who has been given to the other man by the law of God. For this reason, if anyone should take any woman as wife on the command of God, it would not be adultery or fornication. The same argument can be made about stealing, which is taking the property of someone else. When someone takes anything on the command of God, who is the Lord of the universe, such a person does not take it against the will of its owner, which is stealing. In human affairs, whatever is ordered by God is right, by that very fact; and the same is true in nature, for whatever God makes to happen is in a way natural, as has been said.[5]

---

1 *ST* I-II, Q. 94, A. 4, pp. 178–80.
2 Genesis 22:2.
3 Exodus 12:35–36.
4 Hosea 1:2.
5 *ST* I, Q. 105, A. 6, Reply to Obj. 1 (not included in this volume).

OBJECTION 3

Isidore of Seville says that "the possession all things in common and the liberty of all people belong to the natural law."[1] We see, however, that these have both been changed by human laws. The natural law, therefore, is changeable.

REPLY TO OBJECTION 3

There are two ways in which something can be understood to belong to the natural law. In one way, something belongs to the natural law because nature inclines to it, as, for example, we should not harm another person. In another way, something belongs to the natural law because nature does not incline us against it, as, for example, we might say that being naked is part of the natural law, because nature does not provide clothing but human skill does. In this sense, "the possession of all things in common and the liberty of all people" belong to the natural law, because private property and slavery do not come from nature but are devised by human reason for usefulness in human life. In this way, the natural law is not changed except by addition.

Article 6: Can the Natural Law Be Abolished from the Human Heart?

THOMAS'S ANSWER

As was said above,[2] the natural law contains, in the first place, some very common precepts, which are known to all; it also contains some secondary precepts that are more proper or specific, and these are like specific conclusions drawn from the principles. The first common principles of the natural law cannot be erased from human hearts in general. The natural law, however, is erased in individual operations, when reason is blocked from applying the common principle to some particular operation, on account of sense emotions or some other passion, as we have explained.[3]

---

1 Isidore of Seville, *Etymologies*, Bk. 5, Ch. 4. On Isidore, see p. 36.
2 *ST* I-II, Q. 94, AA. 4–5, pp. 178–82.
3 *ST* I-II, Q. 77, A. 2 (not included in this volume).

As to the secondary precepts, the natural law can be erased from human hearts, because of bad moral advice (just as we can also make mistakes in scientific reasoning about necessary conclusions), because of bad practices and corrupt habits (as some people do not consider piracy to be wrong), or because of vices against nature, as the Apostle says.[1]

---

1   Romans 1:24.

Appendix A: Anselm's Ontological Argument

From Anselm, *Proslogion* (1077–78), in *S. Anselmi Cantauriensis Archeopiscopi Opera Omnia*, edited by F.S. Schmitt, 6 vols., Nelson, 1946–61, vol. 1: 101–04

[St. Anselm (1033–1109) was a Benedictine philosopher and theologian. He was a monk, prior, and eventually abbot of the Norman monastery at Bec in Normandy, France, from 1060 to 1093. In 1093, Anselm became Archbishop of Canterbury, which made him the ecclesiastical leader of the entire Church in England and brought him into conflict, in his effort to protect the freedom of the Church, with two kings, William Rufus (r. 1087–1100) and Henry I (r. 1100–35). In 1077–78 he wrote his famous *Proslogion*, an excerpt from which is translated here. The *Proslogion* contains the most famous argument of all for the existence of God, an argument that Kant called the "Ontological Argument." This argument formed the basis of later mediaeval discussions, Bonaventure accepting a version of it, Thomas rejecting it in favour of various cosmological arguments, and Scotus providing an ingenious combination of both ontological and cosmological arguments. Briefly, an ontological argument is one that seeks to prove the existence of God solely on the basis of what is known about the idea, definition, or meaning of God. By contrast, a cosmological argument argues from some effect in the world to the existence of God as the cause of that effect.]

Chapter 2

You, Lord, who give understanding to faith, give me what you know I need to understand that you exist, as we believe you do, and that you are that which we believe to exist. We certainly believe that you are that-than-which-nothing-greater-can-be-thought. Or, is there perhaps no such nature, because, "the Fool has said in his heart, 'there is no God'"?[1] Surely, however, even the Fool himself, when he hears this thing that I say, "something-than-which-nothing-greater-can-be-thought," understands what he hears. And what he understands is in his intellect, even if he does not understand that it exists. It is, of course, one thing for something to exist in the intellect, and another

---

1 Psalms 13:1; 52:1.

to understand that the thing exists. For example, when a painter thinks about the picture he is about to paint, he has the picture in his intellect but he does not yet understand that what he has not yet made exists. When, however, he has painted it, he both has it in his intellect and he understands that what he has made exists. Even the Fool, therefore, is convinced that something-than-which-nothing-greater-can-be-thought exists at least in the intellect, because he understands what he hears, and whatever he understands is in the intellect. Surely, however, that-than-which-a-greater-cannot-be-thought is not able to be in the intellect alone. For if it is at least in the intellect alone, it can be thought to exist also in reality, which is greater. If, therefore, that-than-which-a-greater-cannot-be-thought is in the intellect alone, this very thing than-which-a-greater-cannot-be-thought is something than which a greater can be thought. But surely this cannot be. There exists, therefore, without doubt something-than-which-a-greater-cannot-be-thought, both in the intellect and in reality.

Chapter 3

This being so truly exists that it cannot be thought not to exist. It is, of course, possible to think of something that cannot be thought not to exist, which is greater than whatever can be thought not to exist. If, therefore, that-than-which-a-greater-cannot-be-thought is able to be thought not to exist, that very thing-than-which-a-greater-cannot-be-thought is not that-than-which-a-greater-cannot-be-thought. This clearly cannot be. Therefore, something than-which-a-greater-cannot-be-thought so truly exists that it cannot be thought not to exist.

This is you, Lord, our God. You thus so truly exist, Lord, my God, that you cannot even be thought not to exist. This is as it should be. If some mind were able to think of something better than you, the creature would ascend above the creator and would pass judgement on the creator, but this is clearly absurd. Indeed, whatever exists other than you alone is able to be thought not to exist. You alone, therefore, of all things have being most truly and therefore to the highest degree. Anything else does not have being so truly, and therefore has less being. Why, therefore, has "the Fool said in his heart, 'there is no God,'" when it is so obvious to a rational mind that you exist most greatly of all? Why, indeed, unless because he is stupid and a fool?

Chapter 4

In what way has the Fool actually said in his heart what he could not think? Or, in what way could he not have thought what he said in his heart, since to say in the heart and to think are the same? If it is true, or rather, because it is true that he both thought, because he said in his heart, and he also did not say in his heart, because he could not think, there is more than one way in which something is said in the heart or thought. In one way, a thing is thought when the word signifying it is thought; in another way a thing is thought when the very thing itself is understood. In the first way, it is possible to think that God does not exist, but not at all in the second way. No one, to be sure, who understands what God is can think that God does not exist, although someone might say such words in the heart, but without any or with some irrelevant meaning. God indeed is that-than-which-a-greater-cannot-be-thought. Whoever understands this certainly understands that this being so exists that it cannot even be thought not to exist. Whoever, therefore, understands God in this way cannot think that God does not exist.

I give you thanks, Good Lord, I give you thanks, because what I first believed from your gift I now so understand from your illumination that, even if I should refuse to believe that you exist, I could not possibly understand such a claim.

Appendix B: Bonaventure Argues that God's Existence Is Indubitable

From Bonaventure, *Commentaria in Quattuor Libros Sententiarum Magistri Petri Lombardi* (1251–54), in *Opera theologica selecta*, Collegium S. Bonaventurae, 1934–64, vol. 1: 118–21

[St. Bonaventure (1221–74), Franciscan theologian and philosopher, was a contemporary of Thomas at the University of Paris. Bonaventure became a Franciscan in 1243, taught in Paris from 1248 until 1257, when he was made the Minister General of the Franciscan Order, and in 1273 became Cardinal Bishop of Albano, Italy. Bonaventure was not only a scholastic theologian/philosopher but also a very effective administrator at a time of serious controversies involving the mendicant orders, a Church leader (taking an important role in the Council of Lyons, where he died in 1274), and a spiritual writer of enormous influence.

The passage below is taken from Bonaventure's *Commentary on the Sentences*, his major theological synthesis, which he wrote between 1250 and 1253. This passage is Bonaventure's scholastic version of Anselm's claim that it is impossible for humans with a correct understanding of God to think that God does not exist. Bonaventure agrees with Thomas that Anselm's claim amounts to a claim that the existence of God is self-evident, but he parts company with Thomas in holding that such a claim is philosophically knowable to us in this life. Bonaventure also regards the existence of truth as evidence of the existence of the First Truth.]

Book 1, Dist. 8, Part 1, A. 1

Question 2: Is This a Property of the Supreme God, that the Divine Being Is So True that It Cannot Be Thought Not to Be?

Arguments in Favour

a. It seems that the answer to this question is yes, because Anselm[1] says that the common concept of the mind is that God is "that than which nothing greater is able to be thought." That which cannot be thought not to exist is greater than that which can be thought not to

---

1 Anselm, *Proslogion*, Chs. 2–3.

exist. Therefore, since nothing greater than God can be thought, the divine being so exists that it cannot be thought not to exist.

b. John of Damascus says that a knowledge of the existent God is naturally impressed upon us,[1] but natural impressions do not change and cannot be contradicted. Hence, the truth about God is indelibly impressed upon the human mind. Therefore, God cannot be thought not to exist.

c. There is more truth in the divine being than in any axiom of thinking or science. Any axiom, however, is so true that it cannot be mentally contradicted, as, for example, the axiom "every whole is greater than its part." Hence, the truth of an axiom cannot be thought not to be. It will be even truer, therefore, to make this claim about the Primary Truth.

Bonaventure's Answer

I answer that something can be thought not to exist in two ways. In one way, because of some falsity, as when I think this: a human being is a donkey. To think this is merely to understand the words that are said. In this manner, the truth about the divine being can be denied. In another way, thinking involves assent, as when I both think that something does not exist and also believe that it does not exist. In this latter way, to think that something actually existent does not exist can come about either through a defect on the part of the person understanding or from a defect on the part of the thing understood. The defect on the part of the person understanding is blindness or ignorance, on account of which the person thinks that the thing does not exist precisely because of ignorance about the thing.

There are two kinds of knowledge about any being: knowledge of *whether it exists* and knowledge of *what it is*. Our intellect is deficient in knowledge of what the divine truth is, but it is not deficient in knowing whether it exists. Hugh of St. Victor says, "God so implanted a knowledge of himself in human beings from the beginning that, just as what God is can never be comprehended, so also the fact that he exists can never be ignored."[2] Since, therefore, our intellect is never deficient in the knowledge of whether God exists, it cannot be completely ignorant that he exists, nor can it think that he does not exist.

---

1   John of Damascus, *An Exposition of the Orthodox Faith*, Bk. I, Ch. 1.
2   Hugh of St. Victor, *On the Sacraments of the Christian Faith*, Bk. 1, Part 3, Ch. 1. On Hugh of St. Victor, see p. 36.

Because, however, our intellect is deficient in the knowledge of what God is, it frequently thinks that God is something non-existent, as when it thinks that God is an idol, or it thinks that God is not what God is, as when it fails to think that God is just. Because the one who thinks that God is not what he is (just, for example) consequently thinks that God does not exist, it is therefore by reason of a defect in the intellect that God or the Supreme Truth can be thought not to exist. Such cannot be thought simply in itself, but only as a consequence of some other falsity; for example, when one who denies that blessedness is found in God also denies that God exists. This is the mistake in the arguments that conclude that some intellect thinks or is able to think that the divine being does not exist.

In another way something can be thought not to exist because of a defect on the part of the intelligible object, and this sort of defect can come about either as a defect in presence or a defect in evidence. A defect in presence occurs when the intelligible object does not always exist, or does not exist everywhere, or does not exist fully everywhere. What does not always exist, sometimes exists and sometimes does not exist. Thus it sometimes can truly be thought not to exist. Likewise, that which does not exist everywhere, by the same reason by which it can be thought not to exist here, can also be thought not to exist elsewhere. Likewise, the same argument can be made concerning that which is partially present and partially absent. God, however, exists always and everywhere, and exists fully always and everywhere, and therefore he cannot be thought not to exist. Anselm gives this reason in his book *Against the Fool*.[1]

Something can be thought not to exist not only because of a defect of presence but also because of a defect in the evidence, as when something is not evident in itself or not evident in argument. The truth of the Divine Being, however, is both evident in itself and in argument. The truth of the Divine Being is evident in itself in just the way that we know principles from a knowledge of their terms, that is, the subject includes the cause of the predicate. So it is in the proposition in question, for God or the Supreme Truth is his very being, than which nothing better can be thought. Therefore, he is not able to be thought not to exist, for the predicate [being or existence] is included in the subject [God].

Not only is the existence of God evident in itself, but also in argument. Every truth in created nature proves and concludes that the Divine Truth exists, because if there is a being through participation and from another, there is a being existing essentially and not through

---

1 Anselm, *Proslogion*, "Reply to Gaunilo," Ch. 1.

another. Every right understanding also concludes that the Supreme Truth exists, because the knowledge of the Supreme Truth is impressed upon the soul and all knowledge is through it. Again, every affirmative proposition concludes this, because every such proposition affirms something. When something is affirmed, it is affirmed to be true. When something true is affirmed, Truth is affirmed, which is the cause of every true thing. A negative proposition, however, implies the existence of Truth sophistically, as is said. From the claim that nothing exists or that no truth exists, one cannot conclude or infer that truth does exist. This proposition, "nothing exists," destroys all truth. No affirmation can follow upon it, and therefore this is false: "if nothing exists, it is true that nothing exists." If it should be said that every proposition implies the truth of what it claims, this is true, but if nothing exists, no proposition exists, nor does anything else. Augustine gives this sort of argument for the sake of discussion, not as an argument he agrees with.[1]

We must grant, therefore, that the truth of the Divine Being is so great that it cannot be thought, with assent, not to exist, except through the ignorance of what is meant by the name of God. The arguments that support this conclusion should be granted, although some are sophistical.[2]

OBJECTION 4

That which is most hidden can most easily be thought not to exist. The truth of the divine being, however, is most hidden, because "God dwells in unapproachable light" (I Timothy 6:16).

REPLY TO OBJECTION 4

To the objection about what lies most hidden to us, the response is clear, because the "what it is" is most hidden to us, although the "whether it is" is most obvious.

OBJECTION 5

I ask what it means to say that God is not able to be thought not to exist. If it means that this can be thought neither truly nor falsely, clearly such is not the case. If it means that it cannot be thought truly, then we should have to argue just the same thing about the soul or about the heavens or about other such things.

---

1 Augustine, *Soliloquies*, Bk. 2, Ch. 2, ¶ 2.
2 The initial "Arguments in Favour," pp. 189–90.

REPLY TO OBJECTION 5

To the objection, "what does it mean to say that the Divine Truth cannot be thought not to exist?" I say that it means that someone cannot believe that God does not exist while thinking rationally. It is not the same concerning creatures, because even if it is certain that one creature is present to another, this cannot be certain to all, for no creature is of such power to be present equally to all others, as the Primary Truth is.

OBJECTION 6

Whatever one can express one can also think. One can, however, express that the Divine Being does not exist; therefore, one can also think it. That such is possible is obvious when one says, "God does not exist," and in general, "nothing exists." It is obvious that neither of these propositions implies that God exists, because one opposite does not imply the other. Also, if we affirm nothing we imply nothing, but neither of these propositions affirms anything.

REPLY TO OBJECTION 6

To the objection about what one can express and think, it ought to be said that "thinking" can be taken generally for an act of the mind, whether the mind is in error or not, whether it assents or not. In this broad sense, the objection is correct; but it is false concerning thinking with assent, because one can contradict axioms in their exterior expression, but not in their interior meaning, as Aristotle says in the *Posterior Analytics*.[1]

---

1 Aristotle, *Posterior Analytics* 1.10, 76b26–27.

Appendix C: Scotus's Proof of the Existence of God

From John Duns Scotus, *Ordinatio* (1300–08), in *Joannis Duns Scoti Opera omnia*, edited by Scotistic Commission, Vatican Press, 1950, vol. 2: 148–73

[John Duns Scotus (1266–1308), a Franciscan theologian and philosopher, was educated at Oxford and later taught there. Thereafter (in 1302), he was sent to study and teach at the University of Paris, and he finally taught at Cologne (1307). Scotus developed a compelling metaphysical position, reflecting both a foundation in Aristotle and also a number of themes from Augustinian, Avicennian, and Franciscan sources. The following passage is taken from one of Scotus's versions of the *Commentary on the Sentences* (there were at least three), called the *Ordinatio*.

Scotus regards the concept of "infinite being" as the best philosophical way of capturing the reality of God. He sets out to prove the existence of an infinite being, but he does so by arguing for a first being in three ways: a first efficient cause, a first final cause, and a first being in perfection. These three "firsts" are, as Scotus argues, but one being, which he calls the "Triple Primacy." The arguments for each of the firsts are cosmological arguments, in that Scotus argues in each order that there cannot be an infinite series and therefore there must be some first, uncaused being. Crucially, however, Scotus at that point is arguing only for the *possibility* of a first. His argument for the *actuality* of the first turns on an Anselmian consideration that the first being by definition cannot have been caused. Scotus denies that he is arguing from any actual, contingent effect to the cause of that effect, although he shows the possibility of the first being from consideration of cosmological causal sequences or sequence in perfection. In examining the possibility of such sequences, Scotus thoroughly shows the impossibility of an infinite series of essentially ordered causes or beings.]

Bk. 1, Dist. 2, Part 1, Q. 1
Demonstration of an Infinite Being

It is not possible *for us* to demonstrate the existence of an infinite being by arguing from cause to effect, even though *in itself* such a demonstration is possible. For us, the proposition that an infinite being exists can be demonstrated by arguing from effects to the cause. Further, the properties of an infinite being that are relative to creatures are used in the premises of a demonstration from effect to cause, and the absolute properties are not. Thus, the existence of an infinite being can be more immediately demonstrated from the relative properties than from the absolute ones, because from one relative property the existence of its correlative property follows immediately. Accordingly, I shall first demonstrate the relative properties of the infinite being and thereafter I will demonstrate the existence of an infinite being, because the relative properties can only belong to an infinite being. Accordingly, there will be two principal articles.[1]

In the first article, I say that the properties of an infinite being relative to creatures are properties either of causality or of perfection; and there are two kinds of causality, efficient causality and final causality. (The "exemplar cause" is sometimes added, but this is really no different from the efficient cause; otherwise there would be five kinds of causes. The exemplar cause is a kind of efficient cause, because it is an agent acting through understanding, as distinct from a purely natural agent.)

In the first principal article I shall show three things. First, I shall show that something actually exists that is absolutely first as efficient cause, as final cause, and as the most perfect being. Second, I shall show that whatever is first in one of these orders of primacy is also first in the other two orders. Third, I shall show that the triple primacy belongs to one nature only, such that it cannot belong to more than one nature differing in kind or in essence. Hence, there will be three subsections to this article.

Subsection 1

The first subsection includes three main conclusions, one for each of the three primacies. Furthermore, each of these conclusions is itself dependent on three conclusions: first, that something is first; second, that what is first cannot be caused; and third, that this first thing actually exists. Hence, in this first subsection there are nine conclusions, but three main ones.

(1) The first[2] of the nine conclusions is that something is able to be an efficient cause that is absolutely first such that it cannot be caused

---

1   Only the first article is included here. The second article is a demonstration of the infinity of God. The relative properties of God here discussed are those of being first efficient cause, first final cause, and first being in perfection. The absolute property of God is infinite being.

2   The second conclusion of the nine occurs on p. 200 below, after a long argument for the impossibility of an infinite series in essentially ordered causes.

and it does not have its causal power from anything else but itself. Proof. Some being can be caused. It can be caused either by itself, by nothing, or by something else. It cannot, however, be caused by nothing, because nothing is the cause of nothing. It cannot be caused by itself, because nothing can make or generate itself, as Augustine says.[1] Therefore, it could only be caused by something else. Suppose that something else is A. If A is first, in the sense explained above, then I have my conclusion. If it is not first, then its causal power is derivative, because it can be caused by another thing or by the power of another, because the negation of a negation results in an affirmation.[2] Let us suppose another cause and call it B; the argument about B will be just the same as that about A, and so on to infinity. Any one of these causes will be second with respect to its prior cause, until the chain comes to a stop in some cause that does not have a prior one. Because an infinity in ascending causes is impossible, therefore a first is necessary, having no prior cause and being posterior to nothing posterior to it (for a circularity in causes is also impossible).

There are two objections to this argument. First, some philosophers say that an infinity in ascending causes is possible, and they cite the example of eternal past generations, in which no generation is first and each one is second to some other. There is no circularity implied in such causes.

Second, this argument seems to be based on contingent claims and is not, therefore, a demonstration. The premises of the argument assume that the being of something is caused, but any such causality happens contingently.

I shall refute the first objection by saying that philosophers do not think that an infinity is possible in essentially ordered causes, but only in accidentally ordered causes, as Avicenna says in the *Metaphysics*, when he talks about the infinity of individuals in a species.[3]

In order to make this clearer, the distinction between essentially and accidentally ordered causes must be made. Note first that the distinction between essentially and accidentally *ordered* causes is not the same as the distinction between merely essential and accidental causes. In the second distinction the comparison is made between one cause and its effect: the essential cause is a cause by its own nature and not from anything accidental to it; an accidental cause is just the reverse. In the first distinction, the comparison is between two causes insofar as some effect comes from them.

---

1 Augustine, *On the Trinity*, Bk. 1, Ch. 1, ¶ 1.
2 This is, if it is not uncaused, it is caused.
3 Avicenna, *Metaphysics*, Bk. 6, Ch. 5, 22.

Essentially ordered causes differ from accidentally ordered causes in three ways. The first difference is that in essentially ordered causes, the second cause depends for its causality on the first cause. In accidentally ordered causes, there is no causal dependence, although there might be some other kind of dependence (in being or in something else).

The second difference is that in essentially ordered causes there is always a causality of different kinds of causes that are at a higher and a lower level, because the primary cause is at a higher level than any secondary cause. In accidentally ordered causes there is no such distinction of levels. This difference follows from the first difference, because no cause depends essentially on a cause of the same kind; in causing an effect, one cause of any given kind is sufficient.

The third difference is that all essentially ordered causes must necessarily be simultaneous in causing, otherwise some essential part of the causality would be lacking to the effect. In accidentally ordered causes, however, there is no such requirement of simultaneity in causing.

From these three differences, three conclusions can be shown, namely, (a) that an infinity in essentially ordered causes is impossible. Likewise, a second conclusion can also be shown, namely, (b) that an infinity of accidentally ordered causes is possible only on the supposition of a finite number of essentially ordered causes. Hence, an infinity of essentially ordered causes is impossible in every way. (c) Even if an essential order of causes is denied, an infinity is still impossible. In any way, therefore, there must be some first being able to cause necessarily and absolutely.

Proofs of these three propositions: (a), (b), and (c).

Here is the proof of (a): a proof that an infinity of essentially ordered causes is impossible. First, the entire series of essentially ordered causes is from some cause that is not part of the series, because otherwise it would be the cause of itself. The entire series of dependent causes is itself dependent on what is not a part of the series. Second, an infinite number of causes would have to be both simultaneously in existence, which is a requirement of the third difference given for essentially ordered causes, but no philosopher would grant the possibility of a simultaneous infinity. Third, since whatever is prior is nearer to the beginning, as is said in the *Metaphysics*,[1] therefore, if there is no beginning, nothing is essentially prior to anything else. Fourth, since a higher cause is more perfect in causing, as was said in the second difference, therefore, an infinitely higher cause would be

---

1 Aristotle, *Metaphysics* 5.11, 1018b9–11.

infinitely more perfect. An infinitely perfect cause, however, would consequently be a cause independent of any other cause, because any dependent cause would be imperfect, insofar as it is dependent on some other cause. Fifth, what is able to cause necessarily implies no imperfection; it is therefore able to exist without imperfection. If, however, there is no cause without a dependence on some prior cause, then no cause will exist without imperfection. Therefore, the ability to be an efficient, independent cause can exist in some nature, and it is absolutely first. Therefore, the ability to be an absolutely first efficient cause is possible. This is a sufficient conclusion because from this it will be concluded below[1] that, if such a being is possible, it must exist in reality. Thus we have five arguments to support (a).

Here is the proof of (b): a proof that an infinity of accidentally ordered causes is impossible, except on the supposition of a finite number of essentially ordered causes. If an infinity of accidentally ordered causes is posited, it is clear that this could not be simultaneous but could only be successive, such that one cause would come after another and in some way the later cause would flow from the earlier one. Such causes, however, would not be dependent on one another in causing, for one would be able to be a cause when the previous one was no longer existing, as the son is able to generate offspring just as well after his father has died as when his father was alive. Such a successive infinity is impossible unless it comes from some nature existing always, on which the entire succession and any individual cause is dependent. No changes in form are possible except in virtue of something permanent that has no part in the succession, because all successive causes within the series are causes of the same nature. Some cause, however, is essentially prior, because whatever is part of the succession depends upon a cause that is at a different level from the cause that is merely prior in succession. Hence, (b) is clear.

Here is the proof of (c): a proof that even if essential order is denied, an infinity is still impossible, which presupposes the premise that nothing is able to come into being from nothing. If the essential order of active causes is denied, it will follow that some nature is able to be an efficient cause and that it can do so in virtue of nothing other than itself. Although this cause might be supposed to be caused in some individual case, nevertheless it is not caused in some other case, which is what I am trying to show about this nature. If, then, it is supposed to be caused in every instance, a contradiction immediately arises by the fact that essential order has been denied. This is so because no nature can be supposed to be caused in every instance

---

1   See p. 201.

such that there is an accidental order in causes below it and no essential order of it to the other nature [that caused it].

The second objection given above is that my argument is based on contingent claims and is not, therefore, a demonstration. I respond in one way thus. Some nature has been caused because something has been changed, and the change has begun to be realized in the thing; hence that change or newly composed thing has been produced or caused. Therefore, given the law of correlatives, there has been some efficient cause. In this way I could argue for the first conclusion as manifestly true, but contingent. On the other hand, it is possible to argue for the first conclusion in this way. This is true, "some nature is able to be caused; therefore, some cause is able to cause it." The antecedent is proved, because some things can be changed, since in some respects things are possible as opposed to necessary. The same can be argued about things that exist necessarily. In this way, the proof of the first conclusion is about quidditative being or possible being, and not about actual existence.[1] At this point the possibility of the first cause is being shown; in the third conclusion its actual existence will be shown.

(2) The second conclusion about the first efficient cause is this: the first efficient cause is absolutely uncaused. This is proved because that which is able to be an efficient cause independently cannot be made. This is clear from what has come before, because if something is able to be an efficient cause because of the power of another or if it can be caused by another, then either there will be a chain of causes to infinity or the causal chain will be circular or it will come to a stop in some uncaused independent efficient cause. I call that uncaused independent efficient cause the first cause, and it is clear that some other cause is not first, from what has been conceded. We have, therefore, further consequences: if the first efficient cause cannot be made, it cannot be caused at all, because it could not have a final cause, nor a material cause, nor a formal cause. The first consequence, that because the first efficient cause cannot be made, it cannot have final cause, is proved because the final cause does not cause except insofar as it moves (though not literally so) the efficient cause to action. This is the only

---

1 Scotus distinguishes *quidditative* or *possible* being from *actual* being. The word "quidditative" comes from the Latin *quid*, which is used in questions when we ask, "what is it?" To talk about quidditative being is to talk about what something is, that is, its essence or its nature; one can talk about the nature of something without being committed to its actual existence. The point that Scotus makes here is that his argument is based on a consideration of the nature or essence of God (what God is), without begging the question of God's actual existence, which he is attempting to prove.

way a final cause can be received from some prior cause. If the effect does not depend essentially on the prior cause, the cause is not an essential cause. The other two consequences, namely, that if the first efficient cause cannot be made it does not have a material cause or a formal cause, can be proven together. If something does not have an extrinsic cause, it cannot also have intrinsic causes. Having the causal power of an extrinsic cause implies perfection without any imperfection, but having the causal power of intrinsic causes necessarily implies imperfection, because an intrinsic cause is partially an effect. Hence, the nature of an extrinsic cause is prior to that of an intrinsic cause. If, therefore, we deny the prior, we must also deny the posterior. These two consequences can also be proved in another way. Intrinsic causes are caused by extrinsic causes, either because the extrinsic causes cause the being of the intrinsic causes or because they cause the whole composite or because they cause in both ways. The intrinsic causes cannot by themselves cause the composite being to exist without some extrinsic agent. From all of this, the second conclusion is sufficiently proven.

(3) The third conclusion about the first efficient cause is this: the first efficient cause actually exists, and this truly existing nature is actually causing. If something by nature cannot have its being from another, such a being, if it can exist, can exist only from itself. The nature of the first efficient cause absolutely cannot have being from another, as the second conclusion has made clear. Further, this same first efficient cause is able to exist, as is clear from the first conclusion, where the fifth proof for proposition (a) was given.[1] This fifth proof provides a restricted but demonstrative conclusion. The other four arguments for proposition (a) do indeed deal with the existence of the first efficient cause, but they do so from premises that, though they are evident, are contingently true; or these other four arguments may be understood to be about the nature, quiddity, and possibility of the first efficient cause, and in these senses to be based on necessary truths. The first efficient cause, therefore, absolutely can exist from itself. What does not exist from itself cannot exist from itself, because otherwise a non-being would bring something into being, which is impossible. Further, if the first efficient cause were the cause of itself, it would not be absolutely uncaused. This same conclusion, that the first efficient cause does exist, can also be shown in that it is not fitting that the universe lack the highest possible being.

From the three conclusions demonstrated about the first efficient cause, we can draw a corollary that includes the three proven conclu-

---

1 See p. 199.

sions. The corollary is that the first efficient cause is not only prior to other things but it is also that to which nothing can be prior without a contradiction; thus, the first efficient cause exists. The proof of this follows the previous pattern: the nature of the first efficient cause implies that it cannot be caused, as the second conclusion has shown. If, therefore, it is able to exist, because its existence implies no contradiction, as the first conclusion showed, it follows that what is able to exist from itself also does exist from itself.

Following the same pattern that I used in the three conclusions about the first efficient cause, I now give three similar conclusions about the first final cause.

(4) The first conclusion[1] is that something able to be a final cause is absolutely first, that is, it is not ordered to anything else nor can it by nature be the final cause for other things by virtue of something else. This is proven by five reasons similar to those used for the first conclusion about first efficient cause.[2]

(5) The second conclusion is that the first final cause cannot be caused. This is proven because, if it does have a final cause, then it is not the first final cause. By the same reasoning, it cannot be caused by an efficient cause. This consequence is proven because every essential agent causes acts for the sake of a goal, as is said in the *Physics*.[3] Aristotle intends this to be true about natural agents, and it is even truer about agents with intention. If there is no essential efficient cause for something, that thing cannot be made. What is accidental can never be first in any category, as is clear in what I have been arguing. This is especially clear in the case of accidental efficient causes, which are chance and fortune and which, according to Aristotle,[4] are necessarily derivative from essential, prior causes, which are nature and intellect (or intention). If there is no essential efficient cause of something, there is no efficient cause of it at all. If something does not have a final cause, then it cannot have an essential efficient cause. It will not be possible for such a being to be made, for that which can have a final cause is surpassed in goodness and perfection by its final cause. The rest follows, as it did concerning the first efficient cause.[5]

(6) The third conclusion is that a first final cause actually exists and this primacy belongs to some nature that is actually existent. This is proved in the same way as I argued about the first efficient cause.[6]

---

1   The fourth conclusion of the nine.
2   See pp. 198–99.
3   Aristotle, *Physics* 2.5, 196b17–22.
4   Aristotle, *Physics* 2.6, 198a5–13.
5   See pp. 200–01.
6   See pp. 201–02.

A corollary follows that the first final cause is first such that it is impossible that anything is prior to it, and the argument for this corollary is the same as that made for the first corollary.[1]

I have given three conclusions for both kinds of extrinsic causality; I shall now give three similar conclusions for the perfection of the first being.

(7) The first conclusion is that some perfect nature is absolutely first in perfection. This is clear because there is an essential order among essences. According to Aristotle,[2] forms are ordered like numbers. The order of forms is finite, which is proved with five arguments like those given above against an infinite regress in efficient causes.[3]

(8) The second conclusion is that the supreme nature cannot be caused. This is proved because, since it cannot have a final cause, as was shown above,[4] therefore it cannot be made and, further, it cannot be caused. These two consequences have been proved in the second conclusion about efficient causes above.[5] It can also be proved that the supreme nature cannot be made, because anything that can be made has some essentially ordered cause, as is clear from the proof of the proposition (b) in the first conclusion about the first efficient cause.[6] An essentially ordered cause is superior to its effect.

(9) The third conclusion is that the supreme nature is something actually existent, and this is proved in the same way as above.[7]

The corollary to this is that the existence of some nature more perfect or superior to the most perfect being implies a contradiction. The argument here is the same as those concerning the first efficient and first final causes.[8]

Subsection 2

I say that the first efficient cause is also the ultimate final cause. The proof is that every efficient cause acts for the sake of a goal, and the prior efficient cause acts for the sake of the prior goal. Therefore, the first efficient cause acts for the sake of the ultimate goal. The first efficient cause, however, acts mainly and ultimately for nothing other

---

1 See pp. 201–02.
2 Aristotle, *Metaphysics* 8.3, 1043b33.
3 See pp. 198–99.
4 See p. 202.
5 See pp. 200–01.
6 See p. 199.
7 See pp. 201–02.
8 See pp. 201–02 and p. 203.

than for itself; hence it acts for itself as for a goal. Therefore, the first efficient cause is the first final cause.

Likewise, the first efficient cause is the first in perfection. The proof of this is that the first efficient cause does not have the same univocal meaning as the other natural efficient causes; rather its meaning is equivocal. It is, therefore, more perfect and more noble than they. The first efficient cause, therefore, is the most perfect being.

Subsection 3

In the third subsection I show that, since the triple primacy belongs to the same thing, because whatever has one of the natures has also the other two, there is also a triple identity such that the first efficient cause is only one in quiddity and nature. To show this, I will show first a preliminary conclusion and then the main conclusion.

The preliminary conclusion is that an efficient cause that is first in this triple primacy necessarily exists from itself. The proof is that this first efficient cause cannot be caused in any way, for it implies a contradiction that something exists prior to it in the category of efficient or of final cause, and consequently in any category of cause. It is, therefore, completely uncaused. From this I argue that nothing can be non-existent, unless something incompatible with it can exist in it either positively or privatively. The conclusion, therefore, follows. The major premise is evident, because no being can be destroyed except through something incompatible with it, either positively or privatively. The minor premise is proved because that which is incompatible with its nature can exist either from itself or from another. If it exists from itself, two incompatible things will exist simultaneously, or neither of them will exist, because each will destroy the other. If the incompatible thing exists from another cause, against this it can be said that no cause is able to destroy a being because of a repugnance of the effect to that destructible thing, unless it should give more perfect and more powerful being to its effect than the being of that destructible thing. The being of whatever is from another and caused by another is always less noble than the being of what is necessary from itself, because every effect has dependent being, but what is from itself has independent being.

I proceed now to prove the unity of the first nature, which is the main purpose of this Third Subsection. This will be shown with three arguments.

First, if two natures are both necessarily existent beings, they must be distinguished from each other by some real properties of their natures. Let us call these different properties *A* and *B*. These properties are either formally necessary or not. If they are formally necessary, then each will be necessarily existing because of these two properties, which is impossible, because neither of the two properties includes the other, and each property alone would be necessarily existent. On the other hand, if neither of the properties that distinguish the two are formally necessary, then those properties are not properties of necessary existence, and thus neither one is included in necessary existence. Whatever being is not necessary being is, of itself, possible being, but nothing that is possible is included in necessary being.

Second, it is not possible that there be two most perfect natures in the universe; therefore, neither can there be two first efficient causes. The proof of the antecedent is that species are related to each other like numbers, as is said in the *Metaphysics*.[1] Consequently, two species cannot exist at the same level; therefore, it follows even more that there cannot be two first causes or two most perfect beings.

Third, the same conclusion follows from the nature of the final cause, because if there were two ultimate final causes, there would be two orders of beings in relation to these final causes. The result of this would be that the two orders of beings would have no order in common nor a goal in common, because the beings that are ordered to one ultimate final cause could not be ordered to the other. It is impossible that there be two total and complete causes in the same order of the same effect. In such a case, an essential cause in one order might not be causing and yet the effect would still result. Therefore, the beings ordered to one goal would in no way be ordered to the other, and neither, consequently, would they be ordered to the other order of beings, with the result that the totality of beings would not constitute a universe.

This can be commonly confirmed, because no two beings can provide the goals upon which one and the same being is completely dependent, because if this one should provide a goal on which others are dependent, even if this one were removed, the dependence would still remain, and thus there would be no real dependence on it. The dependence, however, on the efficient cause, the final cause, and the perfect being is essential. Therefore no two natures are able to be first in setting goals for other beings according to the triple primacy of dependence. There is, therefore, exactly one nature providing the goal for beings according to the triple dependency, and thereby having the triple primacy.

---

1 Aristotle, *Metaphysics* 8.3, 1043b33.

Appendix D: Ockham's Proof of God's Existence

From William of Ockham, *Questiones in Libros Physicorum Aristotelis* (before 1324), edited by Stephen Brown, in *Guillemi de Ockham Opera philosophica*, St. Bonaventure UP, 1974–84, vol. 6: 762–69

[William of Ockham (1287–1347) was a Franciscan who lived a much more colourful life than the other scholastics considered in this volume. His education and teaching were entirely in England, at Oxford and London Franciscan houses of study. Suspected of heresy, Ockham was called to the Papal Court in Avignon in 1324. Allying himself there with the Minister General of the Franciscan Order, Michael of Cesena, he eventually came to regard the Pope (John XXII) as heretical and lacking authority. He and Michael fled from Avignon, incurring excommunication and expulsion from the Order. They obtained protection from the Holy Roman Emperor, who protected them in Munich, where Ockham eventually died.

Ockham's philosophical position, characterized by (1) nominalism, (2) an insistence on logical possibilities determined by the absolute will of God, and (3) the principle of parsimony ("Ockham's Razor"), was in many ways a radical departure from the scholasticism of the thirteenth and fourteenth centuries. Nominalism, as opposed to realism, is the position that universal terms or universal concepts have no reality outside of speech or the mind. The nominalist's world is a world of individuals, and natures or essences have no reality in things, or no foundation in things. Logical possibilities determined by the absolute power of God are possible beings or states of affairs that, however bizarre or counterintuitive, Ockham must grant as possible. God's absolute power can do or make *anything* that does not involve a logical contradiction. These philosophical possibilities become important for Ockham in limiting the claims that we can make about the world. Ockham's razor is the principle that beings should not be multiplied beyond necessity. Philosophers are given to supposing the reality of metaphysical entities in order to explain the world. Ockham's razor is intended to expunge all such entities from philosophical vocabulary, except for those that are absolutely necessary. These three characteristics are ways in which Ockham's philosophy adumbrated the empiricism of later philosophical positions from his part of the world.

The selection that follows is taken from a series of *Questions on Aristotle's Physics* that Ockham wrote in London or Oxford before 1324. In this selection, Ockham argues for a distinction between whether a temporally first cause can be proven and whether a first being in conservation can be proven. According to Ockham, an absolute first in time cannot be proven, but it is possible to prove that there is a first cause that is now conserving all things in being. In making this distinction, Ockham is in accord with Thomas, Bonaventure, and Scotus, although Ockham takes issue with parts of Scotus's argument, especially the argument against the possibility of an infinity in essentially ordered causes. Furthermore, Ockham's proof of a first conserving cause is not a proof that there is one God causing all things, for the heavenly bodies may be the needed first cause.[1] On the general problem of proving God's existence, however, Ockham sides more with Thomas than with Anselm, Bonaventure, or Scotus in that he insists that any argument for God's existence must be cosmological.]

Question 135: Can It Be Proven Sufficiently that There Is a First Efficient Cause of the Production of Things as Distinct from Their Conservation?

An argument to the affirmative: some being can be made. It cannot be made by itself, therefore, it is made by another. I ask whether that cause is the first efficient cause or whether it, too, has been made. Since there cannot be a series of causes to infinity, therefore, there must be a first efficient cause.

An argument against this: among causes of the same nature, there can be a series of causes to infinity; therefore, there is no proof of a first efficient cause.

Scotus's Arguments to the Affirmative[2]

The first proof is this: the universe is the effect of essentially ordered causes; therefore, the universe is caused by some cause that is not a part of the universe, for otherwise something would be the cause of itself.

Second, the entire universe of effects is dependent, and dependent on nothing within the universe. Otherwise, any thing would be dependent upon itself.

Third, if there were an infinity of essentially ordered causes, it would follow that such an infinity would be all in existence simultane-

---

1   On this point, see Armand Maurer, *The Philosophy of William of Ockham in the Light of Its Principles*, Pontifical Institute of Mediaeval Studies, 1999, p. 177.

2   See John Duns Scotus, *Ordinatio*, pp. 196–202. The eight arguments that follow are Ockham's version of Scotus's arguments.

ously, because essentially ordered causes occur simultaneously. Therefore, etc.

Fourth, whatever is prior is nearer to the beginning. If, therefore, there is no beginning, nothing is essentially prior to anything else.

Fifth, since a superior cause is more perfect in causing, therefore, an infinitely superior cause is infinitely perfect. Such a cause, however, does not cause with the aid of anything else. Therefore, etc.

Sixth, an efficient cause does not imply any imperfection. The ability to cause, therefore, can exist in something without imperfection. If, however, the ability to cause is in every cause with a dependence on something prior, such an ability exists nowhere without imperfection. Therefore, a first efficient cause is possible.

Seventh, if there were no first efficient cause, an infinity in accidentally ordered causes would be impossible, because such an infinity would not exist simultaneously but only successively, one cause following another and the second cause being caused by the first. The second cause, however, does not depend upon the first in causing, because the son can generate offspring whether the father is dead or alive. Such an infinity cannot exist unless it is caused by some nature existing eternally, on which the whole succession depends and everything within it.

Eighth, no change of form can be caused except by the power of something that remains the same and is not a part of the change, because all successive things are of the same nature. There is, therefore, something essentially first on which everything in the succession depends and which is the immediate cause of the succession.

Ninth, the first and second arguments above have been strengthened by another scholar.[1] He argues about the entire multitude of all of the things that have been caused. If that multitude is finite, then it has an efficient cause, which itself does not have an efficient cause; it is, therefore, the first, uncaused cause. The first assumption is clear, because, since every part of the multitude is caused, therefore, the entire multitude is caused. This is so, because to say that the whole multitude is caused is nothing other than to say that every member of it is caused. Scotus's second assumption is clear, because the prior cause of the whole multitude is not a part of the multitude, for if it were, it would not be a prior cause and it would not be uncaused.

---

1 Walter Chatton, *Lectura* I, Dist. 2, Q. 1, A. 1; *Reportatio* I, Dist. 2, Q. 1, A. 1.

[Ockham Argues against Scotus's Arguments in General]

These arguments of Scotus are not sufficient to demonstrate the production of things, as distinct from their conservation. I especially reject the first, second, and the last arguments.[1]

First, this argument implies that God would not be able to make a world that exists eternally into the future. Consider an entire multitude of future days, each one of which would have a day following it in duration. From this, it will follow that the entire multitude has something posterior to it, because each part of it has something posterior to it in duration. That posterior day would be last, because it has no day posterior to it and because it is not a part of the multitude. There is, therefore, a contradiction in the supposition of a perpetual succession into the future.

Second, the argument equally proves that a line is composed of points and that time is composed of instants. Let *a* be the first point of a line; I show then that there is an entire multitude of parts in the continuum, each one of which has a part prior to itself outside of point *a*. I then argue that this multitude of parts does not have something after it outside of *a*, because it would then be part of the entire multitude. It is, therefore, outside of *a* immediately. It would not be divisible, because then one part would be prior to another. [One] indivisible [point], therefore, is immediate to [another] indivisible [point].

Third, Scotus's argument equally proves that there cannot be an infinite series of interconnected actions. Consider the entire multitude of actions, each one of which is posterior to some other. I argue thus: this entire multitude of actions has an act posterior to it, because each action has an action posterior to it; that last act does not have another action posterior to it, because it would then be part of the multitude.

[Ockham Refutes the Nine Arguments Above]

Against the first argument, I concede that the universe of caused things is caused. One could deny, however, Scotus's conclusion, because one could say that one effect is caused by another thing that is part of the multitude, and it by another, and so on infinitely; such is the case for accidentally ordered causes, according to the Philosopher,[2] one of which can exist and can be caused by another, as, for

---

1   That is, Ockham especially rejects the first, second, and last arguments above attributed to Scotus. The three arguments that follow are general arguments intended to imply that, on Scotus's principles, an eternally existing world would be impossible, but such an eternal world was generally recognized to have been a possibility.

2   Aristotle, *On Generation and Corruption* 2.11, 338b5–19.

example, one human being is caused by another, and that one by another, and so on, to infinity. The contrary of this cannot be proven, so long as we are talking about the production of things. It does not thus follow that "the same thing is the cause of itself," because the entire multitude is not caused by some one cause. Rather, one thing is caused by another, and it is caused by yet another, but all are within the multitude.

Against the second argument, I say that for the production of things it cannot be sufficiently proved that the entire universe is simultaneously dependent, but only for the conservation of things. The reason is that whoever would not suppose the conservation of things, would say that one single thing in that universe depends upon another that is part of the multitude, and it in turn depends upon another, and so, on to infinity, as far as the first production of things is concerned. Given this, there is no dependence except upon that which is conserving things, but this is not at issue in this argument. Further, it does not follow that something would be dependent on itself, because the entire multitude does not depend on some one thing, but, rather, one thing depends on some other thing, and it on something else.

Against the third argument, I say that, although whatever conserves another—whether immediately or mediately—is simultaneous with the thing conserved, nevertheless not everything that produces something—immediately or mediately—is simultaneous with what it produces.[1] In producing causes, therefore, there can be an infinite series without any actual infinity. Hence, as is clear from before,[2] not all essentially ordered causes concur simultaneously in causing, although sometimes they do concur simultaneously in conserving.

Against the fourth argument, I say that, when we are considering only the production of things, it cannot be proven that something is essentially prior but only accidentally so.

Against the fifth argument, I said above[3] that the superior cause is not always a more perfect cause in its nature, and frequently it is less perfect.

---

1 Something that conserves something else in existence might do so immediately or mediately. "Immediately" means that the cause acts on the effect with no intervening instrument or other cause; "mediately" means that the cause acts on the effect with some intervening instrument or other cause. One might say that God conserves all creatures in existence immediately (acting all by himself); or, one might say that God conserves all creatures in existence mediately, through the action of the sun, for example, which provides heat and energy.

2 Ockham, *Questions on Aristotle's Physics*, Q. 134.

3 Ockham, *Questions on Aristotle's Physics*, Q. 133.

Against the sixth argument, I say that when we are considering the production of things it cannot be sufficiently proven that an efficient cause does not imply imperfection. The reason for this is that from production alone it cannot be sufficiently proven that an infinite series of efficient causes is impossible.

Against the seventh argument, I say that an infinity of accidentally ordered causes is possible without some nature that exists eternally and on which the entire succession depends. The reason is that, if we are considering production alone, it cannot be sufficiently proved that the complete efficient cause of one human being is not some other human beings. It could be said, therefore, that one human being depends completely on another, and that one depends on another, and so on infinitely, and there is no dependence on some eternally existing thing. The opposite of this cannot be proven through a consideration of production, although it can be proven from conservation.

Against the eighth argument, the same sort of response can be made, namely, that the succession is perpetuated because one member of the series depends completely on some other member of the same nature. It cannot be proven by a consideration of the production of things or of the whole succession that an infinite series is not possible. The reason is that for production it is sufficient that one human being completely depends on another as the efficient cause, and that one depends on another, and so on infinitely.

Against the ninth argument, I concede that the entire multitude is caused, but not by some one cause. Rather, one thing is caused by another that is part of the multitude, and that one is also caused by another that is part of the same multitude, and so on. I therefore concede also the first assumption and its proof, but in this sense: when we are considering the initial production of things, nothing other than the natural sequence of causes can be proven. Against the second assumption, I say that it cannot be proven sufficiently that the entire caused multitude has itself been caused by something else.

Against the main argument I say this: if we are considering the initial production of things, it cannot be proven sufficiently that an infinite series of efficient causes is impossible, one of which is successively caused by another. No actual infinity follows from this, as is clear from what has been said.

Question 136: Can It Be Proven Sufficiently that There Is a First Efficient Cause of the Conservation of Things?

An argument on the negative side: to conserve something is to make it. It is not, however, possible to prove a first efficient cause, and therefore neither is it possible to prove a first cause of conservation.

An argument on the other side: all conserving causes concur simultaneously in conserving the effect. If, therefore, there were an infinite series of conserving causes, there would be an actually infinite number of them, but this is impossible. Therefore, etc.

[Ockham's Opinion]

I shall briefly argue the affirmative side of this question. The proof is as follows. Whatever is really produced by something, is really conserved by something, as long as it remains in actual being. This is clear. It is certain, furthermore, that some effect is produced, and therefore it must be conserved by something, as long as it remains. I ask, then, about that conserving cause: it is either produced by another or not. If it is not, then it is the first efficient cause by being the first conserving cause, because every conserving cause is an efficient cause. If, however, that conserving cause is produced by another, I ask about that other cause, as I did before, and thus either there is an infinite series or it is necessary to come to a stop at something that is the conserving cause and is not conserved itself in any way. Such an efficient cause will be the first efficient cause. There cannot be an infinite series in conserving causes, because there would then be an actual infinity, which is impossible. The reason is that whatever conserves another thing—whether immediately or mediately—is simultaneous with the thing conserved. Hence, whatever is conserved requires all conserving causes to be in actual existence, but not all produced effects require all of their producing causes in actual existence—either immediately or mediately. Therefore, although there can be an actually infinite series in producing causes without there being an actual infinity, there cannot be an infinite series in conserving causes without an actual infinity.

[Objection to Ockham's Position]

On the contrary, it seems that the same argument should be made about the initial production of things as is made about their conservation. The argument about production is this: something has been produced. I then ask about the producing cause, whether it has not been produced; if so, I have my conclusion. If, on the other hand, it has been produced by another, though not through an infinite series of causes, there must, therefore, be a stopping at some producing cause that is not itself produced. The assumption of this argument is proved in the case of essentially ordered causes: on the one hand, because in essentially ordered causes all causes are required simultaneously for producing the effect. If there were an infinite number of such causes, there would be an actual infinity. On the other hand, because the entire multitude of effects is essentially caused, and not by something within the multitude, for then something would cause itself, therefore, it is caused by some uncaused thing that is outside of the multitude of effects. Likewise, in accidentally ordered causes it is clear that the entire multitude of effects has actually been caused, and not by something belonging to the multitude, for then it would have to cause itself in causing the multitude. The multitude, therefore, is caused by something outside of the multitude, and that cause is either not caused, which is my conclusion, or it is caused by causes essentially ordered, and then the first part of this argument brings us to the same conclusion.

[Ockham's Response to this Objection]

I respond that if we are considering only the initial production of things, it cannot be sufficiently proved that there is not an infinite series of causes, neither in accidentally ordered causes, nor in essentially ordered causes, formally considered. Against the argument about essentially ordered causes, as was shown above,[1] I say that not all essentially ordered causes concur in the initial production of an effect. Against either subsequent argument, I say that the entire multitude, whether essentially or accidentally ordered, has been caused, but not by some one thing that is part of the multitude or outside of it. Rather, one thing is caused by another within the multitude, and it by another, and so on infinitely. From a consideration of the initial production of things the opposite of this cannot be sufficiently proven. Thus, it follows neither that some one thing causes the whole multitude nor that the same thing is the cause of itself, because no one thing is the cause of all.

To the main argument, I say that, if we are considering the efficient causality by which a thing first receives being after non-being, it cannot be proven that there is a first efficient cause. On the other hand, if we consider the efficient causality by which a thing is maintained or conserved in being, this can very well be proven. The answer to this question is now clear.

---

1 Ockham, *Questions on Aristotle's Physics*, Q. 134.

Appendix E: Ontological Argument for the Existence of God

From René Descartes, *Meditations on First Philosophy* (1641), edited by Andrew Bailey, translated by Ian Johnston, Broadview, 2013, pp. 73–76

[René Descartes (1596–1650) wrote his best-known work, *Meditations on First Philosophy*, in 1641. The *Meditations* are a kind of *Summa* of Cartesian philosophy, and they contain three proofs for the existence of God, two in the Third Meditation and one, given below, in the Fifth Meditation. Proving the existence of God is absolutely essential to Descartes's philosophical project: without such a proof, Descartes is reduced to solipsism and scepticism. With the existence of God, Descartes is able to justify common-sense truths and, more importantly, the truths of science. Proving the existence of God is thus not an act of piety on Descartes's part, although it might well have been that, too. Rather, the existence of God in Cartesian philosophy is the foundation of all truth beyond the bare affirmation of the existence of the thinking subject.

In the Fifth Meditation, Descartes formulates an ontological argument, which is given below. This argument is ontological because it is an argument from the idea of God alone. As Descartes tells us, he has a clear and distinct idea of God, and this idea includes all perfections. Existence is a perfection, and therefore the idea of God includes the idea of existence. When we think about God, therefore, we must include existence in the idea of God or, in other words, we must think of God as existing. The claim that existence is a perfection is the claim that led to Kant's famous criticism of the Ontological Argument, that existence is not a predicate.[1]]

But if it follows from the mere fact that I can draw the idea of some object from my thinking that all things which I perceive clearly and distinctly as pertaining to that object really do belong to it, can I not also derive from this an argument which proves that God exists? For clearly I find the idea of Him, that is, of a supremely perfect being, within me just as much as I do the idea of some shape or number. I know that [actual and] eternal existence belongs to His nature just as clearly and distinctly as [I know] that what I prove about some shape

---

1   Immanuel Kant, *Critique of Pure Reason*, 2nd Division, Bk. 2, Ch. 3, Sect. 4, translated by Norman Kemp Smith, St. Martin's, 1965, pp. 500–07.

or number also belongs to the nature of that shape or number. And therefore, even if all the things I have meditated on in the preceding days were not true, for me the existence of God ought to have at least the same degree of certainty as [I have recognized] up to this point in the truths of mathematics.

At first glance, however, this argument does not look entirely logical but [appears to] contain some sort of sophistry.[1] For, since in all other matters I have been accustomed to distinguish existence from essence, I can easily persuade myself that [existence] can also be separated from the essence of God and thus that I [can] think of God as not actually existing. However, when I think about this more carefully, it becomes clear that one cannot separate existence from the essence of God, any more than one can separate the fact that the sum of the three angles in a triangle is equal to two right angles from the essence of a triangle, or separate the idea of a valley from the idea of a mountain. Thus, it is no less contradictory to think of a God (that is, of a supremely perfect being) who lacks existence (that is, who lacks a certain perfection) than it is to think of a mountain without a valley.[2]

Nonetheless, although I cannot conceive of God other than as something with existence, any more than I can of a mountain without a valley, the truth is that just because I think of a mountain with a valley, it does not therefore follow that there is any mountain in the world. In the same way, just because I think of God as having existence, it does not seem to follow that God therefore exists. For my thinking imposes no necessity on things, and in the same way as I can imagine a horse with wings, even though no horse has wings, so I could perhaps attribute existence to God, even though no God exists.

But this [objection] conceals a fallacy. For from the fact that I cannot think of a mountain without a valley, it does not follow that a mountain and valley exist anywhere, but merely that the mountain and valley, whether they exist or not, cannot be separated from each other. However, from the fact that I cannot think of God without existence, it does follow that existence is inseparable from God, and thus that He truly does exist. Not that my thought brings this about or imposes any necessity on anything, but rather, by contrast, because the necessity of the thing itself, that is, of the existence of God, determines that I must think this way. For I am not free to think of God without existence (that is, of a supremely perfect being lacking a supreme perfection) in the same way that I am free to imagine a horse with wings or without them.

Suppose somebody objects: Agreed that once one has assumed that God has every perfection it is in fact necessary to admit that He exists

---

1 That is, clever-sounding but deceptive reasoning.
2 That is, an upslope without a downslope.

(because existence is part of perfection), but it is not necessary to make that assumption, just as it is unnecessary to assume that all quadrilaterals [can] be inscribed in a circle. For if one assumed that, one would have to conclude that any rhombus could be inscribed in a circle—but this is clearly false.[1] But this objection is invalid. For although it may not be necessary for me ever to entertain any thought of God, nevertheless, whenever I do happen to think of a first and supreme being, and, as it were, to derive an idea of Him from the storehouse of my mind, I have to attribute to Him all perfections, even though I do not enumerate them all at that time or attend to each one of them individually. And this necessity is obviously sufficient to make me conclude correctly, once I have recognized that existence is a perfection, that a first and supreme being exists. In the same way, it is not necessary that I ever imagine any triangle, but every time I wish to consider a rectilinear[2] figure with only three angles, I have to attribute to it those [properties] from which I correctly infer that its three angles are no greater than two right angles, although at that time I may not notice this. But when I think about which figures [are capable of being] inscribed in a circle, it is not at all necessary that I believe every quadrilateral is included in their number. On the contrary, I cannot even imagine anything like that, as long as I do not wish to admit anything unless I understand it clearly and distinctly. Thus, there is a great difference between false assumptions of this kind and the true ideas which are innate in me, of which the first and most important is the idea of God. For, in fact, I understand in many ways that this [idea] is not something made up which depends upon my thought but [is] the image of a true and immutable nature: first, because I cannot think of any other thing whose essence includes existence, other than God alone; second, because I am unable to conceive of two or more Gods of this sort, and because, given that I have already assumed that one God exists, I see clearly that it is necessary that He has previously existed from [all] eternity and will continue [to exist] for all eternity; and finally because I perceive many other things in God, none of which I can remove or change.

But, in fact, no matter what reasoning I finally use by way of proof, I always come back to the point that the only things I find entirely persuasive are those I perceive clearly and distinctly. Among the things I perceive in this way, some are obvious to everyone, while others reveal

---

1 Quadrilaterals are four-sided figures. A figure can be inscribed in a circle
   when a circle can be drawn that passes through each corner. Rhombuses are
   figures with four sides of equal length. Squares (a type of rhombus) can be
   inscribed in a circle, but rhombuses not containing four right angles cannot.
2 Formed by straight lines.

themselves only to those who look into them more closely and investigate more diligently, but nevertheless once the latter have been discovered, they are considered no less certain than the former. For example, even though the fact that the hypotenuse of a right triangle is opposite the largest angle of the triangle is more apparent than the fact that the square of the hypotenuse is equal to the sum of the squares of the other two sides, nonetheless, after we have initially recognized the second fact, we are no less certain of its truth [than we are of the other].

But where God is concerned, if I were not overwhelmed with prejudices, and if images of perceptible things were not laying siege to my thinking on all sides, there is certainly nothing I would recognize sooner or more easily than Him. For what is more inherently evident than that there is a supreme being; in other words, that God exists, for existence [necessarily and eternally] belongs to His essence alone?

Appendix F: Scotus on the Immortality of the Soul

From John Duns Scotus, *Ordinatio* or *Opus oxoniense* (1300–08), in *Opera omnia*, vol. 20, edited by Luke Wadding, Vivès, 1894, pp. 44–49

[In this passage, Scotus argues that no philosophical demonstration of the immortality of the human soul can be given. Probable arguments are the best that can be given to show this conclusion. Scotus is arguing here against the position of Thomas.]

Bk. 4, Dist. 43, Q. 2
Proposition 2: The Intellectual Soul Is Immortal[1]

I will discuss this second proposition, that the intellectual soul is immortal, in the same way as I did the first. I will begin by reporting the philosophical authorities who support this proposition.[2]

Argument 1: Aristotle says that the intellect is separate from everything else, just as what is eternal is separate from what is corruptible.[3] If it should be objected that the soul is only separate in its operation, I respond that this is enough to prove the proposition. According to Aristotle,[4] if the soul can be separate in its operation, then it is also separate in its being.

Argument 2: Aristotle notes a difference between sensation and understanding in that an excessive sense object corrupts the senses, and when that happens the senses are less able to sense fainter things. The same is not true, however, about the understanding; on the contrary, after the intellect has understood the highest things, it is better able to understand lesser things. The intellect, therefore, is not harmed in its operation, and from this fact it follows that it is incorruptible in being.

Argument 4: Aristotle concludes that the intellect alone comes "from outside."[5] The intellect, therefore, does not acquire its being

---

1 The first proposition, not included in this translation, is that the intellectual soul is the specific form of a human being. Scotus argued for that proposition just before this passage.

2 Of the nine arguments given by Scotus, I have translated the first, second, fourth, eighth, and ninth.

3 Aristotle, *On the Soul* 2.2, 413b25.

4 Aristotle, *On the Soul* 2.2, 413b29–31.

5 Aristotle, *On the Generation of Animals* 2.3, 736b28–29.

from natural generation but from an extrinsic cause. Consequently, it does not acquire non-being from natural corruption, nor through some physical destructive power. Its being is not subject to such a cause, because it came immediately from a higher cause.

Argument 8: One teacher[1] uses the words of the Philosopher to argue thus. Whatever is corrupted is corrupted either because of something destructive of it or because of some defect in it of what it needs to maintain its being. The intellectual soul, however, has nothing in it that is destructive of it. Furthermore, the soul's being has no dependence on the body, because the soul has its own essential being, and this being remains the same, whether the soul is in the body or separate from it. The only difference between these two states is that when the soul is joined to the body it communicates its being to the body, which it does not do when it is separate from the body.

Argument 9: Whatever is simple cannot be separated from itself. The soul is simple; it, therefore, cannot be separated from itself. Consequently, it cannot be separated from its being, because it does not have its being from any other form than from itself. The case is otherwise for a composite thing, because it has its being through its form, and such a form can be separated from its matter, which results in the destruction of the composite.

[Arguments against this Proposition]

The Philosopher, however, seems to have held the opposing view, because in the *Metaphysics* he says that all parts that can remain distinct within a whole are elements.[2] These are material parts, as he understands elements. In addition to these parts, it is necessary to recognize some form of the whole, and the whole is what exists. This form cannot exist separately from the material parts, when the whole ceases to exist. If, therefore, Aristotle held that the intellectual soul is the form of the human being, as he clearly did from the proof of the preceding proposition,[3] he cannot hold that the form will remain separate from the matter, when the whole no longer exists.

Further, one of Aristotle's principles seems to be that whatever begins to exist will cease to exist. Hence, in *On the Heavens*, when arguing against Plato, he seems to regard it as contradictory to say that something began to exist and also that it is perpetual and incorruptible.[4]

---

1 Thomas Aquinas, *ST* I, Q. 75, A. 6, Ch. 3, pp. 98–100. Arguments 8 and 9 reflect Thomas's position.

2 Aristotle, *Metaphysics* 7.17, 1041b12–32.

3 Not included in this translation.

4 Aristotle, *On the Heavens* 1.10, 279b31–280a12.

In addition, in the *Physics*, he says that whatever has a beginning also has an end.[1]

[Scotus's Opinion]

Although there are probable arguments to support this second proposition, they are neither demonstrative nor necessary.

The support brought for this proposition from the authority of the philosophers[2] can be answered in two ways. First, what Aristotle really thought on this matter can be doubted. He speaks about it differently in different places, and he advanced different principles—some of which seem to support one side, and others seem to support the other. It is likely that he remained in doubt over this proposition, sometimes seeming to accord more with one side, and at other times seeming to accord more with the opposite. His changes seem to have varied with the subject that he was treating.

A second, and better, response is that not all philosophers' assertions have been proven by necessary philosophical arguments. Frequently their arguments are based on probable opinions or the common views of their predecessors. In this light, when the Philosopher was dealing with two difficult questions in *On the Heavens*,[3] he said that one should say that one position *seems* to be right, and our willingness to do so should be considered modesty rather than rashness if, for the sake of philosophy, we can accept insufficient evidence about which we have many doubts. Insufficient evidence is frequently sufficient for philosophers when they are not able to achieve something better, provided that they do not contradict philosophical principles. In the same chapter, Aristotle notes[4] that the Egyptians and the Babylonians report many things about the stars, and this is our source of much that we believe about the stars. In this way, philosophers sometimes are satisfied with probable arguments and sometimes with assumptions of principles in place of necessary reasoning. However forceful the arguments from authority might seem, this response should be sufficient to show that they do not prove the proposition.

Reply to Argument 1: Aristotle understands this separation only in the sense that the intellect does not use the body in its operation. For this reason, the intellect is incorruptible in operating, and he is talking about the sort of corruption to which a bodily power is subject when its organ is corrupted. This kind of corruption belongs only to a bodily

---

1   Aristotle, *Physics* 3.4, 203b9.
2   Arguments 1, 2, and 4 just given.
3   Aristotle, *On the Heavens* 2.12, 291b25–29.
4   Aristotle, *On the Heavens* 2.12, 292a7–9.

power. According to the Philosopher,[1] if an old man were given the eye of a young man, the old man would see just as well as the youth. The power of vision, therefore, is not weakened or corrupted because of its operation, but only because of its organ. The intellect, however, is not liable to this corruption because it does not have an organ through the corruption of which its operation could be corrupted. It does not follow from this that the intellect would be absolutely incorruptible in its operation, such that it would then follow that the intellect would be incorruptible in being, as was argued. It *only* follows that it is incorruptible in operating, unlike bodily powers. In fact, the Philosopher indicates in *On the Soul* that the intellect is absolutely corruptible.[2] The intellect is corrupted in us when the interior senses are corrupted. This is so because the intellect is taken to be the principle of operation for the entire composite being in its proper operation. The composite, however, is corruptible, and, therefore, its operative principle is also corruptible. Aristotle seems to say that the intellect is the principle of operating for the whole composite and that the intellect's operation is the operation of the whole.[3]

Reply to Argument 2: An excessive sense object corrupts the senses accidentally, because it corrupts the organ by disrupting the proper proportion of a well-disposed organ. The intellect, however, is different because it does not have an organ that can be corrupted by an excessive object. From this it does not follow that the intellect is incorruptible unless it should be proven that it does not depend in being on the whole composite, which is corruptible.

Reply to Argument 4: What Aristotle thought about the origin of the intellectual soul is extremely doubtful. If Aristotle did not think that God immediately does anything new, but only moves the heavens with an eternal motion, and if God does this as a remote cause, from what separate agent would Aristotle have thought that the intellectual soul was produced as a new thing? If you say that the soul was caused by some Intelligence,[4] there are two problems. One problem is that such an Intelligence cannot create a substance, as I have argued above.[5] A second problem is that an Intelligence is not able immedi-

---

1 Aristotle, *On the Soul* 1.4, 408b22–23.

2 Aristotle, *On the Soul* 3.5, 430a23–25; 1.1, 403a7–10.

3 Aristotle, *On the Soul* 1.5, 411a23–b13.

4 Scotus refers here to the theory, deriving from Avicenna and others, that between the first cause of the heavens and earth there are a series of spiritual beings called "Intelligences" that cause motion in the heavenly bodies and events on earth.

5 John Duns Scotus, *Ordinatio* IV, Dist. 1, Q. Unique, Author's Arguments, Third Proposition (*Opera omnia*, vol. 11, pp. 41–42).

ately to produce something new, any more than God is able to do so, according to the Philosopher's principles about the immutability of the agent and its eternity in acting.

Furthermore, it does not seem that Aristotle, following his own principles, could hold that the intellectual soul is the product of a natural agent, because, as it seems in the *Metaphysics*,[1] he holds that the soul is incorruptible and no form that is the product of a natural agent is absolutely incorruptible.

It could be said that Aristotle does hold that the soul immediately receives new being from God, because the fact that it receives being follows sufficiently from his principles. Since he does not suppose that the soul pre-existed eternally without the body nor that it existed in another body, it is not probable without any other presupposition that it could have received such being from any other agent except God. Aristotle, therefore, would have conceded creation.

I answer that this does not follow, because Aristotle did not suppose one production of the composite and another one of the intellectual soul, just as there are not different productions of fire and of the form of fire. Rather, he holds that the animation of the organic body is the accidental production of the soul. We [Christians], on the other hand, hold that there are two productions: one is the production of the soul from non-being into being, which is creation. The other is the animation of the body that was inanimate, and this is the production of the animated body that occurs through change properly understood. Whoever, like Aristotle, holds only the second kind of production does not hold creation.

Again, it might be said that, although I have denied that Aristotle accepted creation, how nevertheless can I explain consistently that an immutable agent produces something new?

The only response I can make is that newness comes from the passive recipient. If an effect is new that is completely and uniquely dependent on an active cause, the only explanation for this is some change in the efficient cause, according to Aristotle. On the other hand, if an effect is new that is dependent both on an efficient cause and on a passive recipient, the explanation for this is some newness in the passive recipient, without any newness in the agent. It could be said, thus, that God changes the organic body to an animated body by natural necessity, as soon as the body is ready for this animation and when the natural causes have made it newly ready. In this way the change to animation is new and is from God.

How, in that case, can this newness be attributed to God, the efficient cause?

---

1 Aristotle, *Metaphysics* 12.3, 1070a25–28.

I answer that, according to Aristotle, just as the first agent is always acting on its passive effect while always remaining completely unchanged, so also if the passive effect can be new and receptive of a new form, and if this is not caused by some secondary cause, God is the immediate cause of this effect even though it comes to exist as something new. For every passive potency there must be some corresponding active cause, and if there is no created active cause, then the immediate active cause will be God.

Reply to Argument 8 (one of the arguments from the teachers): If [this teacher] understands (1) the soul to have essentially the same being in the whole composite as it does outside of the whole (as essential being is distinguished from accidental being), in the same way the form of fire, if it were without matter, would have essential being and hence it could be granted that the form of fire is incorruptible. If, however, he should understand (2) that the essential being belongs to the composite substance, then it is false that the soul without the body has essential being, because in that case its being could not be shared with something else. In the divine persons, for example, essential being understood in this way cannot be shared. In every way, therefore, it is wrong to say that the soul has essential being without the body: if you understand it in the second way, then the antecedent is false; if you understand it in the first way, the consequence does not follow, unless you add that the soul naturally and without a miracle has essential being. This claim, however, is a matter of faith and is not known by natural reason.

Reply to Argument 9: Not every corruption occurs because of the separation of one thing from another. If, for example, we consider the being of an angel that is, as some say, different from its essence, it is not separable from the angel, and yet the angel is destructible, for its non-being could succeed its being.

Appendix G: Ockham on the Human Soul

From William of Ockham, *Quodlibeta Septem* (1324–25), in *Guillelmi de Ockham Opera theologica*, vol. 9, edited by Joseph C. Wey, St. Bonaventure UP, 1967–86, pp. 62–65

[In this passage, Ockham is arguing that it cannot be known that the human soul is the form of the human body, a claim that is fundamental to Thomas's position. For Ockham, it cannot be proven that the subject of an intellectual operation, which is non-bodily, is also united as form to a human body.]

Quodlibet 1, Q. 10: Can It Be Demonstrated that the Intellectual Soul Is the Form of the Human Body?

An argument on the affirmative side: Because we experience that the activity of understanding takes place in us, and understanding is a human operation, therefore, the efficient cause of understanding and the subject doing this are in us. Our understanding cannot be caused by a separate Intelligence, because the operation of such a substance is beyond our possible experience.[1] Further, understanding is not the operation of a composite of soul and body, and, hence, what does this operation is *part* of a human being. It cannot be the material part; it is, therefore, the form.

An argument on the negative side: The intellectual soul is an incorruptible form; it cannot, therefore, be the form of a corruptible body.

Two Difficulties

In this question there are two difficulties. One is the problem of whether we would be able to understand through the intellectual soul if it were not the form of the body. The other difficulty is whether it can be known with evidence, either by reason or by experience, that we *do* understand. By "understand" we mean an act that properly belongs to an immaterial substance, which the intellectual soul is sup-

---

1 Ockham refers here to the doctrine, derived from Avicenna and others, that the cause of human understanding is the activity of a "separated Intelligence," that is, a spiritual being (like an angel) that provides abstracted, universal concepts to the human mind.

posed to be: a substance that is ungenerated and indestructible, and that as a whole is in the whole person and in every part.

Reply to the First Difficulty

The answer to the first question seems to be "yes." The reason is that we often attribute to one thing what really belongs to another, because of some communication of properties between the two, and this communication is neither matter, nor form, nor any part. We say, for example, that something is attributed to another because of an instrument, clothing, and so forth; in this way we call someone a "rower" because of the oars, or a "digger" [because of a shovel]; if someone is dressed, shod, or armed, we say that such a person has touched another because the person's clothing or armour has touched the other. This kind of communication even exists between the Son of God and the human nature that was assumed, and neither one is a form. In the same way, therefore, something can be attributed to a body that has been moved by the mover, without the mover being the form of the body. Another example occurs in the story of the angel who came to Tobias.[1] To help Tobias, the angel took on a human body and moved it, and the angel was said to eat, to drink, to walk, to understand, and to make judgements. Therefore, even if the soul is only the mover of the body and not the form of the body, we can still say that we understand through the intellectual soul.[2]

Reply to the Second Difficulty

If we understand the intellectual soul as an immaterial form that is indestructible, that as a whole is in the whole body, and that as a whole is in every part of the body, it cannot with evidence be known, either by reason or by experience, that such a form is in us, nor that the understanding that belongs to such a substance is also in us, nor that such a form is the form of our body. For the present, I do not care what the Philosopher might have thought about this, because whenever he treated the topic he spoke doubtfully. The three claims[3] about the soul are taken by us on faith.

---

1 Tobias 5:5–10:21.

2 Ockham may not have had Thomas explicitly in mind, but in this paragraph he argues against the position taken by Thomas: *ST* I, Q. 76, A. 1, Ch. 3, pp. 98–100.

3 The three claims are: (1) that the intellectual soul is an immaterial, indestructible form; (2) that it, as a whole, is in the whole body; and (3) that it, as a whole, is in every part of the body. These claims cannot, Ockham says, be proven by philosophy alone.

It is clear that this cannot be demonstrated, because every argument given to prove this relies upon claims that are doubtful to natural reason. This is also not proven through experience, because we only experience understanding, willing, and other such activities. Anyone following reason and experience would say that these are operations and experiences that belong to the form, through which presumably human beings are distinguished from animals. Although according to faith and the truth, this form is the intellectual soul that is an indestructible form, nevertheless such a person of reason and experience would say that this form is extended, destructible, and generable. It does not seem that experience can demonstrate conclusively any other form.

If you should ask whether it can be proven with evidence that this form, which the reasonable person recognizes through experience, is the form of the body, I respond, "yes," with the following probable argument. Any composite thing that differs in species from another composite differs either as a whole or through some part. A human being differs in species from a donkey, but not as a whole, because the human and the donkey share some matter of the same kind. They differ, therefore, because of some part, but not matter; therefore, they differ by form. There are perhaps some doubtful assumptions in this argument.

If it should be supposed, as indeed is the truth, that the intellectual soul, which is the immaterial and indestructible form, is in us and is that through which we understand, then it is more reasonable to suppose that it is the form of the body than merely the mover of the body. Indeed, if it were merely the mover, it would move the body by either local motion or by altering qualities. This first one is wrong, because if it were so, the soul would move the body of a child equally well as the body of an adult. Further, if the soul that is the form of the body is sufficient to move the body in local motion, then it is superfluous to suppose any other mover for the body. The second one is wrong also, because all changes in bodily qualities are sufficiently explained by other bodily agents; the soul as such a mover, therefore, would be superfluous.[1]

Ockham's Conclusion

Anyone following natural reason would concede that we experience the operation of understanding in ourselves, but this is the act of a *corporeal* and *destructible form*. One would consequently say that such a

---

1 Following this paragraph, Ockham raises a doubt, which is omitted in this translation, about how the soul is united to the body; he responds to the doubt later in this work, in Q. 12.

form belongs to the body as an *extended form*. We do not, moreover, experience our understanding as an operation that belongs to an immaterial substance. We do not, therefore, conclude on the basis of our understanding that this incorruptible substance belongs to us as our form. Even if perchance we were to experience the understanding [that belongs to an immaterial substance] as belonging to us, we would only conclude that what is doing this act is in us as a mover, but not as a form.

Appendix H: Scotus on the Sinful Will

From John Duns Scotus, *Lectura* (1298–99), in *Joannis Duns Scoti Opera omnia*, vol. 18, edited by Scotistic Commission, Vatican Press, 1982, pp. 375–84

[In this passage, Scotus explores the nature of wrongdoing. He is discussing the primordial sin of the devil, or of the fallen angels, but this discussion is about sin in general and it thus applies to human sin. Scotus is arguing against a fundamental Thomistic position, although Scotus does not seem to have Thomas explicitly in mind here. Scotus argues that in some sense the primordial sin is an excessive love of happiness and of the self; Thomas, by contrast, thinks that the love of happiness and self is natural and is the foundation of all good acts.]

Bk. 2, Dist. 6, Q. 2: What Sin Did the Devil Commit?

First we will see what sin the devil committed, and second we will see what kind of sin it was.[1]

As to the first question, I say that the act was an act of willing and not an act of rejecting, because every act of rejection presupposes an act of willing. Although an act of rejection is a positive act in the common usage of terms, an act of rejecting is not first. I do not deny that it can be first, but in simply natural cases the first act is the act of willing. Someone rejects something because he or she wills something that is incompatible with what is being rejected. According to Anselm in *On the Fall of the Devil*, "the greedy man does not want money because he wants bread, which he cannot have at the same time as the money."[2] The first act of the will in an angel was the act of willing.

What sort of act, however, was the first act of willing in the devil? I say that there are two acts of willing, desire-willing and friendship-willing. The act of desire-willing is the act by which someone wills what is good for him or herself or what is good for someone else. The act of friendship-willing is the act of willing what is good absolutely when we love ourselves or something absolutely. These two acts are ordered to each other, because the desire-love presupposes friendship-love. I do not will good for myself unless I love myself, and I will good

---

1 This text provides the answer only to the first question, what was the sin of the devil? The second question is about how the sin is to be classified, specifically, was it the sin of pride?

2 Anselm, *On the Fall of the Devil* (*De casu Diaboli*), Ch. 3.

for someone else because I love that person. The will does not desire good for another unless the will is directed to that beloved person.

I say, then, that the first act of willing of the devil was excessive self-love by which the angel loved himself; from this followed excessive desire, by which the devil desired his own good, based on this inordinate love of himself. Augustine says this in *The City of God*, "two loves have made two cities," and so forth.[1] Hence, the root of all sin is the immoderate love of self. Thus, not without reason the Apostle has said, "There will be people in those days who love themselves."[2] The devil is related to his own essence thus: the devil's own essence is more pleasing to the fallen angel than the essence of God, who was his creator, as Augustine says above.[3]

We thus have our first conclusion, that the first act of the devil was an act of willing; and that act was an act of willing love for himself excessively, from which followed excessive and disordered desire.

Let us now see the progression in the angel's sin, by considering desire-love.

I say that there are three kinds of good things (from Aristotle's *Ethics*),[4] namely, the virtuous good, the useful good, and the pleasurable good. One can desire the virtuous good without sin; and no one first desires the useful good by the love of pleasure, but rather something else is desired first and the useful is a means to it. It remains, therefore, that the devil desired the pleasurable good.

Furthermore, Anselm says that there are two kinds of love of the good: the love of what is advantageous and the love of justice.[5] The devil's desire did not come from a love of justice, for if it had, he would not have sinned; it came, therefore, from a love of what is advantageous. Among advantageous goods, the devil sought what was most advantageous for his own nature, excluding all other considerations. This is pleasure.

In line with this, Aristotle approves of the philosopher who said that pleasure is the highest good and is happiness,[6] because it is close to happiness and follows it in a way that makes it difficult to distinguish. Pleasure is sought without considering other things, and nothing is sought if it is sad or without pleasure. The devil's first act of desire, therefore, was for his greatest pleasure and advantage.

---

1   Augustine, *The City of God*, Bk. 14, Ch. 28.
2   2 Timothy 3:2.
3   Augustine, *The City of God*, Bk. 14, Ch. 13.
4   Aristotle, *Nicomachean Ethics* 8.2, 1155b18–20.
5   Anselm, *The Fall of the Devil* (*De casu Diaboli*), Chs. 13–14.
6   Aristotle, *Nicomachean Ethics* 10.2, 1172b9–15.

This is also made clear in this way. Our will is joined to the sense appetite, just as our intellect is joined to the sense image. Hence, just as the intellect understands nothing except by an abstraction from the sense image, so our will wills and seeks nothing unless it is sought by the sense appetite. We can all experience this in ourselves, because whenever our sense appetite is more inclined to something, our will desires more that same thing. In fact, the will as such does not desire except what the sense appetite desires, just as the intellect does not understand except by turning to sense images. Therefore, just as the separate intellect does not understand by turning to the sense images, so, if the will were separate, it would be able to will without a sense appetite. Hence, if our will were separate, it would naturally take delight in that to which the will inclines as will; this is the most desirable thing, which is also the most intelligible thing. In the same way the appetite of taste desires the maximum in taste (the most perfect flavour), and in the same way the appetite of vision desires the most perfect visible object apprehended by sight (the most perfect colour). On the assumption that each sense power has its own appetite, the general point is that the greatest object that can be perceived by any power is the most desirable. Therefore, since an angel has a will that is separate from sense appetite, it will desire what is more and most intelligible to it. The highest intelligible object, therefore, is the most desired thing by it, in which it would take delight in some way. This most desirable and intelligible thing is happiness. The devil, therefore, desired happiness in a disordered way.

This is what Anselm says in *The Fall of the Devil* when the student asked what the devil desired; Anselm responded that he did not know but that the devil desired what he would have had if he had not fallen.[1]

Objection 1: Against this it seems that the angel did not sin by desiring blessedness, but he desired God and he willed to enjoy God as God was present to his intellect. The devil, therefore, did not sin, because as Augustine says, "blessedness is desired by everyone,"[2] and all people desire blessedness by a natural appetite. The natural appetite is always right; therefore, the devil did not sin with respect to the ultimate goal.

Objection 2: The intellect is related to its first principle just as the will is related to the ultimate goal. Therefore, just as the intellect cannot err about the first principle, but does err concerning other things, so the will does not sin by desiring the ultimate goal, although it does sin by desiring other things.

---

1 Anselm, *On the Fall of the Devil* (*De casu Diaboli*), Ch. 6.
2 Augustine, *On the Trinity*, Bk. 13, Ch. 5.

Objection 3: A good angel had a love of what is advantageous just as did the devil, for he desired the good of his own nature. According to Anselm, however, angels were not able to will the love of what is advantageous.[1] If, therefore, the devil sinned because of a love of what is advantageous, it follows that the good angel sinned in the same way.

I answer that the love of justice, whether it is infused or innate, inclines the will to will as it ought to will. The will ought to will in conformity with the divine will as its reason for willing. Since the will, however, is an appetite, it can only desire, with the love of what is advantageous, what is advantageous to itself, and not to other powers. Because the will does not follow the inclination of the intellect, the will is able by its own freedom to will or to reject what it does not naturally will.

I say then that the devil sinned through an excessive love of pleasure, because he loved God more as something to be enjoyed than as God in himself. The devil was also excessive perhaps in willing to acquire happiness too soon, because he sought it right away, but he ought to have wished for it at the appropriate time according to God's law. A third excess in the devil's willing relates to the cause of happiness, because God intended that happiness be given on the basis of merit, but the devil wanted to have it as a natural possession. Finally, a fourth excess is in the goal, because the devil wanted to enjoy God by seeking the greatest pleasure for himself simply for the sake of pleasure.

In these ways the devil could have sinned, and most likely he did sin in this fourth way. I, therefore, say that the devil was able to sin with respect to the ultimate goal, by seeking the ultimate goal not out of a love of justice but out of a love of what is advantageous. This stemmed from an excessive love in one of the four ways just mentioned.

Reply to Objection 1: I concede that there is a natural appetite for happiness. In the natural appetite, however, there is no excess as described above (for example, the devil seeking happiness too soon), because the natural appetite is not any actual act. Excess, on the other hand, arises from the free act of the will (for example, wanting something too soon), because the will as a free power can moderate and regulate its loves. The devil's will has sinned, therefore, in not following the right rule.

Reply to Objection 2: I say that the comparison is not apt. It is not within the intellect's power to understand more or less intensely or to moderate its acts, because the intellect is a purely natural power in

---

1 Anselm, *The Harmony of the Foreknowledge, the Predestination, and the Grace of God with Free Choice* (*De Concordia Praescientiae et Praedestinationis et Gratiae Dei cum Libero Arbitrio*), Q. 3, Ch. 13.

regard to its object (without the control of the will). Whenever some object is present to the intellect, the intellect understands it as much as it can from its own ability. The will, however, should restrain the intellect to prevent it from putting the highest efforts into objects that are not worthy, as occurs in sins and in idle thoughts.

Reply to Objection 3: When it is argued that the good angels had a love of what is advantageous, just as the fallen angels did, I say that the good angels sought God with a moderate love of what is advantageous and with a love of justice, because they loved God as good just in himself rather than as something to be enjoyed by them. The fallen angels did just the reverse. Likewise, the good angels exhibited moderation in the cause and goal of happiness, and they did not seek God to enjoy him for the sake of pleasure, as the fallen angels did.

You, however, will respond: how is it possible that the good angels were able to seek God without also seeking pleasure?

I say that the good angels were able to do this. Just as the will that does not enjoy God's presence still truly wants God to exist (as is the case when our will is properly ordered), so the will that does intellectually enjoy God's presence also wants God to exist, and all the more so because God is present. All of this arises out of a love of justice.

We have, therefore, two acts of the will by which the devils have sinned: an excessive love of themselves and an excessive desire for happiness as the greatest pleasure.

Was their sin consummated?

I say that it was not. The will in sinning begins with the smallest things and proceeds from there to the greater things, for the one who is negligent in minor matters, "little by little falls" into greater ones.[1] The evil is not simply to seek God's presence in order to take pleasure in hating God. Rather, the progression goes like this. In sinning, the devil sought God's presence to himself for the sake of pleasure, and he sought this so that God would be present to him as something due to his nature. In doing so he implicitly wished to be made God's equal, because it belongs to God alone to enjoy his presence as due to his own nature. Since the devil wanted to have happiness as due to his own nature, he did not wish to be subject to God, even though he did not formally seek equality with God. Thereafter, seeing that he could not have this, he was envious of God's greatness, and God's greatness made him sad. From this followed a hatred of God, and the wish that God did not exist. The devil committed all of these sins and evil acts as though progressing on a journey. He did not sin by just one act, for first he loved himself excessively, then he excessively desired happiness from God, next he envied God, and finally he hated God—and at that

---

1 Sirach or Ecclesiasticus 19:1.

point the sin was finally consummated. There were different objects and acts of sin.

Accordingly, I do not understand that the devils sinned with one act at one indivisible instant that was the final end of irredeemable sin. Rather, I say that in all of their sins the devils were as though on a journey and that, when a devil sinned with one sin, if he had in the second instant had grace and had repented, he would have been redeemed. It is clear thus that there is an order in sinning, because the will begins first with the smallest things and proceeds thereafter to the greater. This is what Augustine says in *The City of God*, as cited above: "Two loves have made two cities, for example, the love of one's self leading to the contempt of God."[1]

This concludes the answer to the first question, "What was the act by which the devil sinned?" Some additional clarifications have also been given.

---

1 Augustine, *The City of God*, Bk. 14, Ch. 28. The second love is the love of God, which Scotus does not include in the quotation.

Appendix I: Ockham on the Freedom of the Will

From William of Ockham, *Ordinatio* (1317–18), in *Guillelmi de Ockham Opera theologica*, vol. 1, edited by Gedeon Gál and Stephen Brown, St. Bonaventure UP, 1967–86, pp. 501–07

[In this passage, Ockham argues that the human will enjoys a radical freedom such that, even in the case of willing happiness, the will is free to will or not to will happiness. If it is said that the will has a "natural inclination" to happiness, Ockham will grant this, but only in the sense that for the most part people do will happiness. If one means that the human will by a necessity of nature wills happiness, as Thomas claims, Ockham denies this. On this matter, Ockham insists on a radical freedom of the will that adumbrates certain positions in modern philosophy.]

Bk. 1, Dist. 1, Q. 6: Does the Will Contingently and Freely Enjoy the Ultimate Goal?[1]

Preliminary Distinctions

Distinction 1: The first distinction concerns what is contingent, that is, in enjoying or producing something contingently. For present purposes, there are two senses of this. In one way, in an absolute sense, it is possible to enjoy or not to enjoy something, or to produce or not to produce something. In this way, whatever produces any effect produces it contingently, because God could make it not produce the effect. In a second way, contingency is understood in a cause that produces some effect such that it is within the power of the cause to produce the effect or not to produce it, when nothing is changed on the part of the cause or on the part of any other circumstances; neither one outcome nor the other is determined by the nature of the cause. In this same sense, we can talk about contingency in enjoying something. In the present question, contingency will be understood in this second way.

Distinction 2: the second distinction concerns freedom. Freedom in one way is distinguished from coercion, and in this sense it is under-

---

1 Ockham provides a long discussion and refutation of the position of Scotus, which is omitted from this translation.

stood in its least proper sense, because in this sense the intellect can be said to have freedom. In a second way, freedom is opposed to the slavery of a rational creature, either the slavery of guilt or the slavery of punishment. In this way, the blessed in heaven are freer than we pilgrims on earth, because they are free from guilt and punishment. In a third way, freedom is opposed to the necessity that is the opposite of contingency, in the second meaning of contingency given above. In this sense, freedom is a kind of indifference and contingency, and it is distinguished from an active natural principle. In this sense philosophers talk about freedom and the will, and in this sense active natural principles are distinguished from them, as in the *Physics*[1] and the *Metaphysics*.[2] John of Damascus gives this same distinction, when he proves that animals do not have free choice, because they do not act but rather are acted upon.[3] When he says this, if he means that the *substance* of an animal is acted upon, this is not relevant to our topic, because in this sense neither humans nor angels would have free will, because they, too, are acted upon. If he means that the *acts* of animals are acted upon, because their acts are influenced from the outside and not from the inside, this too is not relevant, because it could equally be supposed that the sense appetite is acted upon in causing its own actions, or that the intellect is so acted upon, or likewise any natural thing that moves itself. Finally, if he means that animals do not have free choice because they are acted upon, that is, because they do not have their acts under their own power and control, this is the relevant sense. Whatever has free choice has control and power over its own actions, which implies indifference and contingency.

Distinction 3: The third distinction, taken from Anselm,[4] is between the love of what is advantageous and the love of justice; there is likewise the distinction between the rejection of what is disadvantageous and the rejection of injustice. These distinctions are found in actual acts of willing or of rejecting, prompted by the command of reason.

Distinction 4: The fourth distinction is between willing a simple thing, which is properly love, and willing something complex, in the broad sense of the term, like willing to have happiness, willing not to exist, or something like this; likewise, there is a rejection of a simple thing, which can be called hatred or detestation, and there is a rejection of what is complex, as when we reject our own existence, wealth, or honours, and yet we do not in such cases hate wealth or honours, except in a broad sense of "hate."

---

1 Aristotle, *Physics* 2.5, 196b17–22.
2 Aristotle, *Metaphysics* 9.5, 1048a5–9.
3 John of Damascus, *On the Orthodox Faith*, Bk. 2, Ch. 27.
4 Anselm, *On the Fall of the Devil* (*De casu Diaboli*), Ch. 12.

Conclusions

The first conclusion will be that the will contingently and freely (in the senses given above) enjoys the ultimate, universal goal, because it can either love happiness or not love happiness, and it can seek happiness for itself or not seek it.

A first persuasive argument for this conclusion: the will can reject whatever the intellect says should be rejected. The intellect can believe that happiness is impossible, because it can accept only what we see to be genuinely possible for ourselves in this life. It can, therefore, reject anything that we see to be repugnant to our present condition, and consequently it can reject happiness. The major premise[1] is clear because, although the will does not necessarily conform to any judgement of reason,[2] it is nevertheless able to conform to both a right and a wrong judgement of reason.

This argument is supported by the consideration that it is possible to reject whatever might possibly not be satisfying. We can believe that we might not be satisfied by any possible outcome for us. It is, therefore, possible for the will to reject whatever is possible for it, and it can certainly reject whatever is impossible for it, and therefore it can reject anything.

A second argument is that whoever can effectively will an antecedent state can will a consequent state, provided that it is known or believed to be a consequent. Someone can effectively will not to exist, and such a person can know clearly that not being happy is a consequence of non-existence. It is possible, therefore, to will not to be happy, and consequently to reject happiness. The assumption in this argument is clear, because many—both believers in a future life as well as non-believers in any future life—make use of reason when they have committed suicide and exposed themselves to death. They, therefore, willed their own non-existence.

This argument is supported by the consideration that some of the faithful, who believe that they are able to attain happiness if they do not sin, nevertheless choose to sin, knowing or believing that they will have eternal punishment as a result. This could not happen if their rejection of happiness were only a rejection of happiness in general and not in their individual cases.

The second conclusion is that a person can reject his or her own individual happiness. Arguments like those above can be given to show this.

---

1 The major premise is, "The will can reject whatever the intellect says should be rejected."

2 Ockham argues for this later: *Ordinatio* IV, Q. 14.

The third conclusion is that someone can reject happiness in his or her individual case; while believing that such happiness is possible, such a person is able to reject having happiness. A persuasive argument for this conclusion is that whatever is commanded by right reason can be an act of the will. Right reason, however, can order that someone lack eternal happiness. It is possible, therefore, to will to lack eternal happiness, and therefore it is possible to reject it for ourselves.

Support for this argument can be gained from the fact that a person condemned to hell, from the standpoint of punishments of the body and of condemnation, can conform to what is known or believed of the divine will. The divine will, however, wills that such a person lack eternal happiness. It is, therefore, possible that this be willed by a will in hell and, consequently, for the same reason, also by a will in this life.

Another argument is that whoever wills something effectively, wills also whatever is believed to be necessary to carry out what has been willed. There are, however, Christians who believe that they cannot attain happiness without living a good life, and yet they do not will to live a good and holy life. They do not, therefore, will happiness effectively, and consequently, for this same reason, they are able not to will it.

The fourth conclusion is that the one who sees the divine essence but lacks the enjoyment of happiness is able to reject that enjoyment. The argument for this is that, as was said above, any will is able to conform to the divine will in what is willed. God, however, is able to will that someone lack the enjoyment of eternal happiness. Therefore, etc.

Another argument is that whatever can be willed or rejected at one time can be willed or rejected forever. A will, however, can reject having happiness at some determinate time, for example, when God wills that it not have the enjoyment of happiness. It can, therefore, will it without restriction.

The fifth conclusion is that someone seeing the divine essence but, through the absolute power of God, lacking the love for God,[1] is able to reject God. This is proven or at least made persuasive thus. Any disadvantageous thing can be the object of rejection, whether it is truly disadvantageous or only thought to be so, and likewise any advantageous thing, whether truly so or only thought to be so, can be the object of willing. God, however, can be disadvantageous, at least in someone's judgement, and therefore God can be the object of rejection. The assumption in this argument is clear, because such a person could be punished by God, both by bodily punishments and by condemnation.

---

1 Ockham treats this later: *Ordinatio* IV, Q. 14.

This argument is supported in that Christ, although he was bless-edly happy, was punished and underwent bodily punishments. What-ever is punitive or harmful to someone can be disadvantageous to that same person, whether truly so or judged to be so. God, therefore, in this way can be considered to be disadvantageous, whether truly so or only in judgement.

There are many questions that may be raised about what I have just said, but these will be considered later when we deal with happiness.[1] For the present, I pass them by.

Response to the Terms of the Question

From what has been said, we can respond to the terms of the ques-tion. The "ultimate goal" can be taken in two ways: it either means the *created happiness* that is possible for the will, or it means the *object* of that happiness. In the first sense of created happiness, it is not allowed that the will enjoys the ultimate goal, using "enjoys" in its proper sense.[2] Nevertheless, it is possible to enjoy such a thing contingently and freely: because, on the one hand, the fact that it is not allowed means that it is possible not to enjoy it; and, on the other hand, it can be enjoyed, because if the will is able to enjoy a created good that is less good, it can all the more enjoy the greatest possible created good. If, however, we take "to enjoy" broadly for any act of seeking, I then say that the will can absolutely will, not will, or reject the ultimate goal, whether it is taken in general or in particular, whether it is in this life or in heaven. The conclusions given above apply to this sense of enjoying the ultimate goal.

Speaking about the ultimate goal in the second way, I say that in this life this object can be either willed or rejected. If, however, this object should be shown to us just in itself in all its clarity, and if God should suspend the operation of the will in willing, the will could reject it. If, however, God should not suspend the activity of the will and should leave it to its own nature, then there are doubts, about which we will speak later.[3]

To the principal argument I say that the will does not incline natu-rally to the ultimate goal, unless "inclination" is taken to mean what happens commonly. Even in this sense, it is not true that whatever

---

1 *Ordinatio* IV, Q. 14.
2 When Ockham says that it is "not allowed" to enjoy the ultimate goal, he means that it is against Christian doctrine to take a created good as though it were the ultimate goal of human life.
3 Ockham, *Ordinatio* IV, Q. 14.

happens against inclination is violent. When it is said that "everything inclines to its proper perfection," this should be denied, in a strict sense of inclination, and accepted only about the perfection toward which an active natural agent tends, but the will is not that sort of thing.

Select Bibliography

Introductory Works on Thomas Aquinas

Aertsen, Jan A. *Nature and Creatures: Thomas Aquinas's Way of Thought*. Brill, 1988.

Brock, Stephen L. *The Philosophy of Saint Thomas Aquinas: A Sketch*. Cascade Books, 2015.

Chesterton, G.K. *St. Thomas Aquinas: "The Dumb Ox."* Random House, 1974.

Davies, Brian. *Aquinas: An Introduction*. Continuum, 2003.

———. *The Thought of Thomas Aquinas*. Oxford UP, 1992.

Feser, Edward. *Aquinas: A Beginner's Guide*. Oneworld, 2009.

Gilson, Etienne. *Thomism: The Philosophy of Thomas Aquinas*. Translated by Laurence K. Shook and Armand Maurer. Pontifical Institute of Mediaeval Studies, 2002.

Jensen, Stephen. *Living the Good Life: A Beginner's Thomistic Ethics*. Catholic U of America P, 2013.

Kenny, Anthony. *Aquinas*. Hill and Wang, 1980.

McInerny, Ralph. *Ethica Thomistica: The Moral Philosophy of Thomas Aquinas*. Catholic U of America P, 1982.

———. *St. Thomas Aquinas*. U of Notre Dame P, 1982.

Nichols, Aidan. *Discovering Aquinas: An Introduction to His Life, Work, and Influence*. Darton, Longman, & Todd, 2002.

Pieper, Josef. *Guide to Thomas Aquinas*. Ignatius P, 1991.

———. *The Silence of Saint Thomas: Three Essays*. Translated by John Murray and Daniel O'Connor. Regnery P, 1957; St. Augustine's P, 1999.

Porro, Pasquale. *Thomas Aquinas: A Historical and Philosophical Profile*. Translated by Joseph G. Trabbic and Roger W. Nutt. Catholic U of America P, 2016.

Stump, Eleonore. *Aquinas*. Routledge, 2003. Arguments of the Philosophers.

Torrell, Jean-Pierre. *Saint Thomas Aquinas*. Vol. 1, *The Person and His Work*. Translated by Robert Royal. Catholic U of America P, 1996.

———. *Saint Thomas Aquinas*. Vol. 2, *Spiritual Master*. Translated by Robert Royal. Catholic U of America P, 2003.

Weisheipl, James A. *Friar Thomas D'Aquino: His Life, Thought, and Work*. Doubleday, 1974.

Some English Translations of Thomas Aquinas's Works

Aquinas on Creation: Writings on the "Sentences" of Peter Lombard, Book 2, Distinction 1, Question 1. Translated by Steven Baldner and William Carroll. Pontifical Institute of Mediaeval Studies, 1997.

Bobik, Joseph. *Aquinas on Matter Form and the Elements: A Translation and Interpretation of the De Principiis Naturae and the De mixtione elementorum of St. Thomas Aquinas.* U of Notre Dame P, 1998.

The Cardinal Virtues: Aquinas, Albert, and Philip the Chancellor. Translated by R.E. Hauser. Pontifical Institute of Mediaeval Studies, 2004.

Commentary on the Book of Causes. Translated by Vincent A. Guagliardo, Charles R. Hess, and Richard Taylor. Catholic U of America P, 1996.

Disputed Questions on Truth. Translated by Robert W. Mulligan, James V. McGlynn, and Robert W. Schmidt. 3 vols. Regnery, 1952–54.

Disputed Questions on Virtue. Translated by Ralph McInerny. St. Augustine's P, 1998.

Disputed Questions on Virtue. Translated by Jeffrey Hause and Claudia Eisen. Hackett, 2010.

The Division and Methods of the Sciences: Questions V and VI of His Commentary on the De Trinitate *of Boethius.* Translated by Armand Maurer. 4th ed., Pontifical Institute of Mediaeval Studies, 1986.

An Exposition of the "On the Hebdomads" of Boethius. Translated by Janice L. Schultz and Edward A. Synan. Catholic U of America P, 2001.

Faith, Reason, and Theology: Questions I–II of His Commentary on the De Trinitate *of Boethius.* Translated by Armand Maurer. Pontifical Institute of Mediaeval Studies, 1987.

McInerny, Ralph. *Aquinas against the Averroists: On There Being Only One Intellect.* Purdue UP, 1993.

On Being and Essence. Translated by Armand Maurer. 2nd ed., Pontifical Institute of Mediaeval Studies, 1968.

On Creation: Quaestiones Disputatae de Potentia Dei, Q. 3. Translated by Susan C. Celner-Wright. Catholic U of America P, 2010.

On Evil. Translated by John A. and Jean T. Oesterle. U of Notre Dame P, 1995.

The Philosophy of Thomas Aquinas: Introductory Readings. Translated by Christopher Martin. Routledge, 1988.

The Power of God. Translated by Richard Regan. Oxford UP, 2012.

Quodlibetal Questions 1 and 2. Translated by Sandra Edwards. Pontifical Institute of Mediaeval Studies, 1983.

Selected Philosophical Writings. Translated by Timothy McDermott. Oxford: Oxford UP, 1993.

Selected Writings. Translated by Ralph McInerny. Penguin, 1998.

Summa contra Gentiles. Translated by Anton C. Pegis (vol. 1), James F. Anderson (vol. 2), Vernon Bourke (vol. 3), and Charles J. O'Neil (vol. 4). U of Notre Dame P, 1975. 4 vols.

Summa theologica. Translated by The Fathers of the English Dominican Province in 1920. Benzinger Brothers, 1948. Reprinted Christian Classics, 1981. Parts of this translation have been printed in numerous editions, for example: Anton C. Pegis. *Introduction to St. Thomas Aquinas.* Random House, 1948; Peter Kreeft. *A Summa of the Summa.* Ignatius P, 1990; Peter Kreeft. *A Shorter Summa.* Ignatius P, 1993.

A Small Sample of Advanced Works on Thomas

Brock, Stephen L. *Action and Conduct: Thomas Aquinas and the Theory of Action.* T. & T. Clark, 1998.

Burrell, David B. *Aquinas: God and Action.* U of Scranton P, 2008.

Davies, Brian, editor. *Aquinas's* Summa theologiae. Rowman and Littlefield, 2005. Critical Essays on the Classics.

Davies, Brian, and Eleonore Stump. *The Oxford Handbook of Aquinas.* Oxford: Oxford UP, 2012.

Dewan, Lawrence. *Form and Being: Studies in Thomistic Metaphysics.* Catholic U of America P, 2006.

——. *Wisdom, Law, Virtue: Essays in Thomistic Ethics.* Fordham UP, 2008.

Feser, Edward. *Scholastic Metaphysics: A Contemporary Introduction.* Editiones Scholasticae, 2014.

Flannery, Kevin L. *Acts Amid Precepts: The Aristotelian Logical Structure of Thomas Aquinas's Moral Theory.* Catholic U of America P, 2001.

Gilson, Etienne. *Christian Philosophy: An Introduction.* Translated by Armand Maurer. Pontifical Institute of Mediaeval Studies, 1993.

——. *Thomist Realism and the Critique of Knowledge.* Translated by Mark A. Wauck. Ignatius P, 1986.

Jensen, Stephen. *Good and Evil Actions: A Journey through Saint Thomas Aquinas.* Catholic U of America P, 2010.

Kenny, Anthony. *Aquinas on Being.* Clarendon P, 2002.

——. *Aquinas on Mind.* Routledge, 1993.

Kerr, Fergus. *After Aquinas: Versions of Thomism.* Blackwell, 2002.

Knasas, John F.X. *Being and Some Twentieth Century Philosophers.* Fordham UP, 2003.

Kretzmann, Norman. *The Metaphysics of Creation: Aquinas's Natural Theology in* Summa contra Gentiles *II.* Clarendon P, 1999.

———. *The Metaphysics of Theism: Aquinas's Natural Theology in* Summa contra Gentiles *I*. Clarendon P, 1997.

Kretzmann, Norman, and Eleonore Stump, editors. *The Cambridge Companion to Aquinas*. Cambridge UP, 1993.

Lisska, Anthony J. *Aquinas's Theory of Natural Law: An Analytic Reconstruction*. Clarendon P, 1996.

Maurer, Armand. *Being and Knowing: Studies in Thomas Aquinas and Later Medieval Philosophers*. Pontifical Institute of Mediaeval Studies, 1990.

McInerny, Ralph. *Aquinas and Analogy*. Catholic U of America P, 1996.

Pasnau, Robert. *Thomas Aquinas on Human Nature: A Philosophical Study of "Summa theologiae."* Cambridge UP, 2002.

Stump, Eleonore. *Aquinas*. Routledge, 2003.

Weisheipl, James. *Nature and Motion in the Middle Ages*. Edited by William E. Carroll. Catholic U of America P, 1985.

Wippel, John F. *Metaphysical Themes in Thomas Aquinas*. Catholic U of America P, 1984.

———. *The Metaphysical Thought of Thomas Aquinas: From Finite Being to Uncreated Being*. Catholic U of America P, 2000.

Analytical Index of Thomas's Texts, Chapters 1–4

Alphabetical Index

Kant, Immanuel, 27, 31n1, 185, 215
  "Ontological Argument," 185, 215
knowledge, 17–18, 25–27, 114–35
  Aristotle's position accepted, 123–25
  Plato's position rejected, 114–23

law, 172–74
  natural law, 31–33, 175–83
Leo XIII, Pope,
  Aeterni Patris, 39
Lombard, Peter, 36, 189
  Sentences, 11, 18, 36

Maimonides, Moses, 10, 36, 81
  The Guide for the Perplexed, 36
matter, 16–19, 23, 26, 45–59, 62, 72, 74–76, 80, 81, 93, 95, 97, 98,
    102–05, 114–16, 118, 121, 122, 126, 128, 130, 131, 143, 144, 166,
    166n2, 168, 220, 224, 226, 227
  prime matter, 18, 49–50, 49n1, 81
Melissus, 36, 37
Michael of Cesena, 207

Nemesius, 35, 37
  De natura hominis, 36, 37

Ockham, William of, 33, 207
  "Ockham's Razor," 207
  Ordinatio, 235–40
    contingency, 235
    freedom, 235–36
    the will is free to will or not to will happiness, 237–38
    the will in relation to the divine essence, 238–39
    the will in relation to the "ultimate goal," 239–40
  Questiones in Libros Physicorum Aristotelis, 207–14
    arguments against Scotus's arguments, 210–12
    proving a first efficient cause of conservation, 212–14
    Scotus's arguments for the existence of a first efficient cause,
      208–10
  Questions on Aristotle's Physics, 207–08
  Quodlibeta Septem, 225–28
    whether the human soul is the form of the human body, 225–28
  Summa logicae, 11n2

Parmenides, 36, 37
  On Nature, 37
Paul, St., 12, 35, 66, 66n2, 96
Plato, 12, 23, 25–26, 31, 34, 37, 58, 59, 94–95, 95n1, 96, 101, 114–15,
    117, 120, 121, 122, 123, 124, 125, 126, 128, 130, 131, 220
  Meno, 120
Platonists, 25, 117, 123, 126, 133
Plotinus, 34

virtues, 30–31, 169–71
voluntariness, 28–29, 149–57

will, free will, 23–25, 105–13, 151–52, 155–56
and necessity, 105–06

Zeno, 36, 37

From the Publisher

A name never says it all, but the word "Broadview" expresses a good deal of the philosophy behind our company. We are open to a broad range of academic approaches and political viewpoints. We pay attention to the broad impact book publishing and book printing has in the wider world; for some years now we have used 100% recycled paper for most titles. Our publishing program is internationally oriented and broad-ranging. Our individual titles often appeal to a broad readership too; many are of interest as much to general readers as to academics and students.

Founded in 1985, Broadview remains a fully independent company owned by its shareholders—not an imprint or subsidiary of a larger multinational.

For the most accurate information on our books (including information on pricing, editions, and formats) please visit our website at www.broadviewpress.com. Our print books and ebooks are also available for sale on our site.

broadview press
www.broadviewpress.com